THE AUTHOR: Hyōe Murakami was born in Japan in 1923 and graduated from the Army Academy. During World War II he first served with the Sixth Imperial Guard Infantry Regiment then was appointed to a position in his old academy. In 1949, he graduated from the Department of German Literature of Tokyo University, and soon made a name for himself as a novelist and critic. His published works include *Sakura to ken* (The cherry and the sword). He served as editor in chief of the Japan Culture Institute from 1973 to 1982.

JAPAN
The Years of Trial, 1919-52

Hyōe Murakami

KODANSHA INTERNATIONAL LTD.
Tokyo, New York and San Francisco

The completion of any book depends on the cooperation of many individuals. The editors wish to express their deep gratitude to all who have helped make the publication of this book possible. Special thanks to John Bester, Theodore Goossen, Thomas J. Harper, Anthony V. Liman, Paul F. McCarthy, and Robert Rolf for the translation; and to the Mainichi Newspapers, Asahi Shimbun Publishing Company, and Kyodo Photo Service for furnishing photographs from their libraries.

The Hepburn system of romanization is used for Japanese terms, which are italicized except for words included in the second edition of *Webster's New World Dictionary*. The Wade-Giles system of romanization is used for Chinese terms, but the Pinyin transliterations are included in the index for the reader's convenience. Japanese and Chinese names, except that of the author, follow the Japanese and Chinese practice of placing the surname first.

This book was published through a grant from the Commemorative Association for the Japan World Exposition.

Previously published by the Japan Culture Institute in 1982.

Distributed in the United States by Kodansha International/USA Ltd. through Harper & Row, Publishers, Inc., 10 East 53rd Street, New York, New York 10022. Published by Kodansha International Ltd., 12-21, Otowa 2-chome, Bunkyo-ku, Tokyo 112 and Kodansha International/USA Ltd., 10 East 53rd Street, New York, New York 10022 and 44 Montgomery Street, San Francisco, California 94104. Copyright © 1982 Hyōe Murakami. All rights reserved. Printed in Japan.

LCC 83-80223
ISBN 0-87011-610-X
ISBN 4-7700-1110-5 (in Japan)

First paperback edition, 1983

Contents

Preface

In the mid-nineteenth century, Commodore Perry delivered the resounding knock that opened Japan's doors to the world after centuries of isolation. The more enlightened Japanese of the day soon became keenly aware that, unless they reformed the feudal state created by the shoguns, at the same time laying the foundations of a modern industry and building up powerful armed forces, the country was in danger of becoming a colony of the West in the same way as almost all other Asian nations. The tale I have told here begins precisely at that point, after the end of World War I, when Japan, having more or less succeeded in modernizing itself, first made its debut in international society as one of the great powers.

As the title of this book suggests, the thirty-four years from 1919 to 1952 were Japan's severest testing-time. The difficulties with which it struggled came from both within and without. Step by step, the nation proceeded along the path toward hostilities, until it finally plunged into the Pacific War. After three years and eight months of bitter struggle, it was defeated and forced to submit to seven years of occupation.

So far as possible, I have told the story as a kind of nonfiction documentary. The principal characters who determined Japan's course during the period in question appear in it, together with the leaders of the powers of the West; and alongside them also appear, under their own names, more than two hundred men and women who, though perhaps only on the fringes of history, were concerned in episodes that bespeak the atmosphere of the age. I have tried to create not a dry, insipid chronology but an accurate account of living Japanese as, moment by moment, they wove the fabric of history.

The fact that Japan became the only great power in Asia gives the story its peculiar lights and shadows. The trials that the nation underwent were due in large part to its situation in Asia and to its late arrival on the international scene. Between Japan and America in particular—two nations on opposite sides of the same Pacific Ocean—mutual misunderstanding, prejudice, and suspicion aroused by mistaken steps taken by both sides were aggravated as the years went by, until they finally led to catastrophe.

Japan was defeated in World War II, yet as a result of that war the countries of Asia achieved independence, to be followed in turn by those of Africa. By now, we live in a different world from before. To say that Japan liberated those countries would be going too far; yet without that great conflict that extended from Southeast Asia throughout the Pacific and that brought Japan down in ruin, those countries would almost certainly not have achieved independence so swiftly. The same goddess of history that punished Japan and the Japanese for their presumption also commanded that the West should stop seeing itself as the sole standard-bearer and arbiter of civilization.

I myself took part in the war as a young army officer, and throughout the postwar years of poverty and ruin I continued to ponder the meaning of what I had experienced. Later still, I avidly read the many accounts of the period and any other related works as they appeared. The present book is the outcome. In presenting it, I pay tribute to the numberless victims of the war, whether friend or foe, soldier or civilian. And at the same time I express my gratitude to the many authors and personal acquaintances—among the latter figures, such as former generals Araki and Kawaguchi, who appear in this book—who have made this work possible. I have set the book mostly in Japan; but I have tried to maintain as fair an approach as possible—to make the work a part of the shared history of mankind.

No one can know what the coming age holds in store. Yet if we look back in tranquillity on the past, carefully scrutinizing the drama enacted by man in all his wisdom and his folly, his humanity and his savagery, then the truths that we elicit thereby will, I am sure, provide valuable lessons for the future as well.

Hyōe Murakami
December 1981, Tokyo

JAPAN
The Years of Trial, 1919-52

1

The Paris Peace Conference

January 11, 1919. Tokyo Station had been thronged with crowds since the early hours of the morning. On that day, Japan's delegation to the Paris Peace Conference, headed by Ambassador Plenipotentiary Saionji Kinmochi, was to leave Tokyo. It was to go by train to Kobe and thence by ship, calling at several Asian ports en route, crossing the Indian Ocean, passing through the Suez Canal, and so finally to France. The journey to Paris would take more than seven weeks.

Tokyo that morning was shrouded in dull gray clouds. The train was scheduled to leave at 8:30. Two hours before that, crowds of well-wishers had begun to pour in. Prime Minister Hara Takashi, nearly the entire cabinet, opposition leaders, members of the imperial family and nobility, generals, admirals—a veritable sea of notables crowded the platform, so that it seemed to sway in a swell of silk hats.

In 1868, Japan, a small island nation in the Far East, had, under pressure from the West, opened its long-closed doors, effected the dramatic "revolution" known now as the Meiji Restoration, and taken its first steps toward becoming a modern nation. Exactly half a century had passed since then. In that time, under the threat of European imperialism and colonialism, Japan had made numerous domestic social reforms, developed modern industries, and built a new military force. Abroad, it had pitted its armed forces first against China, then against Russia, and had won in both cases. It had fought in World War I as a member of the Anglo-Japanese Alliance and was now about to participate in the peace-treaty conference as a recognized world power and one of the victors.

The faces of the members of the delegation and those who came to see them off were animated, as though they were taking part in a festival. For the first time, Japan had been invited to participate in important international negotiations as an equal of the Western nations.

Saionji Kinmochi, his family, and Prime Minister Hara, who was to accompany him part of the way, boarded the spacious observation car. The other members of the delegation boarded the several first-class carriages—except for one young man who had been given a seat in a corner of the observation car. This was Konoe Fumimaro, the eldest son of a family that for a thousand years had been closer than any other to the imperial household. He was a fair-skinned young man, only twenty-seven years old; and though he held a seat in the House of Peers, he had no experience whatever in government. He had asked Saionji to take him along as an "observer" and had been taken on as a special member of the delegation.

Saionji, too, was descended from an old court family. At nineteen he had participated in the revolutionary movement that led to the restoration. Later, around the time of the French Commune, he had studied in Paris. On several occasions he had served as prime minister, and had, as a liberal elder statesman, remained throughout a figure of great importance in Japanese government. Yet he addressed the young Konoe, out of respect for his lineage, as "Your Excellency."

The Paris Peace Conference had its origins in the idealism of American President Woodrow Wilson. The year before the war had ended Wilson had set forth in his State of the Union Message his famous Fourteen Points. Among the more important of these were the abolition of secret treaties, freedom of the seas, reduction of armaments and guarantees thereof, determination of the sovereignty of colonies in a way that took account of the interests of their peoples, as well as certain specific proposals based upon the right of self-determination, such as the independence of Poland. Yet another noteworthy feature was his proposal for the "establishment of a League of Nations' with the aim of guaranteeing the political and territorial sovereignty of all nations, large and small alike."

Japan at the time was in the reign of the Emperor Taishō, the successor of the Emperor Meiji. The press was free, and championship of the people's rights was such that this period would later be known as that of "Taishō democracy." Government in the Meiji era had for the most part been under the strict control of the elder statesmen, the leaders of the Meiji Restoration. However, in the Taishō era a system of government by two major parties was well on the way to establishment. Prime Minister Hara was neither a member of the nobility nor a high-ranking bureaucrat nor a general; having come to power as the head of a political party, he was known as the "commoner prime minister." The right to vote still depended upon the amount of taxes paid, but general elections were already on the cards.

The press was unanimous in its support of Wilson's proposals, and welcomed them as advancing the cause of humanity. However, the response of experienced members of the Foreign Ministry was somewhat more complex. In a word, they were perplexed. These men were accustomed to living by the rules of the jungle of international relations, where might was right and clandestine plotting indispensable. Never before had the "ideals" that Wilson proposed been put forth as fundamental principles of international politics. Justice and humanity were often enough propounded, but always in the service of national interest; for it was, after all, the duty of government to further the interests of its own people. While they felt they could not openly oppose Wilson's idealism, neither could they speak out with any enthusiasm in favor of it. Their hands were tied, and they feared the results would be most disadvantageous to their own country. Would this idealism ultimately become the guiding principle of the post—World War I world? Could they be assured it did not conceal a trap that would hinder the further progress of Japan?

Konoe, though a member of the delegation, was not expected to participate in the conference or perform any duties. However, this philosophically-minded young man who as a student had shown particular concern for questions of social justice, and who harbored serious doubts about the class system upon which his own privileged status was based, had only a short time before published his first essay in the noted magazine *Nihon oyobi Nihonjin* (Japan and the Japanese). It was entitled "Against a Peace to the Advantage of England and America," and in it he challenged openly the "ideals" of Wilson's Fourteen Points.

He sharply criticized Japan's leaders for being deceived by the flowery rhetoric of English and American politicians and for endorsing the ideals of the League of Nations without noting the "egoism of England and America" that lay beneath them. Konoe saw the war in

Europe as a struggle between the established powers and the as yet unestablished powers. Those nations who found the status quo to their advantage advocated peace; those who found the status quo disadvantageous resorted to war. England and America advocated pacifism because it was to their benefit to do so; with the exception of certain progressive provisions, such as the right of self-determination, justice and humanity had nothing to do with their position. Those who stood to profit most from the establishment of the League of Nations were England and America. Other nations might be enticed to participate for the sake of justice and humanity, but they had virtually nothing to gain by it; on the contrary, one could foresee cases in which it would hinder them economically. Following this line of reasoning, he argued that Japan should, at the very least, make its participation in an alliance for peace contingent upon the following two conditions: the rejection of economic imperialism and the abolition of discrimination between the white and yellow races.

Japan, Konoe maintained, had the right to act in its own best interests. This was not to say that Japan could simply ignore other nations, but that it should see their egoism, backed by military and economic power, for what it was. And Japan should resist it for the sake of its own right to exist, which was equally defensible on the grounds of justice and humanity. To the leaders of Japan, who since the opening of the country had pursued a foreign policy based entirely upon learning from the West and cooperating with the West—often to their own humiliation—this was an entirely new concept. It seemed a dangerous proposition, excessively direct and naive.

About twenty years later, Konoe was elected to his first term as prime minister and thereafter held the post twice more before finally relinquishing the position to General Tōjō just before the beginning of the Pacific War. The reader will doubtless notice a striking resemblance between the public statements of the Japanese government in that period and the tone of his early article.

Konoe's article immediately attracted the attention of the *Millard Review*, a Shanghai journal known for its anti-Japanese stance. It translated, printed, and strongly criticized the article, and warned moreover that "the person who propounds these ideas is a member of the Japanese delegation." When their ship called at Shanghai, the matter became the subject of debate, even among the members of the delegation. The elder Saionji reproved Konoe for his "imprudence and immaturity." No record survives telling whether Konoe defended himself or maintained a respectful silence.

However, there was one Chinese who was deeply impressed by the article. When the Japanese delegation arrived in Shanghai, he dispatched a messenger to request an interview. This was Sun Yat-sen, now known as the father of the Chinese revolution. Eight years before this, after several unsuccessful uprisings, the revolution had succeeded and he had been chosen first provisional president of the Republic of China. The Ch'ing dynasty had thus fallen, but power had then passed into the hands of General Yuan Shin-k'ai, and China had entered a period of war among opposing warlords. Sun Yat-sen had failed in attempts at a second and third revolution and for fear of assassination was living in hiding in the French legation.

Konoe's father, Konoe Atsumaro, was an eminent figure known for his nationalism as well as for his knowledge of China. He had protected Sun from the pressures of the Japanese government during his exile in Japan and had supported the revolutionary movement. Konoe Fumimaro boarded a rickshaw and was taken to Sun's hiding place. When Sun saw Konoe, he praised his article, lauded him as the "true son of Prince Atsumaro," and predicted that "the Paris Peace Conference would decide the fate not only of Japan but of all the peoples of East Asia."

Recalling the Russo-Japanese War, Sun said, "I was in Paris when I heard of Japan's victory in the battle of the Japan Sea. On the journey home, an Arab I met at the Suez Canal asked me if I was Japanese. I told him I was, and he said to me, 'I've seen a constant stream of wounded Russian soldiers coming through the canal lately, on their way home. That's real proof that an Asian nation can defeat Russia. And when I realized that, I was happier than if my own country had won that war.' As a fellow Asian, masquerading as a Japanese, I myself had never felt as confident as I did then. And in fact it all happened after that, didn't it—one revolutionary movement after another—in Egypt, Arabia, Persia, Turkey, Afghanistan. . . ."

As soon as Sun began talking of the awakening of Asia, his face flushed, and he went on far into the night. Japan's victory in the Russo-Japanese War had been a beacon of rebellion to the peoples of the world who for the past three hundred years had been ruled by the

West. It had aroused a desire for independence among the oppressed peoples of the world, especially in Asia. India's Jawaharlal Nehru and Indonesia's Achmed Sukarno were both, in their childhood, awakened to their mission in Asia by Japan's victory. The many young intellectuals from Vietnam who came to study in Japan were yet another manifestation of its influence. Ten years earlier, after the Sino-Japanese War, great numbers of Chinese students had come to Japan, reaching a peak of over ten thousand. These students were later to become the core of Sun Yat-sen's revolutionary party. Yet at the same time, following the Russo-Japanese War, the Japanese had subjugated the Korean people, and following the lead of the West, had joined in the division of China. Sun pointed this out with some force, too, at the end of his talk.

"Yes—until thirty years ago, there wasn't a single country in Asia that was entirely independent. Twenty-five years ago Japan succeeded in amending the unequal treaties; this was an eye-opener to the peoples of Asia, a momentous event. But now that Japan has become one of the five great powers it stands at a parting of the ways. Will it participate in the division of Asia, will it act as an agent of the enslavement of Asia; or will it lead the one billion people of Asia and fight by their side? It is unfortunate," he concluded, "that at this crucial time there is neither a true politician nor a true diplomat to be found in Japan." Konoe agreed completely.

Preliminary discussions at the Paris Peace Conference had already begun on January 13, while the Saionji delegation was still in Kobe. The first general session, held at Versailles Palace, opened on January 18 and was attended by twenty-eight countries, not including Germany and the other defeated nations. America's President Wilson, England's Prime Minister David Lloyd George, France's Prime Minister Georges Clemenceau, and other heads of state were in attendance as members of their countries' delegations. Japan had sent as its representatives former Foreign Minister Makino Nobuaki and various of its ambassadors resident in Europe. The Western approach to this conference—attended by several heads of state, who led discussion and rendered decisions on all matters in person—stood in sharp contrast to that of Japan, which relegated details to experienced professionals while the head of the delegation waited until negotiations were well advanced before making his appearance. The fact that Saionji was then an old man of sixty-nine,

Representatives of the twenty-seven victor nations at the opening ceremony of the Paris Peace Conference on January 18, 1919.

who had declined several times to serve as ambassador plenipotentiary, must also have influenced this late departure.

Japan's delegation thus acquired the somewhat unflattering nickname "the silent partner." However, the delegates had been instructed not to involve themselves in European problems, which, since the war had been a European war, inevitably figured largely on the agenda. In the subcommittees, however, Japan's delegates were vigorously involved in matters that did affect Japan. Japan's greatest concerns at the Paris Peace Conference were, first, the inclusion of a clause in the Covenant of the League of Nations abolishing racial discrimination, and, second, the guarantee of its rights to the Shantung Peninsula in China, which had been taken from Germany in the war. As the structure of the League of Nations began to take shape under the guidance of England and America, the Japanese government, like Konoe, sensed the danger of racial bias working to Japan's disadvantage. The government had instructed the delegation that if this happened they should "endeavor insofar as circumstances permit to obtain guarantees against this." As may well be imagined, their most formidable opponent was America, the reason being that America's discrimination in the acceptance of immigrants from Japan and its treatment of Japanese in America had for more than ten years been a point of contention between the two nations and a continuous source of pain to Japan.

Immigration to America from Asia had begun as a result of a severe labor shortage during the development of the west. Entrepreneurs had welcomed Chinese laborers for the dangerous work of mining and building railroads. As travel abroad was prohibited in Ch'ing China, this "coolie trade" constituted a form of smuggling, and the treatment of immigrants on board ships was no different from that of the Negro slaves. They were assembled by violence, abduction, and enticement, and the voyage from Hong Kong or Amoy to California took more than seventy-five days. On some voyages one out of every five died en route. The work was excruciating, and it was said that a Chinese lay buried under every crosstie of the transcontinental railway.

The diligence and low cost of Chinese laborers, as well as cultural differences, ultimately provoked the wrath of white workers. When in 1882 immigration from China was banned, Japanese workers were sought after as substitutes. Since 1868 Japanese workers had been emigrating to Hawaii, where they worked in the sugar cane fields. In 1900, when America annexed Hawaii, the number of Japanese who moved to the mainland increased and ultimately reached a high of eight thousand per year, including those who came directly from Japan.

In California and Hawaii, anti-Japanese sentiment rose markedly. Leaving aside individual acts of discrimination, the first instance of legal discrimination was the segregated-schooling ordinance passed in San Francisco in October 1906. The Board of Education gave as its reason for excluding Japanese children from public schools the fact that they were "vicious, immoral, of an age and maturity too advanced for safe association with the younger American children."

President Theodore Roosevelt, who was shocked to learn of this, sent a message to Congress in which he argued that for the sake of the development of the Pacific Coast, as well as for humanitarian reasons, it was essential to treat the Japanese equitably, even to the point of granting citizenship to "those races who are ineligible for citizenship." His message was welcomed with enthusiasm in Japan, where it was printed in its entirety in the press. Where the leaders of the western states were concerned, however, it was like talking to a brick wall. Protests from California inundated the president's office. It was clear to the president that racial discrimination in the west had deep roots.

Discrimination against the Japanese on the West Coast was, as with the Chinese, based upon resentment of cheap labor and cultural differences, but with an additional element. As one might expect in a situation that had arisen shortly after the Russo-Japanese War, the anti-Japanese leaders on the coast covertly feared the West Coast would be "occupied" by Japan. Thus, the anti-Japanese movement was both politically motivated and well-organized.

In April of that year, the great San Francisco earthquake occurred, and the Japanese people sent contributions totaling $245,000, more than half the amount collected throughout the world. When immediately thereafter the immigration problem arose, it was hardly surprising that the Japanese felt that America was "ungrateful." The president, an old hand at such matters, while on the one hand firmly rejecting this isolationist law, at the same time negotiated a gentlemen's agreement with the Japanese government to send no more immigrants. In view of the growing tension between Japan and America, he staged a display of America's newly reinforced naval power. The War Department's top secret Orange Plan, formulated with war with Japan in mind, dates from the following year.

Anti-Japanese sentiment in California seemed quenched for the moment, but in 1913 it flared up once again. Japanese immigrants at the time worked mainly in agriculture, and many of them had come to own farms of their own. The state legislature, with the aim of remedying this situation, proposed a bill "prohibiting Japanese from owning real estate and limiting their right to rent land to three years." President Wilson sent his secretary of state to attempt to dissuade the governor of California and the legislature, but with no success. In response to the protest of Japan's Foreign Minister Makino, he was forced to reply that this was "not a racial problem, but a purely economic problem."

In 1917, when America entered the war on the side of the Allies, opinion toward Japan took a favorable turn, and there were those who hoped for some relaxation of the California Alien Land Law. Yet when the war ended and the Paris Peace Conference was held, a new and stronger anti-Japanese bill was suddenly proposed, one that would take away even their right to rent land, virtually strangling them economically.

These were the realities that lay behind Japan's attempt at the peace conference to add a clause abolishing racial discrimination to the Covenant of the League of Nations. Wilson, surprisingly, supported the proposal in principle, adding only the qualification that this be accomplished "as soon and as far as practicable." The strongest opposition came from England.

England's delegate, too, felt that since equality of member nations was the fundamental spirit of the League of Nations, Japan's proposal of a racial-equality clause could hardly be denied. However, he opposed the proposal on account of the rigid opposition of the Commonwealth prime ministers, in particular Australian Prime Minister William M. Hughes. Behind-the-scenes negotiations dragged on from the end of January until April. Makino tried every possible tactic: he repeatedly sought the support and cooperation of English and American delegates; he spoke with Henry W. Steed, the chief correspondent of the *Times*, who alerted public opinion in England through his writings; he attempted to persuade Hughes to reconsider his position. All the British Commonwealth leaders tried to persuade Hughes to change his mind, but Hughes, who feared defeat in domestic elections, threatened to withdraw his delegation and refuse to sign the treaty if Japan's proposal was included in any form whatever. South Africa's Prime Minister Louis Botha told Makino, "Strictly between ourselves, I think he is mad."

Japanese had long been working in northern Australia, planting sugar cane and gathering pearls. The first act of the newly established Commonwealth Council in 1901 was to prohibit the entry of Asians.

The new immigration laws required a dictation test given in a European language, which all but completely excluded immigrants from Japan. On the other hand, illiterate Europeans could be excused from the examination at the discretion of immigration officials. Australia's Attorney General Alfred Deakin said of the law, "If restrictions were to be based on race, we would provoke the antagonism of Japan, as one of the civilized nations of the world, and we would not attain our objective." He then went on to say, "The Japanese are extremely enterprising and energetic, and moreover the standard of living they are accustomed to is low. As competitors they are the most dangerous of the Asians, and we must make every effort to keep them out. In short, we exclude the Japanese not because they are an inferior race, but because they are a superior one."

The committee that was to make the decision concerning Japan's proposal of a clause in the covenant calling for equal treatment of nations was convened on the evening of April 11. Wilson was the chairman and there were sixteen other members. The vote was divided as follows: eleven in favor, i.e., two votes each from Japan, France, and Italy, and one vote each from Greece, China, Serbia, Portugal, and Czechoslovakia; and five opposed, i.e., England, America, Poland, Brazil, and Romania. Makino had been advised in advance that because England was opposed America would join it.

Wilson declared as chairman that "since the committee could not reach a unanimous decision, the proposal cannot be adopted." Makino protested that most matters at the conference had been decided by majority vote and was supported in this by several others. However, Wilson dismissed this objection, saying, "I raised this matter on the understanding that such an important matter required the unanimous agreement of the committee, or that at least there be no opposition."

In this way Japan's racial-equality proposal was defeated. News of Japan's frustration in Paris, as well as the exclusion of the Japanese from the Pacific Coast, was reported in detail in Japan. A succession of protest meetings was held, but their efforts were thwarted by the fact that Japan's delegation in Paris could do nothing as long as England and America opposed them. The only way left open to them was to state clearly Japan's intentions for the future.

At the general session at Versailles Palace, when President Wilson presented the draft of the Covenant of the League of Nations, Makino calmly but earnestly proclaimed:

"In the commission that considered the League covenant, believing equality of member nations to be one of the fundamental principles of the League of Nations, I proposed that the covenant be amended to include the principle of equal and just treatment of the peoples of all member nations, regardless of race or nationality. I am aware that there would be many and varied difficulties in implementing this principle, and I do not imagine that the ideal of equality can be achieved immediately. However, I explained in detail that what we proposed was to define the principle clearly and to leave its execution to the individual governments. In other words, the proposed clause was intended as an invitation to the governments and peoples concerned to examine the question more closely and seriously and to devise in a fair and accommodating spirit means to meet it. However, the proposed amendment was not adopted by the commission." He went on: "I proposed again that a phrase endorsing the principle of equal and just treatment of all nations at least be inserted in the preamble of the covenant, yet, although it received considerable support, this proposal too failed to be adopted on the grounds that the commission did not reach unanimous agreement. If it is to be a principle of the League of Nations that certain peoples are not to be given just and equal treatment, this will strike those peoples as odd, and in the future will undermine their faith in the very principles of justice and equality that are supposed to regulate relations between member nations. We will not, however, press for the adoption of our proposal at this moment. In closing, I feel it is my duty to express the deep regret of the government and people of Japan that the principle of fairness was not adopted, and to declare that we shall continue to make every effort to have it adopted by the League in the future."

The Paris press was unanimous in its sharp criticism of the League of Nations plan. *La Victoire* pointed out that it was "outrageous that although a clause recognizing America's Monroe Doctrine was included, the equal-treatment amendment sought by Japan was rejected." *Le Temps* said, "We are deeply sympathetic with Japan's request, and have no doubt that the day will come when we shall have to honor their very proper claims."

The other matter that concerned Japan at the Paris Peace Conference was its right to the Shantung Peninsula. As soon as Japan had entered the war, it had occupied the concession at Tsingtao and other German strongholds. Japan had reached an understanding with England, America, France, and the other allies that upon sending its troops to war, Japan would succeed to these concessions, which at some later date would be returned to China. However, when the conference opened, the Chinese proposed that they be returned immediately, and circumstances seemed to favor their position. There were historical reasons behind Japan's firm adherence to its own proposal.

Japan first acquired rights in China when, following the Sino-Japanese War, it obtained through its victory a concession in the Liaotung Peninsula, including the harbor city of Port Arthur. However, this provoked a strong reaction from Germany, Russia, and France, who argued that Japan's possession of special rights was a threat to peace in Asia. Japan submitted to their pressure. Yet what so sorely angered the Japanese was not this, but the fact that immediately thereafter these three countries, as "rewards" for their intercession, carved out territories for themselves in China. The Liaotung Peninsula, which Japan had just relinquished, was taken by Russia, while Germany and France took, respectively, the Shantung Peninsula and Kuangchou Bay. This humiliation had left an indelible impression on the minds of all Japanese, from the nation's leaders down to the humble farmer. Ultimately, as a result of its victory in the Russo-Japanese War, Japan had regained part of the Liaotung Peninsula and had taken the South Manchurian Railway, which had been built by Russia. Now, in World War I, it was taking possession of Germany's interests.

If these interests were to be returned to China in the near future—Wilson argued—would it not be as well to relinquish them at the conference itself? But Japan was insistent for reasons of national dignity and interest. There was a feeling among the Japanese that they were being manipulated and meddled with by the larger powers. If these interests had to be returned to China—and returned shortly, at that— Japan felt that there should be direct negotiations with China, and it wanted to hold the winning card in these negotiations.

Relations between Japan and China were extremely complex. Virtually every Japanese felt himself to be in league with the Chinese in their determination to prevent European aggression. To this end the modernization and unification of China were essential. The Sino-Japanese War in no way diminished this desire. In 1900 Japan for the first time joined forces with the Western nations in armed intervention in China; yet even then the idea of cooperation between Japan and China remained a strong current in the ideas and activities of the ordinary citizen. Many Chinese students had come to study in Japan, while many Japanese military men had been involved as advisers in the modernization of China's armed forces. While Japan advanced steadily toward becoming a well-ordered modern nation, China was left behind, as disordered as ever, an insignificant state that fell prey to the European powers. Seeing this, Japan's hopes gave way to irritation, while throughout the nation contempt for the Chinese came to prevail. Japan came to feel that, if it was China's fate to be divided up among the great powers, then Japan, its neighbor, who had defended China against the encroachment of Russia, had a right to its fair share of the spoils.

During World War I, while America's and Europe's attention was diverted from the Far East, Japan confronted China with its Twenty-one Demands. These included conditions so harsh that, if accepted, China would become a virtual colony of Japan. China's pride was wounded, and there developed, first among the students, an anti-Japanese movement. America, on the other hand, grew wary of Japan's ambition, which it saw as an attempt to monopolize the China area.

America, unlike the European powers, held no concessions in China. Being rich in capital, it advocated an open-door policy (open ports and equal opportunity) in China. This policy appeared fair, but from America's point of view it was also exceedingly convenient. It coincided with the interests of China, which at that time was attempting to recover its own rights from the various foreign powers. The pattern of foreign policy whereby China attempted to ward off the other powers by joining forces with America dates from this time.

China's delegate at the peace conference, V. K. Wellington Koo, had studied at Harvard and Columbia universities and had many friends among America's leaders. He was a formidable opponent to the Japanese, who were unskilled at debate in a foreign language. One member of the Japanese delegation, who did not stand out in any way on this occasion but was later to play an important role in history, had just returned from America. This was Matsuoka Yōsuke, son of an unsuccessful merchant family, who at the age of thirteen had gone to California and after long and arduous study had graduated from the University of Oregon. He was now press secretary of the delegation. One evening he had dinner with the editor of the *New York World*, and as the night wore on, he told him: "If the Shantung problem is not settled as Japan proposed, the entire delegation will pull out the next day. Preparations have already been made." This was only a bluff; but Italy had, in fact, just withdrawn its delegation in dissatisfaction with the territorial settlement, so the editor cabled his "scoop" to New York at once, and the story appeared in the Paris newspapers almost immediately thereafter.

In the end, the Shantung problem was settled as Japan wished. To what extent this was due to Matsuoka's bluff is not clear, but the fact that Matsuoka himself felt that he had succeeded was to be of great significance in the future. Japan had never before taken such a stance in its foreign relations. Matsuoka had learned his tactics in America, during his ten years on the West Coast, where discrimination against Orientals was most severe. Over and over again he would say, "In dealing with Americans, when you are in the right, no matter how they intimidate you, you must never give in. If you are struck, you must strike back then and there. If you once submit, you will never be able to raise your head again. Anyone who wants equal treatment must stand up to them and act as an equal."

We shall see how this belief fostered in Matsuoka by personal experience was manifested later—when Matsuoka was Japan's foreign minister—in negotiations with Secretary of State Hull on the eve of the Pacific War.

However, at the Paris Peace Conference, Matsuoka's rank was low, and the role he played was a minor one.

The young Prince Konoe thought Matsuoka an interesting person. Throughout the Paris Peace Conference, Konoe neither attended any meetings nor participated in any of Japan's policy decisions. On one occasion he had borrowed a reporter friend's press card and had looked in on one of the general sessions, but the moment Saionji learned of this he reprimanded him sharply for his imprudent behavior. To Konoe, the conference appeared to be ruled from start to finish by power. As a Paris newspaper had pointed out, the fact that Japan's obviously reasonable proposal for the abolition of racial discrimination was defeated, while the obviously unreasonable Monroe Doctrine was added to the Covenant of the League of Nations, could only be attributed to the difference in strength between Japan and America.

World War I changed the world in two major ways. First, it gave birth to the Soviet Union, the first of the new states to be founded on the principles of communism. At the time, this suggested that armed intervention by the once-powerful Russia would diminish, but eventually the great powers came to fear that the new ideas would infiltrate their own nations and lead to revolution. Japan, although powerful, was nonetheless still unsettled internally by the process of development. As a near neighbor of Russia, it was one of the nations that felt its influence most strongly.

Secondly, there was the rise of America. America had had, until then, little power to influence international politics, but as a result of World War I it had become the richest nation in the world and the financial backer of the European nations. It not only became a formidable military power, but also acquired a powerful voice in world politics. Insofar as America often based policies upon ideals—often, admittedly, to its own advantage—it had a different style of diplomacy from that of the European powers.

Europe and America had divided up the world and grown rich on its abundant resources and population. America, with much of its own vast continent still to develop, had in the name of the Monroe Doctrine barred Japanese immigrants from every country within its sphere of influence except Brazil.

Japan had two possible paths of action before it. It could stand up for justice and humanity, to which end it would have to resign itself to sacrificing its special interests in China. It might even have to run the risk of becoming a weak nation. Or, on the other hand, it could adhere to nineteenth-century principles of power, and, with the greatest caution, make its way in the world as a rival of the great powers.

2

The Manchurian Incident

At daybreak on September 19, 1931, Lieutenant Colonel Imamura Hitoshi, operations section chief in the Army General Staff Headquarters, was awakened from a sound sleep by the jangle of a telephone. Lifting the receiver, he heard the voice of Colonel Umezu Yoshijirō.

"The railway near Mukden was blown up last night and the Kwantung Army seems to have marched. I'm going to my office to confirm the cable. I'll send a car to your place; come as quickly as possible."

Imamura's car arrived shortly, while he was changing into his uniform. The morning was still gray, and throughout the thirty-minute ride to the center of the peacefully sleeping city, he was lost in reverie. "If only this incident can be settled locally, without things getting out of hand," he thought. As he saw it, if Japan tried at this point to solve the "Manchurian problem" by military force, the Western powers would show little understanding. Moreover, it was doubtful whether the Japanese people themselves realized the gravity of the problem. He was concerned that if the incident escalated now, there would be no concerted support from the nation, the army would stand alone against the Western powers' intervention, and Japan would be divided.

The Manchurian question was an old yet ever immediate problem for Japan. Manchuria, once the crown territory of the Ch'ing dynasty and for a long time China's border region, had been left undeveloped. The Russo-Japanese War broke out when Russia occupied Manchuria and attempted to extend its influence into Korea. The Japanese army fought on the plains of Manchuria and, with victory, acquired the Kwantung leased territory at the southern tip of Manchuria together with the South Manchurian Railway. The Kwantung Army was established to protect these.

With the railway as the pivot of a Manchurian development drive, which involved opening mines and starting iron and steel industries, Japan conceived the ambitious plan of separating Manchuria from China proper—where chaos continued to prevail—thus creating a stable Japanese sphere of influence. Since the Chinese revolution of 1911 the army and its auxiliary units had attempted a number of plots, but they all came to nothing. Three years earlier, there had occurred the assassination, by bomb, of Chang Tso-lin. The most powerful warlord in Manchuria, Chang was its de facto ruler. Originally a chieftain of mounted bandits, he was used during the Russo-Japanese War by the chief of staff of the Japanese expeditionary force, Major Tanaka Giichi, to harass the Russian rear guard. Later, in both overt and covert operations, the Japanese army continued to groom Chang as part of a scheme to control Manchuria through him. But when Chang became far too powerful, venturing into China proper and taking part in the struggle for supremacy there, a definite rift developed between him and the Japanese. Among those who time and again advised Chang to pay closer attention to the management of Manchuria was Matsuoka Yōsuke, who after the Paris Peace Conference gave up diplomacy and directed the South Manchurian Railway Company as its vice-president. Chang did not heed this advice. When he was defeated in the power struggle in China proper and tried to retreat to Mukden, his armored railway coach was demolished by an explosion and he was killed. The culprit was a senior staff officer of the Kwantung Army, one Colonel Kōmoto Daisaku. Knowing that Chang could no longer be trusted, the colonel resolved to assassinate him and disguise it as a Chinese conspiracy. When the first news of this incident was brought to Japan, old Prince Saionji remarked to his secretary, "I mustn't say this too loud, but I suspect the army."

The elder statesman's observation was correct. The conspiracy that eliminated Chang raised a storm that would eventually lead to the overthrow of the Japanese cabinet itself. Ironically, the prime minister at this time was none other than General Tanaka, the officer who had once used Chang in Manchuria and now headed the Seiyūkai, one of the two largest political parties.

Imamura had assumed the position of section chief of Operations at

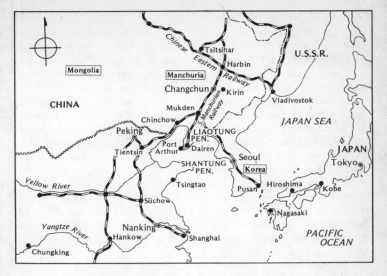

Army General Staff Headquarters less than two months before. When asked to fill this prestigious post, he had at first declined. There was a tangle of complicated political problems in Manchuria and the army had expected that the main theater of war would be there. Because Imamura had served in England and India, he was not familiar with Manchuria. Moreover, though he was confident of his talents as a military strategist, he considered himself incompetent in political matters. He owed the job to the forceful recommendations of many of his senior officers, who were impressed by his ability and sincerity.

Since the spring of that year such headlines as "Manchuria— Japan's Lifeline" had become a frequent feature in the newspapers. Soon after his appointment, Imamura was shown a four- or five-page paper called "A Basic Outline of a Solution to the Manchurian Problem." This plan was compiled by Army Headquarters, and Major General Tatekawa Yoshitsugu, division chief of Operations, was one of those who had drafted it. According to this document, "violation of Japanese interests and anti-Japanese activities in Manchuria, led by Chang Hsüehliang—son of the assassinated Chang Tso-lin—grow fiercer day by day and a time is coming when the situation will have to be dealt with by military force. Yet such a time is at least one year away, and until then, whatever happens, prudence and restraint must be exercised, while we strive to change public opinion and inform the nation fully about the importance of the Manchurian problem."

Imamura had no objections to this policy. Ever since he had been appointed section chief of Operations, tension in Manchuria had grown. An intelligence officer on an inspection tour of Manchuria, Captain Nakamura Shintarō, was killed by the local Chinese troops, and the case was given full coverage in Japanese newspapers. Public sentiment was aroused and the consensus was that China deserved to be chastised. A disturbing rumor even reached the central command that the Kwantung Army would march on its own initiative. To reassert their policy of prudence rather than impetuous action, Major General Tatekawa had left Tokyo for Mukden a few days before. If everything had gone according to plan, he would have arrived at his destination on the afternoon of the previous day. All Imamura could do now was to put his trust in Tatekawa's judgment and leadership.

As soon as he arrived at his office, Imamura went to the room of the man who had telephoned him, Colonel Umezu. Umezu was already there, leafing through a batch of telegrams. He handed those he had already read to Imamura. One said, "South Manchurian Railway blown up north of Mukden. Commander in chief ordered troops out. Securing enemy's barracks and attacking the city of Mukden." This could only mean a full deployment of armed forces.

"Isn't there a telegram from Major General Tatekawa?" asked Imamura impatiently. "Not here," Colonel Umezu replied. "Ask in the telegraph unit." Imamura examined the telegrams scrupulously one by one, but there was not a single piece of news from Tatekawa. Only later did he learn that Tatekawa had arrived in Mukden on schedule. He was met at the station by staff officers of the Kwantung Army and then taken straight to a restaurant. At the welcoming banquet, staff officers plied him with a generous measure of sakè. Late at night, when he had finally collapsed on his bed, the incident broke out.

That night, Consul Morishima Morito was on duty at the Japanese consulate in Mukden. A little after 10 P.M. he received a telephone call informing him that the South Manchurian Railway had been blown up by the Chinese army; Japanese troops were marching, and he was to come to the Army Special Service Agency in Mukden immediately.

When he rushed over to the agency's building near Mukden's railway station, he found a senior staff officer, Colonel Itagaki Seishirō, and his staff working frantically under the harsh light of a lamp. The colonel turned to him and informed him that the army was already marching and that the consul must secure the safety of the Japanese population in the city of Mukden.

About twenty thousand Japanese were living in this central city of southern Manchuria. Most of them had settled on land belonging to the South Manchurian Railway, and only a few lived in the city proper. Moreover, the city center was the stronghold of Chang Hsüeh-liang, whose army was stationed nearby in three sets of barracks.

Consul Morishima challenged the colonel: "Who issued this order?"

"Since this is an emergency," Colonel Itagaki replied, "I gave the order in place of the commander in chief. The commander is in Port Arthur."

"This problem must be settled by diplomatic negotiation," Morishima said. "Impossible," said the colonel, raising his voice. "The army is on the march. This is an act of the Supreme Command. Does the consul intend to obstruct it?"

When Morishima made no reply, the man who stood by his side, a major from the Army Special Service Agency in Mukden by the name of Hanaya Tadashi, suddenly pulled his sword and said threateningly, "There'll be no mercy for those who stand in the way of Supreme Command!"

Morishima by now suspected an army conspiracy, but he merely reported the situation to the consul general and conveyed the order for an emergency evacuation of the Japanese residents of Mukden. Suddenly he heard the boom of artillery through the window.

The Japanese army had opened fire and was attacking Chang's barracks and Mukden city. By this time, Chang, who was in Peking, had already ordered his troops not to resist the attacking Japanese, and the Chinese army was withdrawing without a fight. The Japanese gained control of the city easily, with a minimum of confusion. The commander in chief, General Honjō Shigeru, received the first report at the Port Arthur Command Headquarters, and by dawn of the next day was traveling north, heading for Mukden by train, in the company of staff officer Ishihara and others.

It was this Lieutenant Colonel Ishihara Kanji who had masterminded the Manchurian Incident. His reputation as a brilliant strategist was firmly established throughout the army. After studying for three years in Germany, beginning in 1922, he had conceived the idea of a "last world war," based upon a prophecy that the world's last war would be fought toward the end of this century. The plan was a strange blend of military philosophy, based on his research on Frederick the Great, Napoleon, and World War I, and on his strong faith in the prophecies of the thirteenth-century Japanese priest Nichiren, founder of the Nichiren sect of Buddhism.

The world in which five great powers had emerged as a result of World War I would ultimately be unified, but before lasting peace could be achieved, a last world war might have to be fought. This war would be a struggle for supremacy between the champion of the West, America, and the champion of the East, Japan. Such a war would last only briefly, as the development of decisive weapons and super-long-range planes would make possible the annihilation of the enemy's metropolitan centers in a matter of moments.

In line with his prophecy, Ishihara urged that Japan, in order to maintain its supremacy in Asia in the future, should secure a sphere of influence for itself. His concept depended on the cooperation of Japan, Manchuria, and China. On assuming his post on the staff of the Kwantung Army three years earlier, he had started to study in great detail plans not only for occupying Manchuria but also for the administration of such an occupation.

Ishihara believed that, in view of China's inability to rule itself, a Japanese occupation and Japanese rule of Manchuria would not only bring happiness to its thirty million people but might even accelerate the unification of China proper.

Moreover, the Soviet Union at that time probably would not be able to offer any effective military challenge to a Japanese occupation of Manchuria. The only important opponent could be America, but Ishihara claimed that America, even with the naval power it then had, could not subdue Japan. His senior staff officer, Colonel Itagaki, had deep trust in Ishihara's superior ability as a strategist. The two officers carefully watched the growing unrest in Japan regarding Manchuria, and around midnight of September 18—under Itagaki's leadership—carried out their plan, using the blasting of the railway tracks by in-

Troops leaving for the Manchurian front. At their peak, Japanese forces in Manchuria numbered 700,000 men.

telligence as a pretext. Commander Honjō, who at the time was not fully informed on the real state of affairs, pondered the intentions of Army Headquarters and hesitated to extend the incident. But once troops were on the march and the younger staff officers united under Itagaki and Ishihara, the commander too was swept away by the collective will of his staff. None of them expected that this incident would mark the beginning of an agonizing war for Japan, lasting fifteen long years.

When the cabinet in Tokyo received word of the troops' going into action in Manchuria, its decision was "localization." The war minister and the chief of the General Staff both agreed. But the main body of staff officers was unanimous: this time the Manchurian problem should be solved with no backing out. At this point Imamura too joined their consensus.

The Kwantung Army, of its own accord, was expanding the war. Three days after opening hostilities, on September 21, Japan dispatched troops to occupy the seat of government of Kirin Province, Kirin city, lying 127 kilometers from the railway zone that belonged to the South Manchurian Railway Company. To make up for the resulting shortage of men in patrol units guarding the railway zone, the Kwantung Army asked the neighboring Korean Army (the Japanese army stationed in Korea) for reinforcements; it responded immediately, without waiting for orders from Tokyo. To dispatch troops overseas, imperial sanction was needed, and to go into action without it was a grave violation of the military code.

For several days, the cabinet debated the new situation that had arisen in Manchuria. As before, the prevailing opinion was in favor of localization. The strongest opponent of a military occupation of Manchuria was Foreign Minister Shidehara Kijūrō, the man who had ferreted out the army's conspiracy. He had not only served as ambassador to America but was a faithful follower of the traditional Japanese policy of giving highest priority to cooperation with England and America. Although he would not have objected if Manchuria could be occupied without friction with the Western powers, he concluded that to launch military operations without the acquiescence of England, and above all America, was a dangerous course that jeopardized Japan's very existence.

Both the minister of war and the chief of the General Staff concurred with his opinion. Possibly the Emperor's intentions influenced their thinking too. When Prime Minister Wakatsuki Reijirō first reported the incident to the throne, the Emperor expressed strong approval of the "localization" policy and hoped that the same policy would be maintained henceforth. His words were relayed to the cabinet by the prime minister and had reached at least the upper echelons of the army. The Emperor had no precedent enabling him to veto a decision so long as it had been reported to him according to proper procedure. Nevertheless, to the Japanese people, with their deep feeling of loyalty toward the Emperor, the words of course carried authority, and the matter was thus one that needed to be treated with special caution.

The Kwantung Army was fighting two "enemies." The first was the Chinese army that was stationed throughout Manchuria; but since this lacked the will to resist, real fighting was rare on this front. The second enemy was the one at home—the government, as well as the highest echelons of the army. When the Kwantung Army officers learned that Army Headquarters and the government would not approve their plan to occupy Manchuria, they simply proceeded to their next ploy.

This was a plan to establish a new political regime in Manchuria with the last Ch'ing emperor, Henry Pu-yi, as its figurehead. Henry Pu-yi was at the time residing incognito in the Japanese quarter of Tientsin. This plan to establish a new political regime was also aimed at the influential in Manchuria, particularly the Manchurians. Hsi Chia, a graduate of the Japanese military academy and representative of the government in Kirin Province, responded to the proposal immediately and declared independence for the Kirin provincial government.

The idea of a new political regime shocked the government in Tokyo. Foreign Minister Shidehara in particular raised strong opposition to the proposal, saying it was out of the question and forbidding any Japanese participation in such a plan; unless Japanese troops were withdrawn from Kirin, he would not assume any responsibility for diplomatic negotiations.

After returning to Tokyo from Mukden, Major General Tatekawa reported with some embarrassment, "When I tried to rush out of my lodgings after the affair broke out, one of the staff officers detained me politely—I was, so to speak, under informal arrest, which is why I've come back without accomplishing anything." (Imamura believed this the rest of his life, as he confirms in his memoirs.)

While this may have been true of the evening of the attack on Mukden city, the next day Tatekawa sat relaxed, in close conference with Itagaki and Ishihara. He advised them in a friendly way that their plan for the military occupation of Manchuria was unlikely to be recognized by the upper echelons of the army. Upon returning to Tokyo, he endeavored to secure the approval of the war minister and the chief of the General Staff for the Kwantung Army's action, but he was not successful.

American Secretary of State Henry Stimson kept a close watch on the Japanese army's activities in Manchuria, but since Foreign Minister Shidehara was doing his utmost to restrain the army, Stimson was satisfied that efforts toward localization were under way. At a White House meeting on September 22, he proposed that Japan be made aware of "our surveillance of its activities," and that this be done in such a fashion that Foreign Minister Shidehara's hand would be strengthened in his confrontation with the military. President Herbert Hoover approved his proposal.

In London, a report arrived from Britain's ambassador to Japan, Sir Francis Lindley: "The Chinese are persistently violating Japan's treaty rights; the Japanese army's action in Manchuria may exert a beneficial influence in the protection of Britain's interests." MacDonald's cabinet was just then facing a serious financial crisis and to interfere in the Manchurian problem was judged "totally unwise."

What was Moscow's reaction? The Soviet Union's territory bordered on Manchuria, and it had vested rights in the Chinese Eastern Railway running through Manchurian territory. Two years earlier, China had tried to abolish these rights unilaterally, but when it expelled the Russian employees, trouble had started. An advance unit of the Soviet army crossed the border and invaded Chinese territory, but Foreign Minister Shidehara mediated secretly between the U.S.S.R. and China, and a crisis was averted. It was a military confrontation with the Soviet Union that Ishihara, too, feared most. However, as he had expected, there were no signs that the Soviet Union would embark on aggressive action. The latter could not afford to reduce its strength by fighting the Japanese regular army, although it had power enough to intimidate the weak border troops of China. Moreover, it was too busy building up its own nation.

So for Japan the ultimate battleground was to be Geneva, on the shores of Lake Leman. In the offices of the League of Nations, the council had been in continuous session since September 19, and both Japan and China, who were council members, had set forth their respective claims. China's aim was the evacuation of Japanese troops, to be enforced by the League and carried out under the supervision of observers dispatched by the League. Japan opposed this, in line with Shidehara's instructions that negotiations should be between representatives of the countries directly concerned and that the battle lines of the Japanese army should be shortened insofar as was consistent with the need to secure the safety of life and property of Japanese and other foreign residents of the South Manchurian Railway zone. Contrary to the expectations of Japan's representatives, the council's deliberations developed favorably for the Japanese side. Stimson thought that the proposal to send League observers would weaken Shidehara's position, and restrained England from insisting on it. On the final day of the general assembly, the twenty-ninth, there was a decidedly conciliatory attitude toward Japan in the council. Yet such a mood could continue on one condition only—at some point the Japanese army would have to withdraw.

Having gained time, the government in Tokyo felt greatly relieved. Now as before, its policy was still "localization," but it gave its approval in retrospect to the Kwantung Army's action. At this point, however, the Kwantung Army made a move that amounted to a slap in the face to its own government and to world public opinion. This was the bombing of Chinchow. Having lost Mukden, Chang moved his headquarters to Chinchow, halfway to Peking, and from there resisted the Japanese army.

On October 8, Ishihara and his fellow staff officers sent eleven aircraft to bomb military installations in Chinchow city. The aircraft used were not proper bombers, but reconnaissance planes and captured planes loaded with bombs, and casualties were fairly high among the civilian population. While military results were negligible, the political repercussions were enormous: this show of strength was intended to induce defections among powerful leaders and deal a crushing blow to Chang Hsüeh-liang, who boasted the greatest military force in Manchuria. At the same time, the bombing aroused negative reactions abroad and pushed the Japanese government to the point of no return. This was Ishihara's second great gamble.

The most shocked of all was Secretary Stimson. He called the Japanese ambassador to his office and expressed profound doubts as to whether the Japanese government was in control of its overseas troops at all: was not Foreign Minister Shidehara in effect approving the army's actions? Protests from England, France, Italy, and other countries deluged the Japanese government. Yet the French ambassador added: "Personally, I think China may have to be taught a lesson for once." The Italian ambassador, relatively conciliatory, said,

"If you remove Japanese influence from Manchuria, it will eventually fall under Soviet influence, and that is dangerous for the world." The response of the great powers was based on the logic of imperialism, and the future still held elements of uncertainty.

The council of the League of Nations next met on October 13, and this time deliberations were to Japan's disadvantage. A resolution was introduced calling on the Japanese army to withdraw by November 16. Due to Japanese opposition, this was rejected and the meeting came to an end. Once again Japan had gained time as it stood at the crossroads of its destiny. One way open before it was submission to the opinion of the great powers, which would mean restraining the army and withdrawing from Manchuria. If this were to happen China, triumphant, would suppress Japanese rights and interests further still, probably forcing Japan to give up many of its holdings in the end. The other way would mean taking the risk of fulfilling Japan's old dream of subjugating Manchuria, even at the cost of censure by the great powers.

To say that Lieutenant Colonel Imamura was busy from September 1 would be an understatement. He would usually work in his office until 8 or 9 P.M., frequently staying up all night. Although the main body of staff officers had reached agreement that the Manchurian problem should be settled, they faced continuous trouble with the Kwantung Army. The arbitrary entry of the Korean Army, the bombing of Chinchow, and other such arrogant acts by the Kwantung Army had time and again embarrassed the headquarters staff, making their position very difficult. Even if Japan were to take possession of Manchuria, headquarters wanted to get the Kwantung Army under control and dispose of things in an orderly fashion. To that end, a whole series of orders had been dispatched chiding the Kwantung Army for its excesses —yet all the while headquarters was kept busy clearing up after it. Even among Imamura's subordinates there were sympathizers with the Kwantung Army who tried to obstruct headquarters' control. Such attempts made Imamura's work even more troublesome.

One day in October, as he was having his usual late dinner at home, two captains, strangers, paid him a visit. They reported an important piece of intelligence: plans were under way for a coup d'état, centering on Lieutenant Colonel Hashimoto Kingorō of the Russian Intelligence Section.

While serving as military attaché at the Japanese embassy in Turkey, Lieutenant Colonel Hashimoto became an admirer of Kemal Atatürk and began to advocate the need for a "revolution" in Japan. Founding an association of field-rank officers called the Cherry Blossom Society, he became its leader. He planned a coup d'état for March of the same year, forming a coalition with rightist thinkers and labor-movement activists. The plan, however, was extremely ill thought-out, and the attempt came to nothing. The army hushed up the whole matter, treating it as an internal affair, and the lieutenant colonel received no punishment whatsoever. Now the same Hashimoto was planning another coup d'état.

It was the First World War that had inspired these officers with the urge to "reform." Three Japanese majors who resided in Europe in 1921 gathered one evening in a hotel at Baden-Baden to discuss the reform of the army. In the Great War they had been deeply impressed by the rapid advances in weaponry, changes in strategy, and the concept of total war. They were worried that the Japanese army, if it stayed as it was, would drop to third-rate status. To avoid this, they appealed to their comrades in the officer corps, urging upon them the need to band together to change the ways of thinking of the older upper echelon. As soon as they returned to Japan, they expanded their circle. Among them were Colonel Itagaki, one of the originators of the Manchurian Incident, and the man later to be responsible for the opening of hostilities between Japan and the United States, Lieutenant Colonel Tōjō Hideki.

Before long another group also concerned with reforming the army came into being, with Ishihara and a number of somewhat younger officers at its core. The two groups came to cooperate with each other, their main interest being the "solution of the Manchurian problem." They had long hoped for a powerful state that could accomplish this and an opportunity to accomplish their wish soon presented itself: by the time the Manchurian Incident broke out, their members had reached posts in the Army General Staff Headquarters and the War Ministry, and, with one another's backing, they did all they could to support the Kwantung Army's action. The Cherry Blossom Society, the latest of these groups to be founded, consisted of the youngest officers. They were all influenced by Lieutenant Colonel Hashimoto and their goal was clear: "reconstruction of the national polity."

Japan's military men had a long tradition of avoidance of politics; however, the outlook of these officers was based on a new view of modern warfare as including industrial power and basic resources. What they were aiming for was a "strong Japan." In 1918, Japan had entered on a period of party politics that replaced the institution of the elder statesmen; yet the two conservative parties did little more than vilify each other, seemingly without thought for the country's future. On top of this, a succession of political scandals had shaken the people's trust in politicians. The economy too was faltering; unemployed workers flooded the cities and the farmers experienced extreme poverty and famine. After the Paris Peace Conference the Japanese press had sung the praises of peace, and military men were treated with contempt as useless relics; until recent years they had hardly been able to walk the streets in uniform. Now, though, the times were changing and the soldiers instinctively foresaw that their hour was coming.

When Lieutenant Colonel Imamura received the intelligence that Lieutenant Colonel Hashimoto was plotting another coup d'état, he immediately got a taxi and rushed through the night to Major General Tatekawa's residence.

"I have a report that you're supporting the Hashimoto group. Is it true?" "I thought it worthwhile," Tatekawa replied, "for the younger officers to collect and study a wide range of information in addition to their regular duties; I have, indeed, contributed toward the expenses of the Cherry Blossom Society. But a coup d'état—what a preposterous idea! I'll put an end to it at once."

The next day, Tatekawa called Hashimoto and had a two-hour-long, heated discussion with him. In the end, he persuaded Hashimoto to change his mind. But only a few days later a new urgent report—that Hashimoto's change of mind had been a pretense—reached Imamura. That evening, in the state minister's reception hall at the War Ministry, the vice-minister of war, vice-chief of the General Staff, a group from the army's main officer corps, and the commander of the military police met to confer on countermoves. All present agreed that the ringleaders must be confined at once. The only one who opposed this to the end was Lieutenant General Araki Sadao. It was Araki that the Hashimoto group was planning to make head of a military cabinet. They had not in fact consulted Araki himself, and he had no knowledge of the plot, but he was considered a sympathizer and had gained great popularity among them. He maintained now that before subjecting officers to the ignominy of confinement, every attempt should be made to reason with them. Imamura suggested to him that he might assume an arbitrator's role, and the others agreed. Araki thus went to a restaurant in Tsukiji where the Hashimoto group was meeting and talked to them until late at night. Yet his attempt at arbitration ended in failure, and the ringleaders of the Hashimoto group were put into protective custody.

This incident was later referred to as the "October Plot." The so-called opening of Japan and its modernization had begun with the Meiji Restoration. Yet the men who carried out that restoration were not old men with outmoded ideas but young samurai raising their standard against the older generation. Thus the young soldiers now saw in this a precedent, and tried to justify their own scheme by calling it the "Shōwa Restoration." In fact, though, they plotted to destroy the old establishment without any concrete plans for building a new order in its stead.

Colonel Itagaki of the Kwantung Army and his group now felt that circumstances were developing in their favor. They instigated riots in Tientsin, therefore, and in the subsequent confusion brought Henry Pu-yi into Manchuria. He agreed to the invitation of a secret messenger, Colonel Doihara, who relayed a promise to make him emperor of Manchuria. The rebirth of the Ch'ing dynasty had long been Pu-yi's earnest wish. The Kwantung Army was now supporting warlords hostile to Chang Hsüeh-liang, and, intervening in their internal struggle, occupied Tsitsihar. Simultaneously the administrative governor of the Three Eastern Provinces and the Special District, Chang Ching-hui, severed relations with the Nationalist government and declared the independence of Heilungkiang Province. The seats of government in Manchuria's three eastern provinces, namely, Mukden, Kirin, and Tsitsihar, were now all in the hands of the Kwantung Army.

When Secretary Stimson learned of the occupation of Tsitsihar by the Japanese army, he realized immediately that the Japanese government no longer had any power to control the army and that the objective of the Japanese army was nothing less than the occupation of Manchuria. Although Foreign Minister Shidehara opposed the Kwantung Army's occupation of Tsitsihar and threatened that if this were to happen, the whole Japanese delegation to the League of Nations would have to resign, in actual fact no such thing was done.

Before the League council reassembled in Paris, Shidehara changed his policy dramatically. In his instructions to the Japanese delegate he formulated Japan's position in strong terms. Concerning the evacuation of Japanese troops, he demanded direct negotiations with the Chinese; if the Chinese refused to negotiate, the evacuation would have to wait until local government was stabilized and would then be carried out by Japan at its own discretion. Moreover, in the event of the League's sending observers, their duties should not be restricted to Manchuria but should also include investigation into illegal acts in other parts of China, as well as consideration of whether China was capable of protecting foreigners' lives and property and of putting the treaty into practice. Such conditions of course were an outright insult to China, but the primary concern of the leaders of the League of Nations was the preservation of the organization's own prestige. They avoided matters that might end in idle polemics and focused discussion on how to send an effective commission of inquiry. In the drafting of the plan, Japan's opinions were given full consideration. It looked very much like a Japanese diplomatic victory.

The Kwantung Army was now looking for an opportunity to complete the separation of Manchuria from China proper by seizing control of Chang's stronghold, Chinchow. And army headquarters, which had been giving its recognition, however reluctantly, to a succession of faits accomplis presented by the Kwantung Army, finally agreed to the assault. On December 28, after an operation lasting several days, the Kwantung Army seized the city. Chang's troops retreated in the direction of Peking without a fight. Chang himself feared that if his forces were reduced in a battle with the Japanese army, his status in Peking would be endangered. The Nationalist government in Nanking sent no reinforcements whatsoever to Chang. At that time, Chiang Kai-shek's army was engaged in a great siege operation against the Communist armies along the middle reaches of the Yangtze River. His hands thus being full, he had little interest in the loss of Manchuria, the remote base of Chang Hsüeh-liang.

After the new year, Secretary Stimson published a declaration stating, "Under no circumstances can we condone an alteration of present conditions by military force." He was hoping for European support in this, but the response of the major powers, including England, was cool. They preferred to place their own hopes in Japan's open-door policy, namely, the Japanese government's declaration that foreign participation in Manchurian enterprise would be welcomed. Even Chinese newspapers were cool toward Stimson's note. One paper stated: "A proclamation of this kind was needed at the time of Japan's initial aggression in Manchuria. Now it is like locking the door long after the thief has disappeared with the jewels."

What, one wonders, were the reasons for such a dramatic change of heart in Foreign Minister Shidehara, the one-time champion of the traditional Japanese diplomatic policy of cooperation with England and America? The chief reason almost certainly lay in a change in Japanese public opinion.

Around 1931, when the Kwantung Army provoked the Manchurian Incident, circulation of the four largest Japanese dailies had grown to more than a million copies, giving them a virtually complete monopoly of the news. In the editorials of these papers, the liberalism and internationalism of the twenties was still in evidence, but their arguments had lost much of their persuasiveness; by now, it was sensational reporting, rather, that swayed the public. As soon as the Manchurian Incident flared up, the news agencies all sent their top correspondents and cameramen into Manchuria, vying with one another to secure full coverage of the incident. The Kwantung Army's conspiracy was ignored, and newspapers were filled with stories of how "Japanese soldiers fought gallantly to defend themselves against the unjust aggression of savage Chinese troops."

The papers had long attacked what they saw as Shidehara's spineless foreign policy in the Manchurian crisis. From the very start, the activities of the Ishihara-Itagaki team had appealed to the spirit of the times; and with the execution of their brilliantly conceived plan, they won overwhelming popular support from the nation.

Moreover, the psychological impact of the October Plot on Shidehara cannot be overlooked. He continued to feel that the growing trend to expansionism should be restrained in every way possible, yet at the same time he could not help fearing that if public opinion were

The Lytton Commission visiting command headquarters of the Kwantung Army in Mukden in April 1932.

too much suppressed, emotions concerning China might flare up on the home front and destroy the whole political system.

To divert world attention from the Manchurian question, Itagaki plotted another incident in Shanghai. In that city, anti-Japanese protest campaigns among the people, and particularly the students, were reaching a peak. Japanese residents were resisting and trouble was rife. On Itagaki's orders, a military attaché at the embassy organized a show of force, which in turn led to popular riots, during one of which a Japanese priest was killed. Japanese marines opened fire on the Chinese soldiers and as the fighting grew fiercer, the army was called in.

European attention now focused on Shanghai with an intensity never devoted to Manchuria. Britain and France had complex vested interests in Shanghai, in defense of which they had many times dispatched their warships. Major Tatsumi Eiichi, military attaché at the Japanese embassy in London, was summoned to the War Office almost every day. On a wall there, he noticed a map showing the position of Chinese forces in minute detail, so he committed the information to memory and cabled it to Japan. Britain was doubtless hoping that the Japanese army would strike a swift blow against the Chinese forces, so that British interests would remain unharmed. In contrast with the units of the Manchurian warlords, the Chinese army at Shanghai put up a sturdy resistance. Reinforced, the Japanese army finally crushed Chinese forces in a fierce battle and immediately announced a unilateral cease-fire.

On February 29, the Earl of Lytton, who had been appointed head of the League of Nations' commission of inquiry, arrived in Tokyo via the United States. It was there that he heard the news of the founding of a new Manchurian state, Manchukuo, with Henry Pu-yi as its sovereign. And there Lytton was unwilling witness to one of the outrages that were to disrupt Japanese society, the assassination by terrorists of the leader of the Mitsui zaibatsu, Baron Dan Takuma.

From Japan the Lytton Commission went on to China, and in Shanghai Lytton met Diet member Matsuoka Yōsuke, who had been asked for his opinion on how the Manchurian problem might be solved so as to meet Japan's legal demands while preserving China's dignity. Matsuoka had first heard the news of the Manchurian Incident just as he was reading the proofs of his own book on the situation. He had thrown down his pen in disgust. It was precisely to prevent this sort of thing that he had started writing, but once actual fighting had started, there was no room for diplomacy.

Yet in the space of a few months the situation had changed again. Now that a new state had been proclaimed in Manchuria, Matsuoka had come to believe that "solutions by a third party" were no solution at all. When he met Lytton, he cited Chiang Kai-shek's ineffectiveness and the League of Nations' silence concerning Russia's partition of Outer Mongolia and establishment of a pro-Soviet regime there; had Japan lost courage and withdrawn from Manchuria, he stressed, Russia would almost certainly have taken its place. "Japan is acting in order to maintain peace in East Asia, but, unlike the European countries, it has no supporters or allies in the League of Nations who understand its methods. Japan wishes to stand by the League to the last; but if Japanese security and the preservation of peace in Asia are judged to be in danger, then serious thought may have to be given to withdrawal from the League."

3

The May 15 and
February 26 Incidents

On May 14, 1932, about two months after the founding of Manchukuo, the world-famous comedian Charlie Chaplin landed in the port of Kobe. The next day, he moved on to Tokyo by express train, accompanied by a throng of reporters. The papers were full of articles welcoming him, and Chaplin responded: "The Japanese are the hardest working people in the world and I respect them for it."

It was Sunday, and Tokyo lay under a bright, sunny sky. That afternoon, Prime Minister Inukai Tsuyoshi, relaxing in the Japanese room of his official residence in downtown Tokyo, was reading the evening edition of the newspaper. He had succeeded Prime Minister Wakatsuki toward the end of the previous year. A former journalist, he was on friendly terms with the Chinese revolutionary Sun Yat-sen and was also known for having assisted the Filipino champion of independence, General Emilio Aguinaldo. At seventy-six, he stood out among the politicians of his time as an elder statesman of the highest integrity.

At about 5:30, two taxis suddenly pulled up in front of the residence. In the cars was a party of naval officers and army cadets. Evading the eye of security, the group, led by the naval officers, forced its way inside, heading for the prime minister's room. The prime minister now sat behind a table, surrounded by military men. Riveting his eyes upon them, he opened the lid of a cigarette box, and offered it around without a word. Not one of the officers put out a hand. Inukai then addressed the intruders: "Won't you at least remove your boots?"

"You needn't worry about our boots. You know what's happening," shouted the leader, Lieutenant Mikami Taku, in an excited voice, aiming his pistol. "If you have any last words, let's have it quick."

Inukai calmly retorted, "There's no need to get excited. If we talk this over, we can come to an understanding."

His tranquillity made a strong impression on Lieutenant Mikami and he lowered his pistol, but another lieutenant shouted angrily, "No discussions, shoot, shoot!"

The prime minister raised his hand as though to calm the attacker. At this point a young second lieutenant who had just burst into the room suddenly pulled the trigger. Lieutenant Mikami also fired a shot. The prime minister collapsed face down on the table.

Inukai breathed his last that night. To the last moment he kept repeating in his delirium, "If only we could have talked . . ." At the subsequent trial, the criminals stated that they had had no personal motive for killing Inukai—on the contrary, they thought him an outstanding politician. Their reasoning was that he had to be eliminated because he was the head of a corrupt political party. At the same time, the group had attacked the Keeper of the Privy Seal, Count Makino—one of the plenipotentiaries at the earlier Paris Peace Conference—as well as party headquarters, the Metropolitan Police Office, and the electrical transformer stations; but except for the prime minister's assassination, all the attacks ended in failure. By creating confusion in the capital, which would be followed by a declaration of martial law by the army, the plotters had hoped to create an occasion for establishing a reformist military cabinet. Their object was the destruction of the status quo; what followed, they hoped, could be left to the top echelons of the army.

Their leaflets, disseminated in the vicinity of the Metropolitan Police Office, made the following appeal: "People of Japan! The time has come to take a look squarely at our fatherland! Look at politics, foreign policy, the economy, education, ideas, military matters—where is the true imperial Japan to be seen? The political parties, blinded by their own interests, conspire with the zaibatsu to squeeze sweat and blood out of the common people, while the bureaucrat defends them and oppresses the people; our foreign policy is spineless, our education decadent, our military corrupt, our ideas are perverted, our working class and farmers suffer in direst distress, and vain speeches are made all the while! Japan is on the verge of dying in a cesspool of depravity. Fellow citizens, to arms! In the name of the Emperor, slay the evil courtiers! Kill the enemies of the people—the parties and the zaibatsu! Wipe out the privileged classes! Farmers, workers, people of our country! Defend your Japanese fatherland! Build a healthier new Japan! To reconstruct, first destroy! Demolish the present abominable system totally!"

War Minister Araki, who was in Kamakura that day, rushed to his official residence just as he was, in civilian clothes. Activists of the officer corps and members of the Cherry Blossom Society rushed there too, all in high spirits, and demanded that this opportunity be seized, that martial law be declared in Tokyo and a military cabinet organized at once. Araki paid no attention to them but went to pay a condolence call at the nearby prime minister's residence. Although relieved that the ringleaders of the plot were naval officers, he felt responsible for the army men among them, mere cadets though they were, and thought it might be best to offer his resignation. Araki's confidant, Major General Obata Binshirō, spoke to the young officers on his behalf. "What a pity," he said with an anguished expression, "that military men had to cause this incident just when we were doing our best to put forward a plan for government reform." Obata was one of the three Japanese majors who had met at Baden-Baden in 1921 to discuss army reform.

For regular military men to attack and assassinate a prime minister was something unheard of. The army leadership feared criticism of the army just when, having conducted a successful operation in Manchuria, it was steadily gaining popular support. Yet even the criticism of the newspapers was weak in the extreme. While pointing out that the culprits were denying parliamentary politics, and that there was a touch of fascism in their reaction against political parties, they asserted that "the parties are preoccupied with their own interests and strategems, and it is abundantly clear to any observer how little thought they give to the country; there is no one who feels that matters should be left as they are."

The army chiefs, guessing where the wind of public opinion was blowing, gradually ceased to hide their sympathy for the perpetrators of the crime. War Minister Araki—who, of course, remained in office—announced: "When I consider why these naive youths acted as they did, I cannot hold back my tears. They did not seek fame or advantage. What they did, they did in the genuine belief that it would be for the good of the empire." The navy minister followed with: "We will have to give much solemn thought to what might have caused these naive young men to commit such an error." The punishments meted out by the court-martial were likewise extremely light. There was not a single death penalty, and the prison sentences were commuted one by one in the name of clemency, a clear reflection of the fact that public opinion was on the side of the culprits.

The year of this incident, 1932, was the seventh since Crown Prince Hirohito had acceded to the throne and the era of Shōwa had begun. No sooner had the Shōwa era begun than all manner of hardships befell Japan. In 1927, there was a panic in the financial world; many banks failed, and the Suzuki Company—matching Mitsui and Mitsubishi in size—declared bankruptcy. Before these wounds could heal, the great world depression that had started with the Wall Street crash engulfed Japan. Wages were cut by 20 to 30 percent and record numbers of workers were left unemployed. The peak of the depression came in 1930, just one year before the outbreak of the Manchurian Incident, when the number of unemployed reached four million.

At that time, the city workers still had strong ties with their families in rural areas, and men and women who were out of work sought to avoid starvation by returning to their native places. Minister for Home Affairs Adachi Kenzō remarked that the people who returned to their villages to help with farm work did not count as unemployed, and boasted that "thanks to the oriental-style family system, the depression's impact on Japan is light. To provide unemployment benefits would only create idlers, and such an evil must be avoided."

Nevertheless, the depression was a crushing blow to the rural areas as well. The price of raw silk dropped suddenly and the price of rice, the chief farm product, fell to one-half its production cost. Many farmers had incurred debts, and in order to pay them off were selling their daughters into prostitution. Moreover, in 1931 the northern area was stricken by exceptionally poor harvests, and farmers already barely making a living now faced starvation.

The political parties had failed to enact an effective economic policy. Furthermore, politicians were constantly exposing scandals involving their political opponents; from 1927 to 1931 hardly a day passed that the newspapers did not contain some story of corruption. The words "political party," as the leaflets of the May 15 conspirators showed, came to be used as a synonym for corruption. In order to survive the depression, the great zaibatsu firms—Mitsui, Mitsubishi, and Sumitomo—organized cartels, and while workers and farmers were living in dismal conditions, they alone seemed to thrive, amassing even more wealth than ever.

A desire for change, acute discontent on a large scale—a belief, in short, that until the political parties and the zaibatsu were crushed and a new, truly fair and just government was installed, there could be no relief for the people—was widespread throughout Japan. Those who attempted to respond to this discontent with action were the civilian left and right, together with the radical elements among the military.

With the advent of universal suffrage in 1928, the government had thoroughly suppressed the Communist party and its sympathizers, practically annihilating the leftist movement. As in Italy and Germany, where the fear of communism gave birth to fascism, in Japan too rightist terrorism broke out, as radical factions in the army gradually made their appearance.

There was a reason that the first terrorist acts by military men were carried out by naval officers. It was directly related to the fact that after the First World War, America had assumed the role of world leader. A year after the Paris Peace Conference ended, Japan sought a renewal of its alliance with England and began the necessary negotiations. The continuation of this alliance was earnestly desired by Japan, and England itself was not opposed to it. But America's President Wilson worked to persuade England to end the alliance, which eventually it did. In an attempt to create a friendly atmosphere, Japan dispatched Hirohito, crown prince at the time, to England, but the visit brought no positive results. Blood proved thicker than water —there was no room for Japan to join in the new Anglo-American honeymoon.

In 1921, on American initiative, the Naval Reduction Conference was held in Washington. At this conference, it was agreed to set the ratio of American, British, and Japanese capital ships at 5:5:3. Japan was demanding a ratio of 10:10:7 but was forced to concede to the Anglo-American alliance. The agreement also stipulated that for the sake of peace in the Pacific area, zones with "limited-defense" installations were to be established. America was to designate the Philippines, Guam, and Wake Island, in return for which Japan was to treat various of its home islands as "limited-defense zones," including the

Okinawas and the Ogasawaras. Hawaii was exempt. That Japan had to place parts of its homeland under restriction, while America was free to reinforce its defenses within its dominion, was an extremely unfair arrangement that could not but irritate Japanese public opinion. But Japanese naval authorities countered internal opposition by arguing that purely from the point of view of defense such a concession was not necessarily a disadvantage, and signed the treaty.

At the 1930 London Naval Conference the ratio of the navy's auxiliary craft was determined. Here, too, Japanese demands were refused. The Navy General Staff, which was in charge of naval operations, resisted the treaty until the last moment. The government that signed it placed itself, ironically, in the line of fire: before turning the muzzles of their guns across the ocean, the young men of the navy would first turn them against their own government.

Inukai's death left in its wake a perplexing question: who to choose as the next prime minister? According to the Constitution, Japan was ruled by the emperor, but in reality it was the custom for the emperor to order a candidate recommended by the elder statesmen to form a cabinet. During the Meiji regime such a candidate would be decided upon at a conference of the elder statesmen, but since around 1918, along with the development of political parties, it had become the custom for the head of the majority party automatically to be recommended by the elder statesmen. Thus after Inukai's unexpected demise it was generally understood that the next prime minister would be Suzuki Kisaburō, who had succeeded Inukai as president of the party. The newspapers, on the same assumption, put forward likely lists of new cabinet ministers. The qualifications of those elder statesmen who were to recommend the candidate for prime minister had never been expressly defined by law. By this time the only survivor from the Meiji era whose qualifications as elder statesman were recognized was the eighty-two-year-old Prince Saionji. From his retreat on the warm coast of the Pacific, the prince watched with deep anxiety as Japan gradually fell into the grip of xenophobia.

He had hoped to retire from political life that spring—he was getting too old to concern himself with politics. Yet such an indispensable man as he could not but give in to those around him who urged him to stay active.

When Saionji received the Emperor's summons at his villa and finally appeared in Tokyo, he met with important men of power in all fields of Japanese politics, including Prince Konoe and War Minister Araki, listening to their opinions and turning them over in his own mind before making a recommendation. In the meantime, the staff officers of the War Ministry and the Army General Staff Headquarters were neglecting their principal duties, spending their time instead on grandiose talk of their absolute opposition to a cabinet drawn from the parties. This was reported on the front pages of the newspapers in extra-large type and exerted a strong influence on the public mood. After careful consideration, Saionji settled on Admiral Saitō Makoto, then on the reserve list. Although seventy-three years old, Saitō was much more liberal than the army generals—that and his personal integrity were reasons enough to recommend him. The party politicians, regardless of which faction they belonged to, gave him their unified support and a coalition government was formed. This amounted to recognizing the existing situation as an emergency. The army was satisfied for the time being, and the politicians, who had opposed a military cabinet, were relieved that their positions would not all be occupied by new people.

In this way the immediate political crisis was weathered, but the parties were not to recover their political initiative until the very end of World War II. Despite the fact that they had supplied the assassins of a prime minister—or perhaps precisely because they had—the army and the navy had made the important first step toward manipulating the government as they wished.

The most urgent international issues facing the Saitō cabinet were recognition of the newly established state of Manchukuo and a suitable response to the League of Nations conference in Geneva that was to discuss the Lytton Report.

An overwhelming majority of the Japanese people had already come to support the founding of Manchukuo. The parties were urging the government to recognize the new state as soon as possible. From a strategic point of view, some in the Foreign Ministry felt it would be better to postpone recognition until the Geneva meeting, but this view was swept aside by the torrent of public opinion. The Lytton Report did not recognize the Japanese army's action in Manchuria as self-defense. At the same time, it deemed a return to the conditions existing prior to September 18 of the previous year impossible and proposed an international administration of Manchuria. Most Japanese, however, including liberal intellectuals, did not trust an administration by the League of Nations in Asia. Old memories of Germany, France, and Russia meddling in Japanese affairs were revived as Japan tragically resigned itself to preparing for a state of "national emergency."

Matsuoka Yōsuke was selected as Japan's ambassador plenipotentiary to the special session of the General Assembly of the League of Nations. As a politician, he was a direct rival of Shidehara, the advocate of international cooperation; and his seven years of experience with the South Manchurian Railway also counted in his favor. It was hoped that he would state Japan's position in positive terms. Although criticism by the great powers was anticipated, the Japanese government did not, at the outset, intend to withdraw from the League. Just before leaving Japan, Matsuoka visited elder statesman Prince Saionji at his retreat and was told: "Whatever happens, I won't let the government withdraw from the League." Matsuoka concurred: "Under no circumstances will we leave the League."

The Matsuoka party left Tokyo by train on October 21 and arrived in Moscow via Siberia on November 3, receiving a warm welcome from the Soviet government. The Soviet Union had not yet been allowed to join the League of Nations and was intent on restoring friendly relations with the Western powers. Quite unexpectedly, Foreign Minister Maksim M. Litvinov proposed a nonaggression pact to Matsuoka. Preparations for such a pact did not proceed this time, and Matsuoka would have to wait another nine years before he signed, as Japan's foreign minister, the dramatic Russo-Japanese Neutrality Pact with Stalin.

Among the Japanese delegates were two adjutants, both army officers. One was Lieutenant General Tatekawa, the other Colonel Ishihara. After the military success in Manchuria, Ishihara had accepted personal responsibility for the serious violation of the martial code committed when the Kwantung Army first marched, and he had seriously considered resigning his military post. Yet when his colleagues complained that his resignation would involve not only many of his comrades in arms but the commander in chief, Honjō, himself, his determination was blunted. Although he was transferred to a less demanding post, he became a famous figure in the international military community—which was why the government had decided to send him to Geneva. In Moscow, Ishihara met with the chief of the General Staff, Aleksandr I. Egorov, and during his short stay in London he saw many British officers, thus satisfying their curiosity. But in Geneva, his turn was not to come.

At the League of Nations council meeting convened in November, the Chinese ambassador plenipotentiary, Wellington Koo, and Japan's Matsuoka crossed swords. Matsuoka had known Koo by sight since the time of the Paris Peace Conference, and he was still sufficiently relaxed to greet the speech by the other attacking his own position with a handshake and a "Nice speech, congratulations!" But that was at a time when the entire floor of the general assembly could applaud his fervent claims, "The whole world is trying to crucify Japan." The present situation was more severe.

The transactions behind the scenes dragged on through the new year and into February, but the Lytton Commission's proposal that Manchuria be put under international administration remained firm. Matsuoka requested instructions from home, saying, "There no longer remains any other way to uphold Japan's honor than to withdraw from the League of Nations."

The order to withdraw from the League of Nations reached Geneva on February 20. That evening, Matsuoka invited Colonel Ishihara to a restaurant called Sicily, where they had a Japanese dinner. Although Matsuoka's options were limited from the very beginning, he had done his utmost to achieve a solution that would accord with Japan's demands. Time and again he had delivered earnest speeches in his American English; toward the end he was hoping for a miracle. Of course, a miracle never came. "The decision to withdraw must please you military men," Matsuoka said to his companion, but Ishihara had nothing to say.

In the last general assembly, Matsuoka spoke to the following effect: "The administration of Manchuria by the League of Nations will be but another name for the continuation of the aggression of the major powers that has gone on in China since the nineteenth century. What justification is there for such an attempt on the part of the League of Nations? I cannot see any. Would the American people agree to such control over the Panama Canal Zone? Would the British people permit it over Egypt?"

The vote on the council's proposal was 42 to 1, Japan's being the only vote against. In a League of Nations composed almost entirely of European, South American, and British Commonwealth countries, this result was only to be expected. One country, Siam, abstained from voting.

Finally Matsuoka took the platform again and declared, "The Japanese government now finds itself compelled to conclude that Japan and the other members of the League entertain different views on the manner of achieving peace in the Far East."

Ambassador Matsuoka left the platform and headed straight for the door. The twenty members of the Japanese delegation rose from their seats and followed him. In this way Japan, like America and the Soviet Union, chose to walk alone, outside the organizational structure of the League of Nations. America, with its wealth, its natural resources, and its military power, as well as its Anglo-Saxon blood ties, was able to exert ample influence on world affairs without being in the League. But what did the future hold for Japan, which was well enough equipped militarily, but was still a poor nation, small in land area, with meager resources and not one powerful ally in the world?

Matsuoka did not return directly to Japan from Geneva. Stopping in Rome, he met with Benito Mussolini; and in London he was jeered at by crowds as a "thief." Then he crossed once again to America and met the youthful Franklin Roosevelt, who had just won a landslide victory in the presidential election. The two men were to cross swords eight years later in crucial negotiations that would determine whether there would be war or peace.

Matsuoka also made a brief stop in Portland, where he had lived as a young man. The local newspapers announced the visitor as the "most eminent graduate of the University of Oregon, our greatest alumnus." But the purpose of his call in Portland was a visit to the grave of a Mrs. Beveridge, who had taken care of him in his youth. Matsuoka loved and respected this devout Christian lady of Scottish origin as much as his own mother. The Beveridge family had fallen upon hard times soon after Matsuoka's return to Japan, and it was not even certain where her grave was. Matsuoka had a new tombstone erected in the cemetery and a Japanese cherry tree planted beside it. The following lines were engraved in the stone: "To the memory of Isabelle Dunbar Beveridge raised by the loving hands of Yosuke Matsuoka in token of the lasting gratitude for the sympathy and gentle kindness of a woman who next to his mother shaped his mind and character. April 9, 1933."

Matsuoka also gave public talks to Japanese-Americans in Spokane, Washington, and Hawaii, in which he spoke of the "collapse of European civilization and the advent of the Pacific Era." His point was that this new era must be brought about by a fusion of Eastern and Western cultures in Japan and in America. "You of the second generation have Japanese blood, but there's no need for you to be good Japanese. Rather, be good Americans!" Matsuoka urged in his speeches. The Nisei remembered these words well after the opening of hostilities between the U.S. and Japan, especially the soldiers in the Nisei units who volunteered to fight for America.

Matsuoka's detour through America on his way home was not a mere sentimental journey. He regretted that he had failed in the task of attaining his country's aims through diplomatic negotiations. At the same time, he was worried about what sort of reception the Japanese nation would give him as its plenipotentiary representative. Since the Russo-Japanese war it had often been the fate of Japanese diplomats returning home from important international conferences to be welcomed by rock-throwing crowds; Japan's gains at the negotiating table had always been small relative to people's expectations. This had been so even after victory in war. Matsuoka's fears were by no means groundless.

Yet when he landed in Yokohama on April 27, the Japanese people welcomed him as if he were a victorious general. Matsuoka disappointed the jubilant journalists by again emphasizing the need for international cooperation. Even so the people welcomed Matsuoka as a hero, the man who for the first time had defended Japan's position at the League of Nations with firmness and dignity.

Exactly three years after Japan's withdrawal from the League, in the early dawn of February 26, 1936, an incident of grave importance occurred in Tokyo. There had been a heavy snowfall the day before and the streets of the capital still lay under a blanket of white. Early in the morning, fourteen hundred troops, led by twenty-two young officers, trudged through the snow on their way to occupy the whole of the Nagata-cho governmental district including the prime minister's official residence and the War Ministry, and to attack the prime minister, the minister of finance, and many other key figures.

This time the ringleaders were not the elite officers of Army Headquarters who had failed in one coup attempt after another, but officers in command of units. From their enlisted men, they had gained a first-hand knowledge of the misery in rural areas and felt resentment against the entire political establishment, including the "corrupted" military. They felt that as long as this kind of government continued, they could not with a quiet mind stand in the front line of the country's defense and sacrifice their lives for it.

Passing through the rebels' strict sentry line, War Minister Kawashima Yoshiyuki and his suite entered the occupied War Office. He conducted the first negotiations in the audience hall, surrounded by the officers of the insurrection. Their first demand was an abstract one: that the right of their mission be recognized. But at the same time they insisted on the following condition: General Mazaki Jinzaburō must form a "Reformed Cabinet." The war minister, still bemused by the gravity of this unexpected incident, could not find an answer.

In the meantime, Colonel Ishihara Kanji, now section chief of Operations in the Army General Staff Headquarters, had entered the room. A keen-eyed man among the rebels, Lieutenant Kurihara Yasuhide, noticed him and approached him. "Colonel, isn't your thinking basically different from ours?" he asked sharply. "How do you feel about the Shōwa Restoration?" The young officers were extremely critical of the headquarters elite, referring to them as "staff fascists."

"I don't understand what you're up to," Ishihara answered bluntly. "It seems to me that if Japan arms itself, that in itself is a restoration. There's no need to create an incident."

Lieutenant Kurihara's hand dropped to the pistol on his belt as he hesitated, wondering whether or not to shoot the other man. At this point, Major General Saitō Kiyoshi—the well-known patriotic poet and a sympathizer with the rebels' cause—entered the argument.

"Well, Ishihara, what would *you* do now?"

"Persuade them to withdraw," Ishihara snapped, as bluntly as before. "And if they don't listen, raise the colors and wipe them out."

"Why, you bastard!" A second lieutenant who had been watching the negotiations with the war minister approached Ishihara with drawn sword. Voices came from behind: "Cut him down."

Captain Yamaguchi Taichirō, who had been talking to the war minister, took in the situation and rushed between them.

"Colonel Ishihara, let's talk this over in another room," he said, leading his old friend out into the corridor. "These people are in a mood to kill . . . but you shouldn't have said that either."

"Shouldn't I?" said Ishihara, calmly entering the next room. Then he went out, alone, through the sentry line.

As he was leaving, a car approached the sentry line. It brought General Mazaki. One of the rebel lookouts, a Lieutenant Isobe Asaichi, greeted the general, almost dancing for joy.

"Your Excellency, we've done it at last!"

"I know how you must feel," the general replied with a tense expression.

"We're hoping for your help now, sir."

"Yes, yes."

It was with just such understanding and fatherly vagueness that the general had long listened to the fiery words of the young officers who so resented the corruption of politics and the army itself. Yet he had never pledged his support for any specific plan of action. Entering the audience hall, the general spotted War Minister Kawashima and started berating him loudly: "What are you hanging around here for? You're the one responsible for this. Get off to the Court!"

Apart from the rebel troops, the first to learn of the dawn incident was General Honjō, commander in chief of the Kwantung Army at the time of the Manchurian crisis and now chief aide-de-camp, the Emperor's highest-ranking adviser on military matters. At five o'clock in the morning he had received a phone call reporting the incident from his son-in-law, Captain Yamaguchi. Although the captain was a member of the rebel army, he did not take part in the action, but conducted the negotiations that followed.

General Honjō had his first audience with the Emperor at six in the morning. Three hours later, the war minister arrived. After elaborating tediously on the state of affairs, he declared that the next cabinet must be a strong body that could bring stability to people's lives and build up Japan's military defenses. The Emperor, who had been listening to the minister's exposé with growing irritation and displeasure,

Rebel troops listening to an address by their commander, Lieutenant Kurihara Yasuhide, after occupying the prime minister's official residence.

interrupted him: "You don't need to tell us that. Isn't it rather your duty to determine by what means this rebellion will be quelled?"

The minister was thunderstruck. He had been deeply impressed by the ferocity of the officers who led the uprising—was not at all sure, in fact, that he could dismiss them simply as "rebels." He looked up at the Emperor and mumbled, "I humbly beg your pardon," then lowered his head and hastily retreated from the imperial presence.

Although the Emperor occupied the supreme position in both the government and the military, he could not, according to custom, make decisions or issue orders without a recommendation to the throne from the proper governmental organization. This was how the elder statesmen, particularly Saionji, had educated the Emperor, and he himself observed the rules strictly. However, many of the key figures who would normally have been consulted in this case had been assassinated—only later did it become clear that the prime minister's life had been saved by his brother-in-law, who took his place—and the government organs that should have been serving this function were momentarily paralyzed. For the first time, the Emperor took initiative, deemed the insurrectionist troops a rebel army and issued a resolute order to suppress them. Supported by the Emperor's firm determination, the government gradually recovered from its initial shock and confusion. At dawn the next day martial law was declared. The rebel army, occupying central Tokyo, formally fell under the same command as the troops enforcing the martial law and consequently received food supplies from them—a somewhat anomalous situation. But the army, fearing a clash, tried not to antagonize the rebels in any way. Thus, for a time the rebel army believed they had achieved a "victory." But the government troops, tightening their encircling net bit by bit, first ordered them to return to their units, then finally demanded that they surrender. Seventy-five hours after the incident began, the officers of the rebel army had at last returned their men to the units, while they themselves had either committed suicide or chosen the alternative of arrest and appeal through the courts.

An insurrection of this sort could hardly have been caused by simple outrage against the government and society. For loyal officers to lead their troops in rebellion required a philosophical foundation to support their resolve. The man who supplied these ideas was a thinker by the name of Kita Ikki.

Born in 1883, Kita had begun as a socialist and when he was only twenty-three offered a glimpse of his genius in a major work called *Pure Socialism*, which was immediately banned. He participated in the Chinese Revolution, and in 1919, the year of the Paris Conference, wrote in Shanghai *An Outline of a Proposal to Reconstruct Japan*. This book too was banned, but it became the secret bible of young army men. Its message was, in one word, absolute equality under the emperor, and basic reform of the Japanese establishment that would include the freeing of farm land and wide-ranging restrictions on private property. Kita's egalitarianism applied even to international relations: he called for the preservation of Chinese integrity and sneered at the way the Japanese government insisted on its interests on the Shantung Peninsula. Rather than taking Tsingtao, he argued, take away Hong Kong from England; instead of colonizing Manchuria, the Japanese should set their sights on Australia. These bold and inspiring declarations exerted a strange fascination on young men's minds.

The army suppressed the rebellion but saw no need to treat the ringleaders with leniency as in the May 15 Incident. The court-martial was held in closed session and lasted only a short time. Within half a year thirteen commissioned officers, two former officers, and two civilians were sentenced to death. One of the latter, the philosopher Kita, who took no part in the planning of the rebellion, was arrested as an influential and extremely dangerous person. He went before the firing squad one and a half years after the incident, on a sultry summer day. A certain Lieutenant Nishida Mitsugu who, along with Kita, sat blindfolded against a stake, turned to Kita and said, "Let's give three cheers for the Emperor."

Pausing for a moment, Kita replied, "I'd rather not."

Almost immediately after this exchange, the report of the guns rang out.

It was, once again, the army that profited most from this incident. Men like Araki and Mazaki were forced to retire, and the reins of power were grasped by the hotheaded staff officers—those whom the leaders of the rebel units had called the "staff fascists." Representing these men, Lieutenant Colonel Mutō Akira muscled his way into the building where a new cabinet was being organized and applied pressure not only in the selection of its members, but in the policies it would pursue as well. Thus Japan entered on that perilous road that led toward a semimilitary state.

4

The China Incident

In the fall of 1936 Colonel Ishihara, then chief of the Military Operations Section in Army General Staff Headquarters, visited the Command Headquarters of the Kwantung Army, which was located in the new capital of Manchukuo, Changchun. Exactly five years had passed since the outbreak of the Manchurian Incident. The main purpose of Ishihara's visit was to admonish the army for ignoring orders from Tokyo and acting on its own initiative.

Though the Kwantung Army had had a succession of commanders during those five years, Itagaki had always played a central role, first as senior staff officer, then as chief of staff. His staff officers now had military and political matters in Manchukuo under firm control and were beginning to meddle in the affairs of neighboring areas as well. They aimed to bring Inner Mongolia within Japan's sphere of influence in order to counter Russian control of Outer Mongolia. In northern China they would establish an independent government friendly to Japan. Then, if these plans proceeded smoothly, they would eventually turn these areas into second and third Manchukuos.

To Ishihara, who stood at the heart of Japan's defense network, such acts amounted to playing with fire. He was convinced that the most urgent need at that point was to concentrate on nurturing and strengthening the still-new state of Manchukuo. Inflammatory acts should be stopped immediately. Thus it was that Ishihara, who himself had once acted contrary to orders from Tokyo, now found himself on the opposite side of the fence, enforcing the policies of the central authorities.

Arriving in Changchun, Ishihara was taken immediately to Lieuten-

An infantry unit heading for Süchow trudges endlessly across the vast wheat-growing plains of China.

ant General Itagaki's official residence for a predinner meeting. Among those present were Major General Imamura, recently appointed assistant chief of staff, and Lieutenant Colonel Mutō, who had been transferred from the War Ministry after the February 26 Incident. Ishihara addressed the group in a friendly manner, explaining the aims of the central authorities and expressing his own hopes that the Kwantung Army would show prudence. This prompted Lieutenant Colonel Mutō, the staff officer in charge of operations in Inner Mongolia, to ask with a smile, "Are you merely voicing the opinions of your superiors or do you yourself truly believe what you are saying?"

"That's enough!" Ishihara retorted, his voice suddenly stern. "I'm opposed to any operations whatsoever in Inner Mongolia. Just when the building of Manchukuo is finally under way, you want to risk stirring up trouble with Russia and China with these clumsy plots. Doesn't common sense tell you what the results will be!"

"You amaze me," Mutō said, the smile still on his lips. "At the time when you were so active in the Manchurian Incident, Imamura and I were working at General Staff Headquarters. It was your actions then that opened our eyes; we admired you. We are only putting into practice in Inner Mongolia what we learned from you."

The staff officers laughed in unison when Mutō finished, as if to voice approval of what he had said. Ishihara, shocked into silence, turned to Itagaki, but his old friend and ally made no move to speak. A sudden chill fell over the meeting. Assistant Chief of Staff Imamura stepped in to act as mediator.

"What do you say, sir—" he said, addressing Chief of Staff Itagaki, "it's time to eat, so why don't we discuss this further tomorrow, when there's more time . . ."

"Yes," Itagaki agreed, greatly relieved, "let's move to the dining room and relax."

The following day Ishihara reiterated the aims of the central command to the commander, Itagaki, and Imamura, but he was fully aware they were not listening in earnest to what he had to say. It was Ishihara himself, together with Itagaki, who had created these headstrong tendencies in the Kwantung Army. Now he was partaking of the bitter fruits of a tradition he had helped create. It was like preaching to a blank wall. For the first time in his life, Ishihara tasted defeat. When Imamura saw him off at the airfield, it seemed to him Ishihara was a different man from when he arrived, that a shadow of forlornness had fallen upon him.

These were times of extreme uncertainty and change for the central government as well. Following the February 26 Incident, Prime Minister Hirota Kōki, a veteran diplomat, had formed a cabinet that collapsed after only eight months. An abortive attempt by a reserve officer, General Ugaki Kazushige, to form a new government was thwarted by the strong opposition of both the army and the navy. Another reserve officer, General Hayashi Senjūrō, somehow managed to put together a new government, but this lasted a mere four months. Amid such an atmosphere of political instability, the name of Konoe Fumimaro began to be mentioned. The army had long looked to Konoe's leadership, for they found his reformist principles not so different from their own. Konoe's candidacy was also encouraged by Prince Saionji, though for virtually the opposite reasons; he thought Konoe would be able to check, to some extent at least, the army's growing control of the government.

Konoe adamantly refused to assume the office of prime minister, citing reasons of health. His health was indeed by no means perfect, yet the fact was he lacked confidence in his own ability to exercise total leadership during such troubled times.

When the army openly proposed that War Minister Sugiyama Gen, a lieutenant general on the active list, form the next cabinet, Saionji, playing his trump card, vigorously advocated the candidacy of Konoe. Even so, this did not imply that Saionji found Konoe trustworthy on all counts. On the contrary, the elder statesman saw signs of danger in Konoe's philosophy and detected a weakness of character that could lead him to be easily swayed by others' opinions. Ultimately, however, Saionji decided that Konoe would be better than total surrender of the nation's government to a representative of the army.

Once already Konoe had been ordered by the Emperor to form a cabinet and had declined. He knew all too well, however, that though the first refusal could be forgiven, a second would be seen as unforgivably selfish. In June, 1937, after much painful indecision, Konoe consented to become prime minister.

When the news that Konoe would become prime minister reached the people, it was greeted with universal jubilation. At forty-five,

Konoe was far younger than any of his predecessors and was known for his old and illustrious family pedigree, his attractive personal appearance, and his openness. He was well known to leading figures in all fields, including the political right and the political left, and all who knew him were impressed with his great courtesy. Konoe's decision to take the reins of government was met with applause from the army, the politicians, the business world, and above all, from the uninformed mass of the population.

Ever since the outbreak of the Manchurian Incident Japan had been facing a serious state of affairs both at home and abroad. The mood of the people was chauvinistically patriotic, in reaction against the Meiji era tendency to revere all things European and American; and the voices proclaiming Japan's superiority and Japan's world mission grew shriller and more insistent. Yet at the same time people could not escape the instinctive feeling that hardship lay ahead. When Konoe took office, therefore, he appeared as a star of hope to the worried citizenry

Once he began to form a cabinet the frenzy of popularity began to cool. The army, on the premise that Konoe understood its way of thinking, requested that certain persons be included, and, though Konoe was able to reject some of their suggestions, he was forced to compromise and accept others. The cabinet, therefore, was in the end not significantly changed for the better. At a press conference held just after his cabinet was announced, Konoe stated, "Measures must be taken to alleviate the internal conflicts and rivalries that have caused us to be looked down upon by other nations. It is essential that this cabinet exercise proper leadership to that end."

The principles of leadership he advocated were a "true peace based not on simple maintenance of the status quo but on international justice and a domestic policy based in social justice." Konoe was here emphasizing ideas he had advocated consistently since his first treatise was published in 1918.

Konoe planned to launch his new cabinet with a flourish by declaring a major amnesty. For several years, a steady succession of bloody incidents had led to the imprisonment of numerous persons from both ends of the political spectrum; it was Konoe's dream to create a new "harmony" under the Emperor by commuting the sentences of many of these prisoners. His plan, however, was strongly opposed by both the army and Japan's senior statesmen. For the army, which had come so close to gaining absolute power, those who broke the law were no more than troublemakers. For the senior statesmen—former prime ministers and imperial advisers—to ignore law and order was an act of dire violence. Even the Emperor disapproved of the amnesty plan, delighted though he was at Konoe's advent on the political scene.

Konoe had little time to dwell upon this setback to his somewhat unrealistic idealism, for on July 7, just one month after his cabinet's inauguration, a serious incident occured on the Chinese mainland—a skirmish between Japanese and Chinese troops on the Marco Polo Bridge just outside Peking.

The original confrontation was a minor one. A company of Japanese soldiers on night maneuvers (Japan had had the right to station an army in the area since 1901) were suddenly fired upon by their Chinese counterparts. Japan demanded an apology for this unlawful behavior, but when negotiations grew complicated and further minor conflicts ensued, the scene was set for a rapid escalation of hostilities.

At Tokyo General Staff Headquarters, Ishihara, now division chief of military operations, took the lead in trying to quell the disturbance. One of the staff officers of the Tientsin occupation army stationed in the area was also opposed to expanding the hostilities and worked earnestly to quench the flames before they could spread. Though finally a cease-fire was achieved, the day before the agreement was concluded the army decided to mobilize five additional divisions. Not only did the Japanese government agree to this mobilization, but it announced at home and abroad that it was doing so "with firm resolve."

At this point, opinion within the Japanese army's central command was divided equally. The War Ministry was largely made up of those advocating war, who argued that China would make no concessions unless a blow was first dealt to its armies. This view was based on the optimistic assumption that one full-scale assault would be enough to easily subdue the Chinese forces. War Minister Sugiyama reported to the Emperor that, once mobilized, Japanese military power could settle matters within a month. On the other hand those, including General Tada Shun, the second in command of General Staff, and Major General Ishihara, who opposed the spread of hostilities, maintained their lonely opposition. At first Prime Minister Konoe was pessimistic about the mobilization plans, but in the end he was swayed by the prowar faction's argument that a display of power would quickly subdue any Chinese opposition.

Surrounded by a burning sea of prowar sentiment, General Headquarters staff, led by Ishihara, coolly went about quenching what fires they could. The mobilization plan was limited to say that the purpose of dispatching troops was not to wage immediate war but rather, through a display of power, to force an apology from the Chinese army and to secure guarantees for the future. Should mobilization turn out to be unnecessary, the troops would be withdrawn. However, the news of the decision to mobilize did more than encourage the fighting spirit of Japan's China-based troops. Japan's persistently highhanded posture finally led Chiang Kai-shek to the crucial resolution to fight back.

Despite the open threat to Chinese sovereignty posed by Japan's Kwantung and Tientsin armies, Chiang had continued to show forbearance. Having studied in Japan and served as a cadet in the Japanese army, he had no desire to fight against Japan, despite his active participation in the Chinese Revolution of 1911. In order to realize his long-held dream of unifying and reforming China, he was willing to cooperate with Japan insofar as possible. For him, the primary concern of the moment was the extermination of the Communist army. He refused to cooperate with the student-led anti-Japanese movement, declaring that, whereas the presence of the Japanese army was but a boil on the skin of China, the Communist force was a disease of the vital organs. However, when he saw that the time had come to make a final decision, he left no room for doubt as to his intentions, appealing to the people of China in the following words:

"Six years have passed since the loss of Manchuria, and now the battle is drawing near Peking. Should Peking become a second Mukden, our capital Nanking may well follow. The very fate of our nation depends upon how the Marco Polo Bridge Incident is resolved. Should we be pushed to the point where no further concessions were possible, then sacrifice and resistance would be our only choice. Though our nation is weak, we must protect the lives of our people and sustain the burden of history passed down to us by our ancestors."

Chiang's appeal was an inspiration to his front-line troops. Conflicts with the Japanese grew ever more frequent; then the Japanese army launched its all-out offensive.

As he anxiously watched the situation develop, Konoe's views about the conflict began to shift subtly. He had hoped that, faced with a display of Japanese might, China would quickly submit before the fighting could spread. Now, however, it looked as if there might be all-out war. Ishihara's advice, delivered over the telephone, was that Konoe should go to Nanking and meet personally with Chiang. Konoe seriously considered this idea but in the end did not go. The main reason for his hesitation was that, even if the two heads of government succeeded in their negotiations, Japan's international credibility would be damaged more than helped should Japanese troops break the truce with further arbitrary actions. He suspected that the army had plotted the initial confrontation just as it had in the Manchurian Incident. However, Konoe also recognized that it was essential to take the first steps toward such a meeting; and so, with the agreement of the war minister, he sent to China as secret envoys two civilians whom Chiang trusted. Prowar army officers had learned of the operation, however, and the envoys were arrested by Japanese military police.

The Japanese army advanced swiftly, first occupying Peking and Tientsin, then winning a rapid series of battles in northern China. Almost daily, Japanese newspapers spread glowing reports of the campaign's progress. The people of Japan, flushed with victory, forgot that Japan itself had provoked this "dirty war" without pretext and was bound to be met with desperate resistance from the Chinese people.

This failure to see the realities of the situation not only created a dangerous state of mind in the Japanese people, but was also a dangerous omen from a purely strategic point of view. The army planned to confront the enemy's troops in the field, deal them a crushing blow, destroy their will to fight back, then wrap up its triumph at the bargaining table. In fact, however, the Chinese troops began to fight back as never before. Recognizing the danger of being trapped in the net of Japan's encircling armies, they slipped away to re-form their lines in the rear and resume their resistance. As the battle area broadened, Japan poured more and more troops into the conflict.

The flames of war spread next to Shanghai, where the Japanese met particularly strong resistance and sustained heavy losses. Despite its mass mobilization and victorious advance, Japan's army found its hopes of restricting hostilities to a manageable scale dashed as the war spread throughout China.

The Japanese government clung to the hope that the enemy could be easily subdued, basing its optimism on the capture of Nanking, China's capital city. Had they been prepared to offer generous peace terms at this point, a truce might have been possible, but the rapid advance had left politicians and people alike intoxicated with victory and the sense of their own superiority. The peace terms proposed by the government were harsh in the extreme, demanding that almost all of northern China be turned into the equivalent of a Japanese colony. The intermediary in the peace negotiations, Germany's ambassador to China, Oskar P. Trautmann, doubted from the very outset that such terms would be acceptable.

The government's attitude infuriated Ishihara. He found it especially hard to stomach the contempt for China's fighting spirit that pervaded the government and the army leadership. "As long as China holds sovereignty over a single acre," he said, "Chiang's government will find popular support for protracted resistance." At this crucial juncture, however, Ishihara was transferred to a post outside Tokyo.

Nanking fell to the Japanese army in December of that year (1937). As expected, Chiang established a temporary capital in Hankow and continued the struggle. Nowhere was there any sign of peace. At the new year, the Japanese government once again had to outline its long-term plans for the future.

By this time Japan had already entered a state of readiness for war, having established an Imperial Headquarters as the highest authority on strategic matters in the expanded conflict. There was as yet no declaration of war, for Japan feared that such a declaration would activate America's Neutrality Act, resulting in a suspension of trade. Japan relied on American exports for much of the basic material needed for its war effort, including most of its scrap iron and petroleum. It was decided that this plus far outweighed the minus of American aid to China.

The first days of 1938 saw a direct conflict of opinions as the government and the Army General Staff met in an Imperial Headquarters—Governmental Liaison Conference. Prime Minister Konoe argued that Japan should break off peace negotiations with Chiang's Kuomintang

(Nationalist) government and await the emergence of a new political force more willing to cooperate with Japan. This view was supported by Konoe's cabinet, including War Minister Sugiyama. Yet, though Ishihara was gone, a deep-rooted, intense anxiety about the future of the war remained at Army General Staff Headquarters. Lieutenant General Tada, the second in command, held his ground, emphasizing that negotiations with the Kuomintang should be continued to the bitter end. Like Ishihara, Tada was clearly aware that the plan to bring China to its knees with a single initial blow had already failed. He accordingly harbored a strong sense of dissatisfaction with the peace terms that had been proposed by a government carried away with its initial superficial victories. Should Chiang move his capital again from Hankow to Chungking, maintaining his resistance even as he retreated deeper into China, there was no telling when a solution could be reached. Tada foresaw that the denial of Chiang's authority would eliminate him as a partner in the negotiations, thereby opening the door for almost certain intervention from Russia, England, and the United States. It was essential, Tada stressed, to shift to a more lenient set of peace terms that would save face for Chiang and his government.

In Konoe, however, half a year as prime minister had given rise to a strong suspicion of the army. He still felt that they had dragged Japan into the China war against his will. And he disliked the way, once the war had started and there was no clear prospect of victory, the General Staff wanted to seek a peace settlement even though on unsatisfactory terms. The Liaison Conference lasted from early morning through the afternoon without resolving the disagreement. Finally, just before the night session began, Tada gave in. As a man of good sense, he realized that if he pushed the Army Headquarters' point of view any further the government would inevitably collapse, something he did not wish to happen.

The following day, January 16, 1938, Konoe issued a momentous proclamation, which read: "Beginning today, the government of Japan will not recognize the Nationalist Chinese government. We anticipate that a new political power, willing to cooperate with Japan, will eventually be established in China, and when that happens, we will adjust diplomatic relations and work with them to build a new China."

The war continued to spread. April and May saw the Japanese army mount an offensive on both northern and southern fronts. In Süchow, a large enemy force was surrounded and badly defeated, but any hopes for peace were dashed when China's main force managed to break through the closing net and retreat. In September and October, the Japanese mounted successful drives against distant Hankow, on the middle reaches of the Yangtze River, and Canton in the south, taking both cities. At this point, Japan halted its offensive. Having poured a military force of 1.6 million men into the vast Chinese continent, it nevertheless now found itself able to hold only the strategic points and defense lines of territory it had secured, with few future prospects.

Despite having publicly broken off relations with Chiang's government, in private Prime Minister Konoe continued to pursue negotiations for a peace settlement. Japan's demands were unreasonable, however, and these talks failed from the outset. This failure drove Konoe to the brink of despair, and he began dropping frequent hints of his intention to resign.

Konoe had already composed his resignation letter by late 1938, at which time one of the influential leaders of the Kuomintang, Wang Ching-wei, fled the temporary capital of Chungking and crossed over to Japan. Wang was strongly opposed to the scorched-earth resistance tactics of the Communists, who, though fighting in collaboration with the Kuomintang against Japan, had managed to expand their own power within China. Wang had decided to gamble on the good faith of Japan's proposed Japan-Manchuria-China Cooperation Program. After his defection, however, it became clear to Wang that Japan's demands were excessive, that it was interested only in establishing a completely subservient puppet government.

Japan's army, though searching desperately for a way to end hostilities, was seized with the desire, whenever an opportunity for peace presented itself, to get as much war booty as possible. The cabinet, too, frequently sought to take similar advantage of such situations. Not only did Konoe lack the power to control the army and the cabinet, he lost his enthusiasm for trying to do so.

The Western powers, in the meantime, were spurred to action by Japan's monopolistic economic policies in its now vast occupied territories in China. The League of Nations passed a resolution to apply sanctions to Japan—though each member nation was free to enforce them as it wished—and America condemned Japanese monopolism.

Japan's prohibition, for strategic reasons, of passage on the Yangtze River, a major trade artery, was also a blow to the powers, and America, Britain, and France demanded free access. Japan's response was to call for the cooperation of the Western powers in the construction of a new order in East Asia. Japan, in effect, was proclaiming that it would set all the rules in the Far East, including China.

In America, calls for the prohibition of munitions exports to Japan grew stronger as the news of Japanese atrocities in China spread, and the Roosevelt administration reaffirmed its support of China by announcing financial assistance to the Nationalists.

Japan had been allied with Germany in the Anti-Comintern Pact since the end of 1936. Italy joined the pact in November of the following year, which marked the beginning of the China Incident. Hitler's Germany was expanding into neighboring territories, occupying the Rhineland, and annexing Austria, in defiance of the Versailles order that had resulted from the Paris Peace Conference. Benito Mussolini's Italy was in the process of subjugating Ethiopia by military force.

It was Germany's hope that the Anti-Comintern Pact could be developed into a military alliance, and Japan's army and a number of its politicians responded favorably to this idea. In the forefront was Matsuoka Yōsuke, then president of the South Manchurian Railway, who emphasized the need for a tighter alliance with Germany. As a career diplomat, Matsuoka was particularly concerned about Japan's isolation in the world, not merely from the standpoint of national defense, but also because he saw that the world was forming new economic blocs, one of which would consist of Japan, Manchuria, and China. Who would support this bloc if not the Germans—who, like the Japanese, were aiming at the destruction of the present order?

Germany, however, preparing as it was for war against England and France, hoped that the alliance could be directed not just against Russia but against America, England, and France as well. Japan's army expressed interest in this concept, for in its inner circles it was felt that British aid was the main reason China was proving so difficult to conquer. The navy, however, was staunchly opposed. There was little prospect, it argued, of defeating America and England at sea, for their navies were the world's strongest, whereas the navies of Germany and Italy were negligible.

When the question of the Tripartite Pact threw his cabinet into confusion, Konoe resigned. Other, more important factors were also involved in his resignation, however. Konoe now hated the post of prime minister, for he had come to feel that every one of his policies had reached a deadlock, and he was ready to resign on any pretext.

On receiving word of Konoe's resignation, Prince Saionji remarked, "I haven't the slightest notion what he's been doing since he became prime minister. I know these are difficult times, but there is no excuse for such an act, especially in view of the wisdom of our sovereign. My heart bleeds for the Emperor."

The aged Saionji took no part in the deliberations to choose a successor to Konoe.

5

Japan-U.S. Negotiations

In July 1940, Konoe Fumimaro was chosen to serve as prime minister for the second time. A year and a half had passed since his resignation, during which time three governments had appeared, only to beat a hasty retreat. Though his first cabinet had demonstrated no particular talent, the people's hopes and affection for Konoe had not yet disappeared. This time he had a plan, formed through reflection on his earlier bitter experience as prime minister. His idea was that the government could be strengthened if it could generate a wave of popular support to back it in its endeavor to resist the power of the army. It was just at the time Konoe reached this conclusion that he resumed the office of prime minister.

The state of the world had changed enormously since his departure. In August of the previous year, Germany had invaded and divided Poland one month after signing a nonaggression pact with Russia. Britain and France had declared war against Germany, and the curtain had risen on World War II. May 1940 had seen Germany shift the focus of its attack westward, invading Holland and Belgium, then, in June, forcing the rapid surrender of France. The invasion of England seemed imminent.

In Asia, the Dutch East Indies and French Indochina had in effect become colonies without masters. Preoccupied with preparations for the coming German attack, England no longer had strength enough to defend Asia. Japan's army fairly danced with joy at this chance of a lifetime to extend its power southward. The navy had similar interests, for it saw the opportunity to achieve its own longstanding dream of advancing southward. To the south lay all the resources, especially those needed in wartime, that Japan, Manchuria, and China could not supply: oil, rubber, and nickel, to name but three. From various quarters, there were murmurs of "Let's not miss the bus!"

When Konoe received the Emperor's order to form a new government, he summoned three important prospective members of his new cabinet to his home on the outskirts of Tokyo: Foreign Minister Matsuoka, War Minister Tōjō, and Navy Minister Yoshida Zengo. Matsuoka was to many an alarming figure, for his eccentric personality, his rich imagination and eloquence, and his unyielding stance toward foreign powers were well-known. Something in Konoe, however, was drawn to this powerful personality. He was especially conscious of the need for such a strong figure to counteract the army's power. Lieutenant General Tōjō had been an outstanding vice-minister of war. Officials working under him had nicknamed him "the razor," for his incisive ability as an administrator. Konoe attached special importance to his dominating strength and his firm belief in the strict obedience owed one's superiors.

These four men met to discuss what Japan's subsequent policies should be. The consensus they reached was that the Japan-Germany-Italy Axis should be strengthened, a nonaggression pact concluded with the Soviet Union, and positive action taken to encompass within a new, Japanese-led order the Asian colonies of England, France, and Holland. They further agreed that the way to forestall American intervention was to take a hard line and stick to it.

Once in power, the Konoe government made rapid progress in its negotiations with Germany to establish a military alliance. The failure of plans to invade Britain was making the Germans impatient. It was their hope that an alliance with Japan would keep America out of the war. At the same time, Britain would be shaken by a Japanese attack on Singapore. The thinking of the Japanese leaders was somewhat different. The alliance with Germany was seen in conjunction with a readjusted relationship with Russia. Japan would join the Soviet Union in a nonaggression pact while forming closer ties with Germany. This would strengthen Japan's world position and in turn induce America to adopt a more conciliatory policy toward Japan. And, through America's mediation, a solution to the China Incident might be achieved. So ran Matsuoka's thinking, with Konoe in complete agreement.

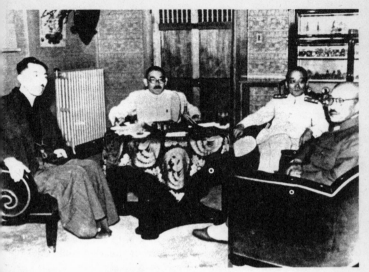

Four ministerial candidates gather at Konoe's private residence. From left: Konoe, Matsuoka, Yoshida, Tōjō.

A special German envoy, Heinrich Stahmer, assured Japan that, with Germany acting as "honest broker," ties between Japan and Russia could be easily established. Konoe was uneasy, however, for he saw that if the Japan-Germany alliance was established before Japan's relations with Russia were settled, Japan would simply be used to Germany's benefit. He counted on the navy to stand in open opposition to the proposed alliance at this juncture, providing him with a needed pretext to drag out the negotiations. Much to Konoe's surprise, however, the navy simply gave its agreement to the proposal. Led by a core of young officers, those favoring alliance with Germany had gained the upper hand even within the navy's leadership.

When the proposed alliance was debated for the last time—at an Imperial Conference, Japan's highest form of governmental council, held in the presence of the Emperor—Matsuoka expressed his views as follows:

"It is not to Germany but to Russia that we wish to extend the hand of friendship. Our ties with Germany are no more than a means to draw Russia closer. If we can ally ourselves with both Germany and Russia, it is unlikely that such countries as America and Britain will wish to wage war with Japan."

Matsuoka next discussed an issue of great concern, namely, the possibility that the proposed alliance would lead to a steady worsening of U.S.-Japan relations.

"American sentiment toward Japan is extremely negative at present," he said. "It cannot be improved through mere recourse to flattery. Rather, the only way to avoid war with America is to maintain our own unflinching resolve."

"Mightn't such an aggressive policy produce the opposite result when applied to such a proud nation as America?" asked one of those present, expressing a concern felt by the Emperor.

"Your question is an apt one," replied Matsuoka, "but we must remember that Japan is not Spain but a great Asian power possessed of a strong navy. America may resist for a while, but I believe it will return to its senses with time. Otherwise, a dangerous situation could develop. In my opinion, both alternatives are equally likely."

Matsuoka's mention of Spain was a historical reference to the Spanish-American War, which had taken place when he himself was living in America. America had taken a strong stand against Spanish colonial policy, and Spain had yielded to the threat, seeking peace through compromise; whereupon America immediately launched an offensive, not only eradicating Spanish influence from the Caribbean Sea, but rapidly deploying its Asiatic Squadron to take possession of the Philippines. The memory of these events was still fresh in Matsuoka's mind. It was his long-held belief that only a firm and uncompromising attitude could establish a basis for negotiating on an equal footing with the Americans.

The Tripartite Pact between Japan, Germany, and Italy was soon concluded—in September 1940, two months after Konoe's government assumed power. Some Japanese, however, were apprehensive about this development, typical among them the Emperor himself. When Konoe went to see him to present the final report on the pact negotiations, the Emperor responded gravely, "Will you share the burden with me if Japan is defeated?" Konoe was deeply moved by this display of trust, and his eyes filled with tears as he pledged to serve with the utmost devotion and sincerity.

In March of the following year, Matsuoka visited Europe, where he was enthusiastically welcomed by Mussolini and Hitler. Relations between Germany and the Soviet Union, however, had grown cold. Germany was already in the mood for war on the eastern front. As German Foreign Minister Ribbentrop told Matsuoka, "To eliminate the source of the evil in Europe, we must attack Russia." Germany's promise to act as an "honest broker" seemed to have been forgotten somewhere along the way.

While urging the Germans to proceed with circumspection, Matsuoka set forth his own ideas. "I am planning to stop in Moscow on my way back, in the interest of better Soviet-Japanese relations," he told Ribbentrop.

"Ah, but that will be difficult," was the reply. "Russia cannot be trusted."

"But if we are successful," persisted Matsuoka, "what would be your response?"

"If you succeed, so much the better," Ribbentrop said, "but I doubt such a settlement is possible."

Matsuoka was warmly received in Moscow as well. Russia was already aware of Germany's planned attack and saw in the Japanese proposals a timely bridge over troubled international waters. Should harmonious relations with Japan be established, Russia's rear would be secure, making preparations against Germany possible. The neutrality pact between Japan and Russia was thus concluded without difficulty. In Japan, Matsuoka's lightning diplomacy was met with an outpouring of praise from an astonished public.

When Foreign Minister Matsuoka embarked on his journey home on the Trans-Siberian Railway, Stalin made a point of accompanying him to the station platform. "We are both Asians," he said, embracing Matsuoka when they parted.

As the train rolled through the vast forests of Siberia, the elated Matsuoka spoke eloquently of his plans for the future to a young journalist accompanying him: "Countries like England and America fear that, now that we have joined the Tripartite Pact and have assured the defense of our northern borders through the Russo-Japanese Neutrality Pact, we will advance toward the south. But this is really the time to negotiate for peace! As soon as I get back, I will rush to Chungking to meet with Chiang Kai-shek. Then, without returning to Japan, I will go with Chiang to Washington, where we will meet with President Roosevelt and together negotiate an end to the East Asian problem. The terms of our agreement will establish a neutral zone north of the Great Wall and require that all Japanese troops be evacuated from the Chinese mainland. In return, America and China will agree to recognize Manchukuo and sign nonaggression pacts with Japan. . . ."

When Matsuoka arrived back in Japan, however, he found an unexpected and unpleasant state of affairs awaiting him. Quite without his knowledge, but with the secret support of Prime Minister Konoe, unofficial negotiations between America and Japan had been under way since the end of the preceding year.

These unofficial negotiations dated from the arrival in Japan of two energetic clergymen, Bishop James Walsh and Father James Drought. While in Tokyo they made the acquaintance of the director of the Industrial Unions Central Bank, Ikawa Tadao, who shared their conviction that a road to peace could be established if men of good will from both sides could but join together. Ikawa, who had lived in America for several years and had an American wife, introduced them to Colonel Iwakuro Hideo, a powerful figure in the War Ministry. As an intelligence expert, he was eminently suited for this sort of task. It had been Iwakuro, in fact, who had persuaded the leaders of the Kwantung Army to admit to Manchuria five thousand Jews fleeing from Hitler.

Iwakuro introduced the two priests to the chief of the Military Affairs Bureau, Major General Mutō, one of the central core of officers at the War Ministry. He was deeply impressed by their idea, and wished them success.

When the two priests returned home to America, they found an ally in Postmaster General Frank Walker, himself a religious man, who arranged for them to meet the president. Roosevelt showed great interest in what they had to say and ordered Secretary of State Cordell Hull to look into the matter. Despite the strong objections of Hull's adviser on Far Eastern affairs, Dr. Stanley Hornbeck, a known Japanophobe, Roosevelt still felt positively about the idea, and instructed Walker to support the project behind the scenes.

First Ikawa, then Iwakuro made the trip from Tokyo to Washington. American sentiment was divided on whether or not America should participate in the war. Those who believed that America's obligation was to join the war effort and give unlimited support to countries standing against the Axis were in the minority, whereas the majority supported the tradition of isolationism espoused by the most famous opponent of the war, air hero Charles Lindbergh.

Father Drought and the two Japanese met for three days in April and drafted a "Japan-U.S. Draft Understanding." Though the content of this document covered the full range of issues, its most crucial section stated that Japan would withdraw all its troops from China if China would recognize Manchukuo and Chiang's government agreed to merge with the government led by Wang Ching-wei in Nanking. Postmaster General Walker read the draft and, fully satisfied, sent a copy to the president. On the Japanese side, in Washington, Ambassador Nomura Kichisaburō and his principal advisers gave the document their approval as well.

In conversations spanning two separate meetings, Hull pointed out to Nomura that the draft still contained several thorny points. Handing Nomura a list of four basic principles, which included the "right of every nation to territorial integrity and respect of its sovereignty," Hull pointed out that these would form the basis of any future reconciliation with the U.S. He asked whether Japan had the will and the ability to abide by them. Hull expressed himself in a cautious and circuitous manner throughout; he did not wish to suggest that negotiations were actually under way. However, Nomura's lack of diplomatic experience, and his own burning desire to reach a negotiated settlement, led him to take Hull's words to mean that the principles of the draft understanding were acceptable to the Americans.

When Konoe received Nomura's telegram, he was both surprised and overjoyed. Those near him had not seen his face glow so in years. He called an emergency meeting that very evening while waiting for the telegram to be translated and printed. All those present at the meeting, including the heads of the army and navy, gave their approval to the draft understanding, and all were in high spirits to think that the way to peace between Japan and America was now open.

Konoe was ready to send a telegram immediately conveying Japan's assent, until the acting foreign minister called his attention to the fact that propriety required that he wait for Matsuoka's return. Konoe agreed. By this time, Matsuoka had completed his European and Moscow visits and was in Dairen, Manchuria.

It was April 22 when Matsuoka's plane touched down at a military airport on the outskirts of Tokyo. He was still ignorant of the Japan-U.S. negotiations now well under way. Knowing Matsuoka's proud and emotional nature, Konoe realized the matter had to be broached delicately. He therefore decided to go personally to the airport to greet Matsuoka in order to break the news himself during the ride back to town. To Konoe's consternation, however, Matsuoka let it be known that he wished first of all to go to make the ritual bows in front of the Imperial Palace. Konoe so loathed this sort of formality toward the Imperial House that he gave up the idea of returning in the same car, delegating the job of explaining the Draft Understanding to the vice-minister of foreign affairs. When he heard of the negotiations, Matsuoka was extremely displeased.

Upon accepting the post of foreign minister, Matsuoka had asked to be given full control of all aspects of foreign affairs, which Konoe, having undergone the bitter experience of army manipulation, had been only too glad to bestow. Notwithstanding these assurances, major Japan-U.S. negotiations had been initiated without the knowledge of the foreign minister.

An Imperial Headquarters—Governmental Liaison Conference was convened at the prime minister's residence the very night of Matsuoka's return. Everyone was in cheerful spirits, expecting the discussion to center on the development of negotiations based upon the Japan-U.S. Draft Understanding. Instead, Matsuoka monopolized the conversation, basking in his own glory as he triumphantly described his trip to Germany, Italy, and the Soviet Union. Those present found it difficult to bear Matsuoka's long-winded eloquence, which had won for him the nickname "Mr. Fifty-thousand Words." When Konoe finally managed to bring up the matter of the draft understanding, Matsuoka suddenly became upset.

"My opinions differ somewhat from yours. I need time to think it over," he said brusquely; then, pleading fatigue from his long journey, he left the meeting.

The next day, Konoe began to attempt to persuade Matsuoka. After a week of almost daily meetings, Matsuoka agreed to examine the draft understanding. Moreover, he made several revisions in the text, emphasizing Japan's obligations to the Tripartite Alliance and deleting the section that renounced the use of force in Japan's southward expansion. Confronted with Matsuoka's absolute confidence in the need to take a firm negotiating stance, Konoe gave way. When U.S. Secretary of State Hull received Japan's proposals, he found not a glimmer of hope for the future in them.

Although talks between Hull and Nomura continued, the negotiations stagnated. Washington formulated a harsh response to Matsuoka's proposed amendments, demanding Japan's withdrawal from the Tripartite Alliance. This document further pointed out that the presence of a certain high-ranking official—clearly referring to Matsuoka—was an obstacle to Japan-U.S. negotiations. Matsuoka saw this personal attack as proof that America regarded Japan as its possession, and was outraged.

The day after Hull handed this document to Ambassador Nomura, another great change shook Europe; an avalanche of German troops swept into Russia; the invasion was finally under way. News of this event had a profound impact on Japan's leaders. Matsuoka predicted the war would last but a short while and would end with Germany's victory. This opinion was shared by both Japan's army and the heads of the U.S. armed services. As Navy Secretary Frank Knox put it, "Hitler should take from six weeks to two months to defeat Russia." Such was the common view of the matter.

Matsuoka, in a sudden policy reversal, now urged that Japan should attack Russia immediately. The army and navy, however, held that there was time enough to study the situation before acting, and that a southern rather than a northern advance seemed more opportune under the circumstances. As soon as France fell, the Japanese government put pressure on the Vichy government, extracting a recognition of Japan's military occupation of northern French Indochina. The army and navy wanted Japan to prepare to advance into southern French Indochina, take control of the now powerless European colonies, and gather up the rich spoils to be found there. Konoe agreed with this view, and in early July decided formally to adopt this policy. The danger of conflict with Britain and America was, of course, anticipated, and for the first time the phrase "War is unavoidable if Japan's national policy is to be fulfilled" began to appear in public documents.

Matsuoka continued his unwavering advocacy of a northern advance, and pressured for an end to the peace negotiations with America. To the Japanese leadership, Matsuoka was clearly a curse upon the government; some even declared that he was quite mad. Konoe, having recommended Matsuoka for the powerful position of foreign minister, felt responsible, and, as before, tendered his resignation. This time, however, it was a trick to get rid of Matsuoka, for after dissolving his cabinet, he was unanimously chosen by the conference of senior statesmen to succeed himself and was given twenty-four hours to form a new government. The only difference between the old and new cabinets was the absence of Matsuoka. In his place as foreign minister was Admiral Toyoda Teijirō, a reserve navy officer who advocated that war with America should be avoided.

After this, southern French Indochina was occupied, as planned, without the use of violence. To get the Vichy government to sign the agreement was as easy as twisting the arm of a baby. The American government, however, had learned of the plan beforehand; it warned that such an incursion would render all Japan-U.S. negotiations ineffectual and tried to restrain Japan by freezing all its American assets. England and Holland followed suit.

Just at the time transport ships carrying occupation troops to southern French Indochina were setting out for Saigon, Konoe summoned former Foreign Minister Shidehara to ask his opinions on recent developments.

"Couldn't the fleet be recalled and stopped at, say, Taiwan?" Shidehara inquired. "Otherwise our negotiations with the Americans are at an end."

"The decision to station troops there has been made and cannot be withdrawn," Konoe answered.

"In that case, I must be frank," Shidehara said. "It will lead to a great war."

"But we are only going to peacefully occupy French Indochina," Konoe said, surprised. "There will be no further challenges to anyone; the army and I have a firm understanding on that point."

"Once you send military forces to French Indochina," Shidehara countered, "the situation will expand. Malaya and the Dutch East Indies will be next. If you want to know my opinion, all I can say is that I am absolutely opposed to the stationing of troops in southern French Indochina."

Konoe paled at this, then buried his face in his hands, lost in thought.

The Japanese military occupation of southern French Indochina did, in fact, have international repercussions. The Roosevelt government totally banned the export of oil to Japan. Since Japan's oil production at the time could barely supply ten percent of its own needs, Japan had to rely on imported oil and depended on America for eighty percent of that. Anyone could see that the embargo would prove a fatal blow to Japanese industry; America's hands had a firm grasp upon Japan's throat.

Japan was now forced to choose between abject surrender or obtaining oil by taking the Dutch East Indies, an act that would mean war. Japan's leadership was violently shaken by this turn of events, for they had not anticipated America's reaction would be so harsh. The shock to the navy was especially keen, since they estimated that their oil reserves would last a mere two years, or one and a half years in wartime. In an audience with the Emperor, Navy Chief of Staff Nagano Osami reported: "Our only alternative under these circumstances is to break the Tripartite Pact and restore friendly relations with the United States." Yet he went on to say, "If war does come, our best policy is to attack first. A head start gives us a chance for victory."

Prime Minister Konoe felt that now only a meeting between the heads of government of Japan and America could avert the impending crisis. The navy gave its immediate approval, but War Minister Tōjō and the army had misgivings about the chances for success. The position they took was to show respect for Konoe's sincerity by supporting the meeting, but on the condition that everyone was prepared to face the inevitability of war if America failed to comprehend Japan's true intent.

Konoe's proposal for a meeting was telegraphed to Washington while President Roosevelt was conferring with British Prime Minister Churchill aboard the warship *Prince of Wales* in Argentia Bay, Newfoundland. Churchill wanted to hasten, if by only a day, America's entry into the war, in order to rescue Britain from its difficulties. Roosevelt agreed on that point, but he wanted no part in a war with Japan. Should Japan become America's enemy, the latter's contribution to the European campaign would, to that extent, be diminished. The two leaders agreed that Japan's entry should, in any case, be delayed as long as possible to gain time to strengthen the defense of Singapore.

When Roosevelt returned to Washington, Konoe's proposal was

waiting for him. Roosevelt took it seriously and expressed great interest. He summoned Ambassador Nomura at once and in great good spirits suggested that the meeting might be held in Juneau, Alaska, and might last about three days. Nomura, excited, cabled the message to Japan that the meeting should by all means be held.

The situation was quickly turned about, however. Cordell Hull, ever suspicious of Japanese intentions, held no hope that the proposed conference would solve anything. Hull's adviser Hornbeck regarded it as a Japanese trick to gain time to prepare for war, and counseled that the leaders should not meet until accord was attained in preliminary negotiations. This argument quickly changed the president's mind.

The time for Japan to make a final choice was drawing close. The newspapers declared that Japan was on the brink of disaster, economically strangled by the ABCD (American, British, Chinese, and Dutch). The question of whether to choose war or peace was discussed at an important Imperial Headquarters—Governmental Liaison Conference on September 3. Many heated words were exchanged in the course of this meeting, which lasted from eleven in the morning until six at night. "Japan is growing weaker by the day," lamented Navy Chief of Staff Nagano. "Before long Japan may no longer be able to survive. If we make up our minds now, we have a chance to win. To advance is our only hope." This was a marked change for the navy, which previously had urged the need to avoid war with America. With Japan's store of war materials, particularly oil, inexorably diminishing, a deadline for making the decision had to be established. Otherwise, Japan would lose not only its ability to wage war but probably even its ability to negotiate for peace. It was decided this final deadline would be in early October.

The third day after the conference, the Emperor received reports from Navy Chief of Staff Nagano and Army Chief of Staff Sugiyama outlining strategic plans for an advance to the south. They estimated that five months would be needed to take the Philippines, Malaya, Indonesia, and the rest. When the Emperor voiced doubts as to whether this strategy would proceed according to plan, Sugiyama's response was, "We are quite confident."

"When you were minister of the army and the China Incident broke out," the Emperor persisted, not willing to let Sugiyama off so easily, "you told me it would be settled in a month. Now after four years it still is not settled."

"That is because China is so vast . . ."

"I know China is large. The Pacific is even larger."

At this juncture, Nagano interceded to rescue the beleaguered Sugiyama. Likening Japan to a sick man in need of an operation, he argued that, though the operation was dangerous, it offered hope for the patient's recovery. The day was fast approaching, Nagano explained, when the decision whether to act or not had to be made.

"We in the military are praying for the success of the diplomatic negotiations."

"You agree that those negotiations must have first priority?"

"Yes."

This answer seemed finally to put the Emperor's mind at ease. At an Imperial Conference the following day, September 6, the Emperor repeatedly reminded those present that the current negotiations had top priority. When Konoe and the others assured him of their agreement, the Emperor took a piece of paper from an inside pocket and recited a poem composed by the Emperor Meiji:

> Though all men
> Across the seas of this world
> Are brothers,
> Why do the wind and waves
> Yet so resound?

"I often read this poem by the Emperor Meiji," the Emperor said, revealing his own feelings, "and I endeavor to carry on his peace-loving spirit."

Everyone sat in solemn silence. Finally Navy Chief of Staff Nagano, who had not yet spoken during the meeting, stood up.

"As we have already stated, we agree that diplomacy is paramount and that war will be resorted to only if it proves to be unavoidable," he said, closing the meeting.

War or peace—already a deadline had been set. That very night Konoe invited U.S. Ambassador Joseph C. Grew to a secret dinner meeting, at which for three hours he fervently urged that a leaders' meeting be convened immediately.

"It would take too long to draw up a detailed agreement. Resentment among the Japanese people caused by economic pressure from the Western powers grows more intense daily. I'm worried that if the agreement takes too long, the mood of the country will change and it will no longer be acceptable. If a consensus between the president and myself were reached right now, it would serve as a goal toward which I could lead the people. General Tōjō too is hoping for a peaceful settlement."

"Since the Japanese government has so often failed to honor its promises," Grew pointed out, "the government of the United States can no longer believe in Japanese assurances and guarantees, but only in deeds and facts."

"This time will be different," Konoe asserted, not arguing Grew's point. "We will definitely live up to our promises. My ship will be outfitted with equipment that can communicate directly between the site of our meeting and Tokyo." Konoe made a further disclosure: "When the president and I arrive at an accord, I have arranged for an immediate report to be made to the Emperor, who will then issue an imperial proclamation ordering a halt to all hostilities."

Ambassador Grew did not doubt Konoe's sincerity. Full of hope, he telegraphed Washington, but the mood there remained unchanged. Grew wrote to Roosevelt privately—they had been friends at Harvard—trying to persuade him to meet with Konoe but, apart from very formal replies, could elicit no new response whatsoever.

Hour by hour, Japan's "final deadline" grew closer. Konoe's despair deepened. In early October, just when Japan's decision for peace or war was to be made (America, of course, had no way of knowing this), Hull's impatiently awaited answer arrived. It was a mere reiteration of what had already been said, that there could be no consideration given to a leaders' conference until both sides had reached a consensus on the basic issues.

For the second time, four men gathered for an important meeting at Konoe's home. Present were War Minister Tōjō, Foreign Minister Toyoda, Navy Minister Oikawa Koshirō, and Konoe himself. Within the navy, the pessimists who believed that Japan was incapable of defeating America had come to the fore once more. However, feeling that to voice this view publicly would reflect upon the navy's honor, they secretly contacted Konoe telling him they would leave the final decision on peace or war to him. When Tōjō heard of this, he felt that, if the navy really had no confidence in victory, then reconsideration was necessary. Although Tōjō questioned the navy minister insistently in the meeting, Oikawa revealed nothing, merely repeating, "We entrust our decision to the prime minister." Tōjō almost lost his temper. Konoe, on the other hand, tried to persuade Tōjō to make concessions regarding the Japanese army's occupation of China, the major point of conflict with America, in order to provide a way out of the impasse with the latter.

"Even if we recognize the principle of immediate and unconditional withdrawal," Konoe told him, "in practice it will be done in stages."

"Such a deception would be absurd," Tōjō said, rejecting the proposal. He went on to remind Konoe that the date he himself had agreed upon to begin preparations for war was approaching. Konoe's reaction was to dissolve the government.

Saionji had already died, and the important role of recommending a successor as prime minister had fallen to Marquis Kido Kōichi, Lord Keeper of the Privy Seal. Kido was a close friend of Konoe, and the most powerful of the Emperor's advisers. With Konoe's approval, he chose Tōjō. Unable to come up with a better alternative, the council of senior statesmen approved the choice as well.

Kido's thinking was that Tōjō did not oppose the continuation of U.S.-Japan negotiations and was the kind of man who would faithfully implement any directives given him personally by the Emperor. In particular, he thought Tōjō was the one man who could forestall an army revolt should Japan commit itself to a policy of peace. Likewise, should the decision be made to go to war, Tōjō would be the one best qualified to carry out the job.

Tōjō was surprised to receive the imperial command to form a new government. Nevertheless, when the Emperor, in an unprecedented order, instructed him to ignore the October deadline and renew efforts to negotiate with America, the new prime minister devoted all his energy to a final attempt to restore relations with the U.S. Even when Chief of Staff Sugiyama repeated the very points Tōjō himself had advocated the previous day as war minister, Tōjō now, as prime minister, silenced him.

Konoe entreated Ambassador Grew to ask Washington not to judge his successor on outward appearances alone. Washington, however, could only see the situation as worse. The news that more Japanese troops were heading toward French Indochina from China further stiffened Secretary of State Hull's attitude toward Japan.

Hull summoned Ambassador Nomura and handed him a note that contained a fresh list of ten items. The note was an arbitrary exposition of America's demands, effectively cancelling all prior negotiations. It amounted to a repudiation of all Japan's policies, demanding that Japan leave the Tripartite Pact, support only Chiang's authority in China, and withdraw all its troops and police from the whole of China and Indochina. Hull assumed that Japan realized that in his opinion "China" did not include Manchuria, so he did not bother to specify this.

A telegram containing the Hull note arrived in Tokyo on November 27, the very day another Imperial Headquarters—Governmental Liaison Conference was to be convened at the Imperial Palace. When the telegram was read at the conference, someone spoke out: "It's a declaration of war!" and none of those present had any doubt that he was right.

6

Pearl Harbor

As events rapidly approached an impasse, the leaders of the American government were fully aware of the deterioration of relations between Japan and the United States. America secretly intercepted and decoded all the important top-secret cables exchanged between the Japanese government and its embassy in Washington, and their contents were promptly delivered to the desks of the secretary of state, the heads of the army and the navy, and the president.

On November 27, 1941, Secretary of State Hull handed Ambassador Nomura the decisive ten-point note, then summoned Secretary of War Henry Stimson by telephone to inform him that peace negotiations between Japan and America were at an end and that matters were to be placed in the hands of the army and the navy. On receiving word from Stimson, Admiral Harold R. Stark, chief of Naval Operations, cabled urgent dispatches to the commanders in chief of the Pacific Fleet and Asiatic Fleet: "This dispatch is to be considered a war warning. Negotiations with Japan looking toward stabilization of conditions in the Pacific have ceased and an aggressive move by Japan is expected in the next few days."

The cables warned that the Japanese army and navy spearheads would probably be aimed at the Philippines, Thailand, Malaya, or Borneo. There was absolutely no mention of Hawaii.

The Japanese task force had already assembled secretly at Hitokappu Bay of Etorofu Island (one of the Kurils) and had sailed eastward, plowing through the stormy seas of the North Pacific. The force consisted of twenty warships and seven tankers, with a nucleus of six aircraft carriers and two battleships.

The strategy whereby the Japanese navy would attack Pearl Harbor in the event of war between Japan and America was not a new one. In 1932, in maneuvers conducted by the American fleet, an "Orange Force" (attack force) commanded by Admiral Harry E. Yarnell approached the island of Oahu completely undetected, launched aircraft from two carriers thirty minutes before sunrise, and dealt a crushing blow to the fleet at anchor and to Hawaii's defense installations. Thereafter, an attack on Pearl Harbor was considered as a serious and potentially effective plan by both Japanese and American military men. Again, in exercises in 1935, an attack force commanded by Admiral John Towers approached Oahu from the north on a Sunday morning and succeeded in a surprise attack on Pearl Harbor.

However, Japan's standard plan for naval operations against America included no provision for a surprise attack on Hawaii. The Japanese navy had planned to lure the American fleet into advancing across the Pacific as far as possible in the direction of Japan and to engage it near the Mariana Islands. In January 1941, the commander of the Combined Fleet, Admiral Yamamoto Isoroku, summoned Vice Admiral Ōnishi Takijirō and asked him to investigate secretly, for the first time, the possibility of an air attack on Hawaii. Yamamoto had been deeply impressed by the effectiveness of aircraft in the exercises he had commanded from the flagship *Nagato* the previous year, and he was preoccupied with the notion of attacking Hawaii from the air.

By May the plan was complete, and even Ōnishi, the man who had drafted it, saw its chances for success as no better than even. Nevertheless, Yamamoto ordered training exercises to be begun.

The success of a surprise attack on the naval base in Hawaii depended upon two conditions. One was the degree of precision of the ultra-high-altitude bombing and the torpedoing of the fleet at anchor; the other was the question of whether the task force could cross thousands of miles of ocean and approach Oahu without being detected by the adversary. The Japanese navy dealt with the former problem with fierce training. The latter—that was a gamble.

Yamamoto had long been opposed to war between Japan and the United States, but he stressed that should a time come when they must fight, Japan should gamble on a daring initial blow. Accomplished poker player that he was, he had said that if the first blow failed, there would be no chance of winning the war. By dealing a mortal blow to

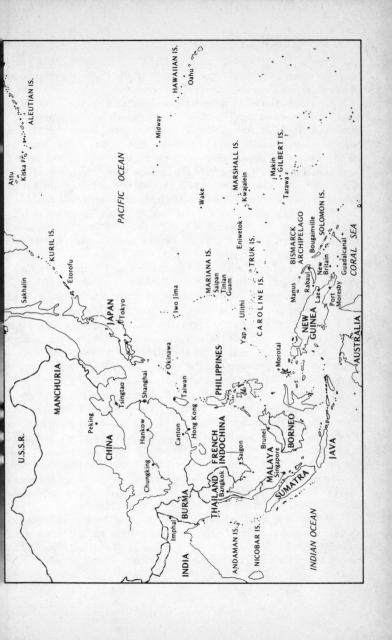

the enemy's Pacific Fleet at the outset of the war, Japan could gain a margin of time to occupy important areas to the south and prepare for the counterattacks of the U.S. forces.

Yamamoto planned to approach Pearl Harbor from the north by the shortest possible route. The North Pacific in winter was a nearly unbroken string of storms; not a single cargo vessel would be in those waters. Stormy weather would conceal the activities of the fleet, but, at the same time, present them with the problem of whether the high seas would permit refueling from the tankers. If they were blessed with clear, calm days, conditions would be ideal for refueling and navigation, but the danger of being detected by the enemy would double.

The Navy General Staff did not readily accept Yamamoto's plan, amounting as it did to a kind of gamble. Nevertheless, after a month of contention, Chief of the Navy General Staff Nagano finally gave approval.

It was at the Imperial Conference of December 1 that Japan finally determined to go to war. The Emperor, who had theretofore repeatedly expressed his desire for peace through diplomatic negotiations, was left with no other course but to sign the documents. He merely made two revisions in the draft of the imperial edict, the public declaration of war. One was to add that the war was not his desire, but the result of unavoidable circumstances, and the other was to moderate the emphasis on the noble purpose of the war, replacing "to enhance the glory of the empire" with "for the preservation and defense of the empire."

Once the Japanese government had determined upon war, the coded message "Climb Mount Niitaka [attack Hawaii as scheduled]" was sent from Admiral Yamamoto aboard the flagship *Nagato* in the Inland Sea to the task force in the North Pacific. Mount Niitaka, on Taiwan, is higher than Mount Fuji; thus the phrase also carried an exhortation to the task force in the daring deed it was to execute. The task force sailed on as instructed through rough seas, and by six o'clock on the morning of December 7, Hawaii time, had managed to approach undetected a point 230 nautical miles north of Pearl Harbor.

The first wave of 183 aircraft left their ships without a single mishap, despite dangerous rolling of the flight decks. The second wave of 167 planes also took to the air with superb skill. It was anticipated that about one hour and fifty minutes would be required to reach Pearl Harbor.

The plan for the surprise attack on Pearl Harbor was known only to a handful of naval strategists; even Prime Minister Tōjō had not been informed. The time schedule had been constructed in strict accordance with the desires of the navy. The likelihood was great that America's Pacific Fleet would be anchored in the harbor on the morning of Sunday, December 7. It was thus arranged that final official notification would be handed to Secretary of State Hull by Ambassador Nomura by 1 P.M. on the seventh, Washington time, one hour before the attack.

Thirteen parts of the fourteen-part notification to be handed to Hull had already been received by the Japanese embassy in Washington on the afternoon of the previous day. They were accompanied by instructions: "As the final part will be transmitted later, decipher these parts first and type them up neatly." That evening, the members of the embassy's communications section finished their work early and left the embassy to attend a farewell party for a coworker who was being transferred. First Secretary Okumura Katsuzō remained until late and typed the deciphered items himself.

The fateful day came. On Sunday morning, December 7, shortly after nine o'clock, the aide to the naval attaché came to work and found a telegram stuffed into the mailbox. It was the final Part 14, and to it were appended the orders "Deliver all 14 parts to Secretary of State Hull by 1 P.M." When presently the communications officer arrived, he set frantically to work translating. Ambassador Nomura made an appointment for a meeting with Hull.

Because of the importance of the contents, the typing of the dispatch was entrusted to First Secretary Okumura; and since he was unaccustomed to typing, the work proceeded slowly. Seeing this, Ambassador Nomura ordered his subordinates to help with the typing and also requested that his meeting with Hull be delayed forty-five minutes.

By contrast with this confusion, work in the American offices proceeded far more efficiently. President Roosevelt had already received the text of the first thirteen parts of the final notification, which had been intercepted at 9:30 the previous night. He read it over, and after showing it to his adviser Harry Hopkins, who happened to be present, said, "This means war."

The contents of Part 14 had reached the U.S. Navy Department by 8 A.M. on the seventh. Ten minutes later it was delivered to Secretary of State Hull, and twenty minutes later to the president. Though by secret means, the leadership of the American government was definitely in receipt of the final notification from Japan. Thus, when Ambassador Nomura proposed a meeting at 1 P.M., Hull was completely aware of both his intent and the contents of the document he would be handed. The only one who did not yet know the full significance of the meeting was Ambassador Nomura.

Nomura had not had time to peruse the document thoroughly. He was not such a fool as not to realize that its contents were of an extremely high level, yet he did not fully realize the importance of the fact that the designated time was "1 P.M." Nonetheless, he stood over First Secretary Okumura and his staff urging them on, virtually snatched away the completed document, which Okumura said, nearly in tears, still contained misprints, stuffed it into his briefcase, and rushed by car to the Department of State. When he arrived in the main entrance of the department, the clock already stood at five past two.

In fact, neither the leaders of the American government nor of the army and navy quite realized the significance of 1 P.M. They had surmised that the Japanese attack would probably begin at that time. It would most likely be in the Philippines, or Malaya, or possibly Guam or Wake Island . . .

One P.M. in Washington would be dawn in Hawaii. There were two men who leapt up as if they had been struck by lightning when they realized that fact. One was Navy Lieutenant Commander Alvin Kramer, who had been involved in the "Magic" operation to intercept and decipher the Japanese cables. He immediately rushed into Admiral Stark's room. Stark took up the telephone to call Admiral Husband E. Kimmel in Hawaii, but then reconsidered. A war alert had already been dispatched on November 27; moreover, he felt it unthinkable that Pearl Harbor should be attacked.

The other man was Colonel Rufus S. Bratton of Army Intelligence. When he succeeded in tracking down General George C. Marshall by telephone, he explained the importance of the "final notification," which the general had still not read. Marshall himself immediately wrote out the text of a cable: "The Japanese are presenting at 1 P.M. Eastern Standard Time today what amounts to an ultimatum. Also they are under orders to destroy their code machine immediately. Just what significance the hour set may have we do not know, but be on the alert accordingly." He then telephoned Admiral Stark:

"What do you think about sending the information concerning the time of presentation to the Pacific commanders?"

"We've sent them so much already, I hesitate to send any more. A new one will be merely confusing."

Marshall hung up, and in less than a minute the telephone rang again. This time Admiral Stark said anxiously, "I'll go along with you in sending that information to the Pacific." And, he suggested, it might be well if the army were to use the navy's emergency telephone too.

"We too have the means to transmit it with sufficient speed," replied General Marshall.

"Then could you," Stark asked, "add orders to cable that this information be relayed to naval authorities in every area, too?" Marshall agreed.

In Washington, it was already well past 11 A.M. Marshall had the order sent immediately. Before long it was in the hands of every commander in Panama, the Philippines, and San Francisco. In Hawaii, however, atmospheric conditions were bad, and there had been no response. The colonel in charge of communications had not thought to use the navy's direct radio communications and had taken the telegram to Western Union.

The very first shots between Japan and America were fired by the destroyer *Ward*. The *Ward* was patrolling the entrance to Pearl Harbor when, at about 6:30 A.M., she spotted what appeared to be the periscope of a submarine advancing through the gray waters into the harbor. She fired and the second round was on target; the submarine began to sink. The *Ward* then dropped depth charges.

The Japanese navy had thought that it might not be able to deal a decisive blow to the fleet in the harbor with air power alone, so it decided to attack simultaneously with small submarines. They were two-man midget submarines, twenty-two meters long; their navigational range was short, but they had considerable speed. Five midget submarines were transported to the mouth of the harbor by large submarines, and there set loose. One of them had kept close behind an American target ship just entering port and had been spotted by the

Ward as it tried to slip through when the antitorpedo net was lifted

The report of the attack on an enemy submarine did not reach Admiral Kimmel himself. Dismissing it as one more mistaken report, of which there had been many in the previous several months, his staff officers put it aside.

Until the previous year, the U.S. navy had assigned a high probability to a Japanese attack on Pearl Harbor. However, as signs of war grew more obvious, they came to regard the idea as fantastic. One reason was that the superiority of the Japanese navy in the Pacific was a recognized fact, and it seemed inconceivable they should risk their superiority in such an improbable venture. Another was that America's excellent intelligence network had been gathering information on Japan's movements; and, on the basis of this, it seemed highly probable that Japan's first blow would be directed at Southeast Asia. The fact that the movements of six Japanese aircraft carriers had not been detected by the intelligence network remained a matter of doubt until the last, yet faith in the intelligence work of the American army and navy lured them into a state of complacency. Thus it was that on the morning of December 7 no one in Hawaii, from the highest ranking general down to the lowliest private, could believe that the Japanese would indeed slip under the many-layered lines of defense around Guam, Wake, and Midway, and suddenly show up at Pearl Harbor.

That morning, a trainee at an army radar site observed on his screen a group of planes approaching from the north. This report was immediately telephoned to the Information Center; it was the time of the changing of the watch, and the duty officer had not yet arrived at his post. The substitute recalled that a squadron of B-17s was due to fly in from California about then. Consequently, no attention was given to this report, and no warning was issued.

At about the same time, an attorney named Royal Vitousek was circling above Oahu in a light plane, teaching his son how to fly, when he suddenly spotted two Zero fighters in the distance. Confirming the red sun insignia on the planes, he quickly landed. The first wave of Japanese fighters had just shot over the airfield. He heard a pilot shouting, "Damnfool Navy—using live ammunition for exercises!"

The Japanese planes continued to fly above the dense clouds, to their great good fortune, undetected. When they arrived at Oahu at 7:48, the clouds scattered and the skies over Pearl Harbor opened up

The battleship Tennessee *in flames after being hit by an 800-kilogram bomb on December 7, 1941.*

bright and clear. The lead commander, Colonel Fuchida Mitsuo, confirmed through his binoculars that eight battleships were at anchor and instantly gave the order, "All units, attack!" First the Zero fighters attacked the three army and three navy airfields. Taken unawares, not a single navy plane could take up the challenge, and the thirty army planes that did finally get aloft were shot down or driven off by the Japanese forces. In great haste, Admiral Kimmel's headquarters sent an unencoded message to the vessels at sea: "AIR RAID, PEARL HARBOR—THIS IS NO DRILL." Having established command of the skies, the Japanese aerial attack force commenced bombing and torpedo attacks on the fleet in the harbor. The bombs and torpedoes struck home with astonishing accuracy and, one after another, the vessels erupted in flames and smoke.

In Washington, the first report of the attack on Pearl Harbor was received by Divisional Chief of Operations Stark. He immediately notified Secretary of the Navy Knox. Knox, unable to believe his ears, said it must be a mistake for the Philippines. Even so, he had to inform the White House.

President Roosevelt was eating lunch; he expressed little surprise at the report. When Secretary Knox suggested it might be a mistake for

the Philippines, Roosevelt quietly said, "No, the cable's probably no
wrong. It's just the kind of unexpected thing the Japanese would do.

Secretary of State Hull was about to leave his office to meet Am
bassador Nomura, who had just arrived at the Department of State—
meeting he viewed with reluctance, since he knew what it held—whe
he received a call from the president. In a calm voice the president in
formed him that Hawaii had been attacked and ordered him to sen
the ambassador away coolly but politely. And, lest the secret of th
"Magic" operation be suspected, he urged upon him the need to pre
tend to know nothing.

Ambassador Nomura had still not caught his breath and was su
prised when Hull neither offered him a chair nor shook the hand h
held out. He could not fathom why Hull would be so angry because h
was an hour or so late for their meeting. Turning to Nomura, Hu
criticized Japan in the severest terms, calling it "shameless"; but, recal
ing the president's warning, finally checked his emotion. Then, sup
pressing Nomura's attempt to speak, he indicated the door with h
jaw. Finally Nomura, still uncomprehending, bid him farewell and pu
out his hand. Hull shook his hand icily and ushered him out of th
room.

In Japan, the first news concerning the war was broadcast by NH
radio at 7 A.M., December 8. It stated simply, "Today, before dawr
Japanese forces commenced hostilities with British and American force
in the Western Pacific." Most people simply felt that the inevitable ha
come. The Japanese were weary of the seemingly unending China Inc
dent. They had come to feel strongly that Japan must, by some mean
break out of the economic encirclement of Europe and America. Th
news of the outbreak of war, as it circulated among the people, had
weighty impact. However, they had not yet had time to digest fully i
import when they were inundated by a rapid succession of radio r
ports of the victory at Pearl Harbor, backed up by the stirring strain
of the "Battleship March." As the hours wore on, the extent of the vie
tory at Pearl Harbor emerged with greater clarity.

Five battleships, including the *Arizona*, and six cruisers and small
ships had been sunk; two other battleships and four cruisers an
smaller ships had been severely damaged. In effect, the Pacific Fleet c
the United States of America had been annihilated. (The aircraft ca

riers that were on duty at sea escaped attack. This was a fact of major significance in the subsequent development of the war but was hardly touched upon at that time.)

In America, too, news of the devastation at Pearl Harbor spread rapidly and caused great shock. For America, it was the worst military blow in its history. The American people could not believe that such a thing could happen and suspected that, if indeed it were true, the navy and the army air corps had been napping. Early on the afternoon of December 8, President Roosevelt addressed a special joint session of the House and Senate. The spectators' seats were packed.

"Yesterday, December 7, 1941—a date which will live in infamy— the United States of America was suddenly and deliberately attacked by naval and air forces of the Empire of Japan," the president stated matter-of-factly. Then, in order to impress vividly upon the memories of his audience that a surprise attack had been carried out while negotiations were in progress, he went on, "I ask that the Congress declare that since the unprovoked and dastardly attack by Japan on Sunday, December 7, 1941, a state of war has existed between the United States and the Japanese Empire."

His address was drowned in a storm of applause, cheers, and shouts. The people had expected the president to speak of the causes of the incredible annihilation of the American forces. He said nothing of that, but the phrase "unprovoked and dastardly attack" had sufficient effect. If the damage in Hawaii had been slight, and if the Japanese forces had incurred corresponding damage in their surprise attack, the people might well have had pause to recall, for example, how, in the Spanish-American War, American forces had made an "unprovoked attack" on the Spanish forces prior to the declaration of war. However, American losses were exceedingly heavy, and the Japanese forces seemed somehow to have escaped unscathed; the president's audience wished to believe that the mighty United States of America could never have cut such a ridiculous figure had it not been for some cunning trick on the part of the adversary. And believe it they did. "Get the yellow bastards!" "Remember Pearl Harbor!"—these became the watchwords of the nation, and the myth of the "sneak attack on Pearl Harbor" was born. And, as Roosevelt wished, that myth roused the nation to solidarity.

The person who slept most peacefully the night he heard the news of the attack on Pearl Harbor was British Prime Minister Churchill. He verified the news of the Japanese attack by a direct telephone call to Roosevelt.

"We are all in the same boat," the president said.

"This actually simplifies things. God be with you," Churchill said, thankful for the turn events had taken.

However, two days later, he, too, would have to confront what he called the greatest blow of his life.

As the situation in the East grew worse, the British navy prepared for the onslaught of the Japanese forces by strengthening its Eastern Fleet; two battleships were sent to Singapore, the *Repulse* and the *Prince of Wales*, both reputed to be unsinkable. When the Japanese advanced upon Malaya, the Eastern Fleet was mobilized. The great unanswered military question was, thus, which would carry the day: the battleships that constituted the core of this fleet, or Japan's aircraft?

On December 10, the Japanese naval air corps, having ascertained the position of the Eastern Fleet, sent up waves of aircraft from airfields in Saigon and the vicinity and attacked the battleships while they were far out at sea. The pom-pom guns with which the British battleships were equipped could fire six thousand rounds per minute; the sky above the fleet was blanketed with shells from the high-angle weapons and antiaircraft guns. At 11:15 A.M. the first bomb hit the *Repulse*, and for two hours thereafter a death struggle was waged on the seas. The *Repulse* took five torpedoes and sank first. The *Prince of Wales* also took five torpedoes and, finally, a direct hit. After ordering all hands to abandon ship, Vice Admiral Sir Thomas Phillips and Captain John C. Leach went down the side of the listing ship and into the ocean.

The news of the annihilation of the American Pacific Fleet, followed by that of the destruction of Britain's Eastern Fleet, stirred the Japanese people into a frenzy of excitement. Since the Meiji era Japan's awe and fear of the West had been deep and prolonged. All the more ecstatic, thus, was reaction to the nearly unblemished record of Japan's early military victories, which, for the moment, allowed Japan to forget the untold hardships looming over the horizon.

At the commencement of hostilities with Great Britain and the United States, the Japanese government declared that it had acted in self-defense and, further, appealed for the liberation of Asia. In a sense, it was correct. As Konoe Fumimaro had once asserted, the world had been apportioned on English and American standards; it was thus historically inevitable that the colonies in Asia would be liberated sometime, by someone. Even so, considering the stance Japan in fact took toward China, its claim to a sacred mission was something of an exaggeration. Just as many governments, in time of war, insist on the absolute virtue of their own cause, the Japanese government too repeatedly appealed, both at home and abroad, to the grand dream of Asian liberation.

Most Japanese believed in this dream, or at least tried to believe—just as most Americans believed they had suffered a "dastardly attack" at Pearl Harbor, and strove to convince themselves of the villainy of Japan. Poets vied to extol the victory with which the gods had blessed the Japanese forces, describing these victories as the sound of the iron chains of colonial control being torn asunder.

Repercussions in Asia were complex. Popular sentiment was still difficult to gauge in the Philippines, Malaya, and Thailand, the countries into which Japanese forces had advanced (the Thais did not fight but accepted the Japanese occupation). This was subsequently to be affected by Japan's power and administrative posture.

Nehru, who had been in and out of jail numerous times in the cause of the Indian independence movement and was later to become prime minister, held scant good will for Japan since its invasion of China. Still, he felt deep satisfaction at the news of the sinking of the *Prince of Wales*, which was only intensified by the unpleasant words of a certain British high official:

"If the *Prince of Wales* could be sunk by the yellow Japanese, I'd rather have let the Germans have her."

Although hampered by the jungle, the advance of the Japanese army was smooth. Having detected that the weak point of the Singapore fortifications was at their rear, the Japanese army landed near the Thai-Malay border at about the same time as the Pearl Harbor attack, crushed the numerically superior British colonial forces, and headed straight south.

The Japanese had neither accurate maps nor sufficient intelligence on the enemy. They simply pushed forward furiously. Their strength was not in their equipment but in their fighting spirit. Lacking sufficient intelligence on their adversary, the British, under severe attack, eventually retreated. Half of the defending British forces were Indian troops, who had no reason to put up a serious fight.

Before commencing hostilities, Army Major Fujiwara Iwaichi contacted members of the secret organization IIL (Indian Independence League) in Bangkok, and they accompanied the Japanese army south, down the Malay Peninsula. At Alor Star, a strategic point in northern Malaya, an Indian battalion was stranded, its route of retreat cut off. Major Fujiwara, alone with only an interpreter, presented himself before the battalion commander, the only Englishman, and advised him to surrender. He agreed. Perceiving the talent of one Captain Mohan Singh, a surrendered Indian officer, Major Fujiwara put him in charge of maintaining public order in the city.

The operations of the IIL expanded with the smooth advance of the Japanese forces. With the backing of the Japanese military, Captain Singh established the INA (Indian National Army) for the liberation of the motherland. Their numbers had surpassed twenty-five hundred by the time the Japanese forces had advanced as far as Kuala Lumpur.

It was the Chinese volunteers who put up the most stubborn resistance in Malaya and Singapore. They did not see the Japanese attack as a liberation. They were resolved to fight together with their motherland, China, and harassed the Japanese forces with the best means at their disposal, guerrilla warfare. Time after time, the Japanese rear units were attacked by guerrillas or, under the latter's accurate guidance, Japanese encampments were showered with shells. When the Japanese arrived at the Johore Straits and attacked Singapore Island, the Chinese, in sharp contrast to the British forces who retreated in avalanche fashion, fought to the last. The Chinese volunteers who defended the northwestern portion of the fortifications died there, to a man, clutching their weapons.

Singapore fell with the surrender of the British forces on February 15, 1942. Two days later, Major Fujiwara took custody of the Indian prisoners of war in Farrer Park. From about noon, the park was inundated with Indian troops; even at 2 P.M. there was still no break in the line of soldiers crowding in. Their number was reported at forty-five thousand.

Major Fujiwara addressed them concerning Indian independence and the significance of the present war and spoke to them of the activities of the INA led by Captain Mohan Singh. The Indian troops

Japanese forces in action in the Burmese oil fields. Lack of shipping hindered the smooth transfer to Japan of Southeast Asian oil.

leapt to their feet and tossed their hats into the air amid a tumult of hurrahs when Fujiwara said, "My Indian soldier friends, if, of your own free will, you join the fight for the liberation and independence of your homeland, the Japanese military will cease to treat you as prisoners of war; we will recognize your freedom to fight and give you full-scale support." These troops, who were to compose the INA, then proceeded to Burma.

The fall of Singapore was a historic event. The principal stronghold of the English, who had ruled in the Orient since the seventeenth century, vanished. In their place, the Japanese assumed the position of masters. The surrendered British forces abandoned resistance; the Malays, for the time being, cooperated with the Japanese. Only the Chinese, still intensely antagonistic, attempted to continue guerrilla warfare. The Japanese military seized a register of anti-Japanese resistance members and arrested sixty-five hundred people on the basis of it; five thousand of these Chinese were executed. This was the largest-scale act of repression carried out by the Japanese military during the war.

Lieutenant Colonel Tsuji Masanobu, an Imperial Headquarters staff officer, is said to have been the person who urged these cruel executions. Tsuji had landed in the vanguard of the unit attacking Malaya, and up to the fall of Singapore he had, forcefully and daringly, directed operations at the front of the battle line, earning himself a name for bravery. The opinions of a man of his stature and his powerful personality carried such force that even the army commander could not reject them.

Hong Kong fell a little more than two weeks after the war began. Japanese forces opened their attack as soon as word was received of the successful landing of the Malay attack force. The division commander in charge of the attack estimated that it would require a week to breach the "Gin-Drinkers' Line," the British line of defense on the Kowloon Peninsula. However, an officer on a scouting mission, Lieutenant Wakabayashi Tōichi, noticed that the enemy's defenses were extremely thin, and, leading a platoon, he slipped through the barbed wire at night, infiltrated deep into enemy territory, and attacked unexpectedly. The British forces wavered, and under continuing Japanese attack the defense line collapsed in a day.

After intense shelling and bombing, the Japanese made a night landing on Hong Kong Island and secured a foothold. A week of fighting ensued, and on Christmas night the British surrendered. The Union Jack, which had flown over the land since the Opium War, was lowered, and the Rising Sun raised in its place.

The Japanese attack against the Philippines was launched on December 8 with an aerial assault by two hundred fighters and bombers, which had crossed eight hundred kilometers of ocean from their bases in Taiwan. No other fighters in the world were capable of flying such distances to battle—a fact that, as in the attack on the *Prince of Wales*, attested to the superior performance of Japanese aircraft.

The Army Air Corps commander in the Philippines, Major General Lewis H. Brereton, received a telephone call from Washington telling him that Pearl Harbor had been "caught napping" and that he was not to repeat the same blunder. The principal base, Clark Field, in the suburbs of Manila, was not napping, but in the middle of lunch when it was attacked. The American airmen did not seriously believe a

Japanese could pilot a plane properly. But even the P-40, the latest American warplane, was no match for the Zero in a fight. Many aircraft were destroyed on the ground, and those that did get into the air were struck down like flies. The first Japanese strike partially paralyzed the American air forces, and with the second strike on the following day the destruction of the American air unit was nearly total.

Having gained command of the skies, Japanese forces landed at Lingayen Gulf, then, overcoming stubborn American and Filipino resistance, headed south, straight for Manila. In the Philippines, too, the Japanese were outnumbered—three to one—but in fighting spirit and training they were vastly superior, and the war turned in favor of the Japanese.

The commander of the U.S. Army Forces in the Far East, Lieutenant General Douglas MacArthur, sent a cable to America, requesting that warplanes be rushed by carrier to Philippine waters. The reply from America, now fighting on two fronts, Europe and the Pacific, was "impossible." It became clear that his plan to drive the Japanese into the sea was now purely theoretical. For some time the American plan had been to carry out a protracted defense relying on the jungles and mountains of the Bataan Peninsula, should Luzon Island become endangered. MacArthur scorned such passive strategy but now had no choice.

The Japanese soon learned through aerial reconnaissance of the American withdrawal to Bataan. The first-line divisional commander Tsuchihashi Yūichi recommended on six occasions that they should cut off the Americans' route of retreat, outflank them, and wipe them out. The army commander, Lieutenant General Honma Masaharu, paid no attention whatsoever to his suggestion, for the orders he had received from Imperial Headquarters were to occupy Manila as quickly as possible. Imperial Headquarters preferred the effects of a political demonstration to tactical gains. The American forces' evacuation was a leisurely one; in the end, the Japanese forces were to have a hard time subduing them.

At 2 A.M. on March 1, 1942, Lieutenant General Imamura Hitoshi was transferring from a transport ship to a landing craft. There was a moon, but the sky was faintly clouded. Imamura had been at Army General Staff Headquarters at the time of the Manchurian Incident and had

had a hard time trying to get the situation under control. Thereafter, he had held several posts and risen in rank and was now commander of the forces attacking the island of Java.

Suddenly, there was a loud explosion; the ship rolled and began to list. It appeared they had been attacked by a torpedo boat. Imamura slid across the tilting deck and down into the sea. He was wearing his life vest, so there was no fear of sinking. He drifted awhile, looking at the deep black silhouettes of the coconut palms growing along the Javanese shore in the distance. Eventually, a motorboat came to his rescue. Peering through the moonlight, the helmsman recognized him:

"Aren't you the army commander, sir? If only you had called out, we would have rescued you first. My apologies, sir."

"It's the young ones who're going to do the fighting. You should rescue them first," replied the army commander.

Such accidents notwithstanding, the conquest of Java proceeded smoothly. A mere week later, the Dutch army, one hundred thousand strong, had surrendered to a Japanese force of twenty-five thousand. It had been frightened by rumors of a landing by two hundred thousand Japanese troops, and the Indonesian soldiers had no will to fight, choosing instead to desert or to retreat. Even the local inhabitants who had been ordered to obstruct the Japanese forces, far from obeying, willingly cooperated with the Japanese.

General Imamura invited Achmed Sukarno, leader of the independence movement, who had been freed from a Sumatra prison, to the study of his Batavia quarters and told him:

"The future of Indonesia is something that will be decided by the Japanese government in consultation with the leaders of this country; I myself have no authority. However, I can definitely promise that we will raise the political position and welfare of the Indonesian people above what it was under Dutch rule. You are free to cooperate with the army, or to observe events from a position of neutrality. However, if you intend to interfere with the military government, your freedom will be restricted. Even so, we will guarantee completely your honor, your life, and your property—and we will not send you to jail."

Four days later, Sukarno visited Imamura with his reply.

"I trust your words; I will cooperate with the military government. However, I must point out that I do not abandon my freedom to choose my own course of action after the war has ended."

As many Indonesians as possible were appointed to the governmental organizations the Dutch had occupied. A supreme military advisory body was organized, with five Japanese and ten Indonesians as members. Those chosen included Sukarno, who would later become president, as well as others who were to become vice-president and cabinet members at the time of Indonesian independence.

The military government of Java proceeded extremely peacefully, and order was maintained completely. The Indonesians were friendly to the Japanese troops, and, here, the Chinese did their best to ingratiate themselves with the Japanese. Criticism arose among military leaders and the government in Tokyo that Imamura's administration was too liberal, but an inspection commission approved his policies as they stood. Indonesia, like Burma in the early days, was one of the few places where the people actually felt that they had been liberated by the Japanese military.

At about the time Imamura was taking Java, Japanese troops also advanced into Burma, where they routed the British and Indian troops, and steadily went about their mopping-up campaign. In the Pacific, Japanese forces had occupied the American bases on Guam and Wake islands in the early days of the war, then, in the following year, made further military gains in the west, in New Guinea and the Bismarck Archipelago.

Five months after hostilities began, Japanese forces held in their grasp an extensive area stretching from east of India to the South Pacific. Although their victories had been flawless and their campaigns had proceeded smoothly, the Japanese forces had hardly once faced a battle that had severely tested them. Only in the Philippines were they still harassed by American and Filipino resistance on the Bataan Peninsula. Imperial Headquarters, which had at first given priority to the occupation of Manila and had relegated the taking of Bataan to a later occasion, now urged Army Commander Honma to go ahead with this task.

MacArthur, who had been commanding the Bataan campaign from the fortress of Corregidor Island, south of Bataan, had escaped by PT boat by March 10, ordered by the president to withdraw to Australia to reorganize an offensive. Major General Jonathan M. Wainwright was appointed as his replacement; MacArthur's parting words to him, after ordering him to fight to the last, were "I shall return." And, he added, "If you're still on Bataan when I get back, I'll put you up for lieutenant general."

In early April, having been reinforced, the Japanese began a concerted general offensive. After a week of fierce fighting, they reached the southern tip of the Bataan Peninsula. The Japanese had not been fully aware of the fact that the American and Filipino forces were exhausted, starving, and wracked by malaria and dysentary, their morale nearly destroyed. They had estimated the number of the enemy entrenched on Bataan at twenty-five thousand but were astounded to discover that the number of American and Filipino troops who came down the mountains in droves, white flags in hand, had swelled to seventy-six thousand.

The Japanese still had to cross the water to attack the Americans defending Corregidor. Japanese trucks were needed, first of all, to transport men and materials to the front. The prisoners were thus forced to withdraw on foot, over sixty kilometers of road from the southern tip of the peninsula to San Fernando. By the standards of a soldier of the Japanese army, that was a two-day journey, no distance at all.

The American and Filipino soldiers, however, who were not only accustomed to being moved by vehicles but had been fighting while plagued by malaria and malnutrition brought on by four months of supply difficulties, dropped one after the other beneath the blazing sun. It took four or even five days for most of them to trudge to the internment camp. Attitudes toward the prisoners among the Japanese soldiers who passed them in trucks headed for the front were varied. One might take pity on them and give them food, the next might beat the marching prisoners over the head with a plundered golf club. The prisoners met a variety of fates. Some were fortunate enough to be driven by truck the entire route; others fell beneath the blows of the guards, never to rise again; many drew their final breath soon after the relief of having found their way into the internment camp at last.

Lieutenant Colonel Tsuji of the Imperial Headquarters General Staff, visiting Bataan to encourage morale, treated the throng of prisoners with undisguised contempt, inciting acts of cruelty. There are no indisputable witnesses, but the story is told that Tsuji once said, "This is the way to treat bastards like this," pulled out his pistol, and shot to death one of the prisoners. Seven thousand prisoners, a third of them American, are said to have died in the Bataan Death March.

Tsuji, of his own accord, also ordered the execution of influential Filipino politicians.* Colonel Kawaguchi Kiyotake, commander on the island of Cebu, received the order from military headquarters in Manila to execute Chief Justice José Abad Santos, who had been seized, as well as his son. Kawaguchi, an officer from the "old days," prided himself on the humanitarian treatment he had given German prisoners when he had served at a prisoner of war camp in World War I. He flew into a rage, exclaiming, "Such an act is contrary to the way of the warrior, Bushido," drove out of the room the staff officer who had brought the order—one of those who had been greatly influenced by Tsuji—and wrote a letter of protest to military headquarters. Nevertheless, two weeks later a telegram ordering the executions came again, and Kawaguchi finally had to make up his mind. Promising Santos that he would at least not fail to safeguard his son, he enforced the order of the military.

General Honma was shocked when he read the report from Kawaguchi, since he had not intended that at all, nor had he received any reports on the matter until then. The execution order was in fact issued by staff officers under the sway of Tsuji. Honma was of a literary bent, a man of common sense, who had served a long time in England; he had come to realize that American rule in the Philippines was relatively unexceptionable for a colonial regime. His policy was to treat the Filipino people with affection and to govern still more liberally than the Americans had.

Former Speaker of the House of Representatives Manuel Roxas, who had been captured on Mindanao, was one who narrowly escaped execution. General Ikuta Torao, the local commander, was reluctant to become involved in the execution order when he received it from Manila, and delegated its disposition to general staff officer Lieutenant Colonel Jimbō Nobuhiko. Jimbō considered Roxas a talented man who could be of use if allowed to cooperate with Japan; moreover, he was loath to execute him for humanitarian reasons. He persuaded General Ikuta that they should at any rate keep Roxas hidden away. On a visit

* A staff officer did not have the right to issue an order, but he could exert pressure to have one drawn up.

to Manila, Jimbō appealed to General Wachi Takaji of the military headquarters, revealing the facts to him. General Wachi was surprised, for he too knew nothing of any such orders. He notified General Honma at once, and Roxas, destined to become the first president of the Republic of the Philippines after the war, was released unharmed.

Indonesia and the Philippines offer a contrast. In the former, the Japanese military was welcomed as a liberating army; the occupation was peaceful, with no serious trouble occurring. The Philippines, however, had already been promised independence by the United States, and so felt the Japanese invasion as interference. The Philippines are unique in the history of Asia. Before they had yet developed into a nation, they were under Spanish rule, then the Spanish occupation was taken over in turn by the United States. The ruling classes of the Philippines had been educated in America and felt very close to the United States; conversely, they found it difficult to get along with the Japanese. As a result, the administration of the Philippines was a headache for Japan from the start, and these early problems aggravated the estrangement.

Although, as an individual, General Honma was a perfect gentleman, there was doubt whether he was a soldier with a capacity for discipline. Like Imamura, Honma advocated a relatively liberal military rule; however, not only was this viewed unfavorably back in Japan, but he was also made a scapegoat for the bungling of the capture of Bataan—notwithstanding the fact that most of the responsibility lay with commands from Imperial Headquarters. He was recalled to Tokyo, and removed from the active list.

7

Two Islands:
Midway and Guadalcanal

Colonel Iwakuro Hideo, who had participated in the campaign against Singapore as a regimental commander, was transferred back to Tokyo after the capture of that stronghold. There he met with Ikawa Tadao, a director of the Industrial Unions Central Bank, with whom he had worked during the Japanese-American negotiations. They agreed that it was necessary to begin peace negotiations with the United States. Both men were aware of the extreme difference in industrial power between the United States and Japan and were concerned about the future course of the war. But the leaders of the government, navy, and army, already tasting the sweet fruits of victory, did not take their concern seriously.

The navy, flushed with success, urged an invasion of Hawaii. This plan was blocked by the strong opposition of the army. The navy then proposed an attack on Australia, which was again opposed by the army. It was obvious that it would be impossible to keep supplies moving to such a distant area; and it would have required at least ten army divisions to occupy such vast territory. The army had no manpower reserves on that scale. The army's long-range strategy was to build up the various battle fronts and strengthen the occupation of the already conquered territories, to increase levels of production, and to adopt a cautious policy of waiting for the fall of Britain and a weakening of America's morale. In contrast, the navy urged an aggressive policy of seeking to conquer the entire area from the Pacific to the Indian Ocean, in effect dividing the world between Japan and Germany.

Admiral Yamamoto strongly urged massive attacks on the U.S. naval fleet with the aim of bringing the war to an early conclusion.

113

Yamamoto's fighting spirit was even more aroused after the B-25 air raid on Tokyo led by Lieutenant Colonel James H. Doolittle on April 18, 1942. The Tokyo air raid did little actual damage, but it heightened the fighting spirit of the American people and demonstrated to the Japanese leaders that the capital of Japan was open to attack at any time.

To Yamamoto it was intolerable that enemy planes had been able to fly over the Imperial Palace, the very heart of the Japanese Empire. To prevent this happening again, he wished to extend further Japanese Pacific lines of defense, judging that if the U.S. navy then attacked those lines, it would present an excellent opportunity for a decisive naval battle.

The army and navy, in fact, differed on every issue: not only with regard to strategy, but even over the division of such spoils of war as whiskey and the like.

Relations between the U.S. army and navy were likewise strained. President Roosevelt thought it advisable to have a unified Pacific command under a single authority and proposed General Douglas MacArthur for the position. However, the navy regarded the Pacific as its own preserve and vigorously opposed MacArthur's appointment. In the end, the Pacific region was divided in two, with Admiral Chester W. Nimitz as commander in chief of the Pacific Ocean Area and General MacArthur in command of the Southwest Pacific Area. MacArthur was highly dissatisfied with this arrangement. On his own authority, he decided to call himself Commander in Chief in the Southwest Pacific. Thus the U.S. army and navy were to find themselves at odds over everything from general strategy to the distribution of jeeps.

The American people's dissatisfaction and anger over the series of military defeats on various fronts came to be directed against Japanese-Americans, especially those living in California. The Japanese-Americans had established themselves as honest, hard-working citizens of their communities in the face of considerable legal and personal discrimination. Now, with the beginning of the war, days of real hardship began for them. The leading members of the community were arrested by the FBI. There were incidents of Japanese-Americans being spat upon and beaten up in the streets, and of shots being fired into their homes. They were dismissed from their jobs at such places as the

Los Angeles City Hall. It was widely rumored that the Japanese army would invade the West Coast and that the Japanese-Americans would guide and assist them.

The demand that the "dangerous Japanese" be removed from the coastal areas to the interior spread from the West Coast throughout the nation, receiving strong support from politicians and the military. Major newspapers declared that America was threatened both from without and from within. With the exception of those in Hawaii, the Japanese-Americans lived almost entirely on the West Coast. Two-thirds of them were Nisei with U.S. citizenship; the rest were still Japanese subjects, having been denied the opportunity to apply for U.S. citizenship.

If one leaves aside the minority who had gone back to Japan to be educated, one may safely say that the adult Nisei were the most loyal of Americans. They had not forgotten Ambassador Plenipotentiary Matsuoka's advice to "be good Americans, rather than good Japanese."

As the crisis of impending war between America and Japan deepened, the Japanese-Americans had, as a matter of course, declared their loyalty to the U.S. The first-generation Issei's feelings were doubtless more complex than the Nisei's; given their previous experience it was only to be expected that they would hope for a Japanese victory. But they loved their children and hoped that in time they would be better accepted by American society. In addition, many felt grateful to America, which had given them the chance of a better life, at least on the economic level. Thus most of the Issei were determined, insofar as they lived in America, to act in accordance with American law.

Such facts, however, were ignored by the average American. Lieutenant General John De Witt, head of the Western Defense Command, stated: "A Jap is a Jap. . . . Loyal or not, they are extremely dangerous. Regardless of whether they are citizens or not, they are Japanese."

The White House at first issued sensible warnings against the ill-treatment of Japanese-Americans. But by February 19, 1942, when President Roosevelt signed Executive Order 9066, the more extreme politicians and the army had gained control of public opinion. The order authorized those responsible, "whenever . . . necessary or desirable, to prescribe military areas . . . from which any or all persons may be excluded, and with respect to which, the right of any person to enter, remain in, or leave shall be subject to whatever restrictions the Secretary of War or the appropriate Military Commander may impose in his discretion."

California, Washington, Oregon, and parts of Arizona were so designated, and an announcement urging the voluntary evacuation of all Japanese-Americans to the interior of the country was issued under Commander De Witt's name.

However, several states in the interior refused to admit Japanese from the West Coast: Nevada even placed guards at the state line to turn back any Japanese coming from California. In the end, many Japanese-Americans preferred to be officially and forcibly evacuated rather than suffer the pains and indignities of "voluntary evacuation."

Internment camps—euphemistically termed Reception Centers— were built at ten scattered sites: Tule Lake and Manzanar in California; Poston and Gila River in Arizona; Granada in Colorado; Heart Mountain in Wyoming; Jerome and Rohrer in Arkansas; Minidoka in Idaho; and Topaz in Utah. Some one hundred and twenty thousand Japanese-Americans were given twenty-four hours after receipt of the order to evacuate. They had to make arrangements for their houses and possessions; many had time only to gather their personal possessions and move as ordered.

The American government had stated both to its own citizens and to the outside world that the war was being fought in defense of democracy against totalitarianism. That claim was, in a sense, true. Yet the internment of the Japanese-Americans in accordance with Executive Order 9066 made it clear that democracy was for whites only, while Asians had no right to enjoy its benefits. The Japanese-Americans were sent off to internment camps, but Italian and German residents of the United States were left untouched.

May 27 was the anniversary of the brilliant Japanese naval victory in which Admiral Tōgō Heihachirō attacked the Russian Baltic Fleet in the straits of Tsushima during the Russo-Japanese War. Around that date, the Japanese navy left port and began moving east across the Pacific. The Northern Squadron, which included two aircraft carriers, planned to attack the islands of Attu and Kiska in the Aleutian chain. The First Task Force, with four carriers as its core and led by the same Admiral Nagumo Chūichi who had participated in the attack on Pearl Harbor, was to attack Midway Island. It was followed by the main force under the direct command of Admiral Yamamoto, the commander of the Combined Fleet. In all, three hundred and fifty warships, one thousand airplanes and over one hundred thousand men were mobilized for this operation. It was the greatest attack force ever seen in world naval history.

What of the American Pacific Fleet, which had to confront this mighty force? All its battleships had been either sunk or damaged at Pearl Harbor; of its five carriers, the *Saratoga* had been badly damaged in a submarine attack and was under repair. In the Battle of the Coral Sea in early May, the carrier *Lexington* had been sunk and the *Yorktown* badly damaged. Only the *Enterprise* and the *Hornet* were left for the defense of the Pacific. If in the coming battle these two ships were lost, the Pacific·would become a Japanese lake.

Yet the American side, apparently so weak, had one advantage: the Americans had cracked the Japanese naval code, just as they had cracked the Japanese Foreign Ministry's code during the American-Japanese negotiations. The U.S. navy had recovered Japanese code books from battleships sunk at Wake Island and other Pacific sites; using them, Admiral Nimitz could infer the general movements of the Japanese naval offensive. Even so, the American side could not be sure where the attack would come: in other words, what "AF," the code word for the main objective, meant. Accordingly, Lieutenant Commander Rochefort of Naval Intelligence had an uncoded message sent from Midway Island stating that its water distilling facilities had broken down and that there was a shortage of drinking water. Two days later, U.S. code specialists intercepted a Japanese navy telegraph transmission stating that "AF is short of drinking water." Thereupon Nimitz decided to take the entire Pacific Fleet to Midway to lie in wait for Yamamoto's fleet. Repairs on the *Yorktown*, which were to have taken some three months, were completed on an emergency basis in two days, and the *Yorktown* was rushed to Midway.

The first aircraft-carrier battle in history had already taken place in the Coral Sea. On that occasion, the opposing vessels never came within sight of each other; only the respective air squadrons fought, and the result was fairly even. The lesson to be learned from this engagement was that the side that struck first was almost certainly assured of victory.

Rear Admiral Raymond A. Spruance, commander of the U.S. task force, had fully absorbed this important lesson. Stressing to the officers and men under his command that "success in the coming battle would be of the highest service to the nation," he ordered, first, the use of surprise attack methods and, second, that the carriers always stay within sight of each other—in other words, that the greatest possible use be made of concentrated air power.

In contrast, Yamamoto cannot be said really to have learned the lesson of the war in the Pacific, despite the fact he had demonstrated the superiority of planes over ships and successfully commanded naval battles that stunned the world. At Midway, he disposed his carriers at some distance from one another and placed his main-force fleet some three hundred nautical miles behind the task force.

On the morning of June 4, Lieutenant Howard Ady, captain of a reconnaissance seaplane, was startled to discover a great fleet virtually covering the ocean below him; it was as though he was witnessing the first act of the "greatest show on earth." Nagumo's squadron spotted Ady's aircraft and sent up fighters. At the same time, flight squadrons took off one after another from the four carriers on their way to attack the U.S. base on Midway Island. Lieutenant Ady dived into a bank of clouds and relayed an urgent report of his sighting of the enemy carriers. The chance for a first strike lay with the U.S. side.

In the skies above Midway, twenty-six fighters that had been sent aloft in response to the lieutenant's urgent warning met the oncoming Japanese planes. But here again the U.S. air force was no match for the Zero fighters. The Japanese attackers bombed at will, destroying the base and calling for a second attack wave.

At this point, Admiral Spruance ordered an attack on the Japanese carriers by all 149 planes from his own three carriers, leaving only a very small number of planes in reserve. It seemed a highly reckless gamble. If the allied carriers, left without defending fighters, were attacked by the enemy, they would be easy prey. But Spruance was determined to use all the forces at his command to destroy the enemy, even at great risk to his own fleet.

The Nagumo Squadron was waiting for the arrival of the U.S. task force. Eighteen attack planes had been armed with torpedoes and stood in readiness on the deck. However, when the message from the first attack squadron at Midway came, urging another attack wave, Admiral Nagumo ordered the planes' bombing equipment to be converted to use for land attack.

Japanese scout planes spotted Spruance's task force about one hour after the U.S. planes took off. Then another thirty minutes elapsed as the Nagumo Command tried to identify what class of warships comprised the task force. Rear Admiral Yamaguchi Tamon, commander of the flight squadron, urged an immediate attack on the task force with all available planes. Yamaguchi, like Spruance, recognized the crucial importance of being first to strike. But Nagumo chose to follow the advice of air staff officer Commander Genda Minoru instead. Genda urged that the warplanes of the first attack squadron just returned from Midway be refitted once again with torpedoes for a full-scale fight to the finish with the enemy.

Through a rift in the clouds, a group of U.S. torpedo planes spotted the four Japanese carriers, frantically engaged in preparations for the planes' takeoff. The U.S. planes dived down to attack the Nagumo Squadron. However, the Japanese task force's defenses were strong; thirty-five U.S. planes were almost immediately downed and not a single torpedo hit its target. It seemed that Spruance's luck had run out.

The decks of the four carriers were covered with fighters, torpedo planes, and bombers readied for takeoff. The order to take off for the attack was given, and the lead fighter rose swiftly into the air. But just at that moment lookouts on board the carriers saw, from between the clouds, the U.S. dive bombers shooting down like gleaming arrows aimed directly at the Japanese ships. One after another the bombers attacked, braving heavy antiaircraft fire; and time after time the bombs hit their targets. Within thirty minutes explosions had reduced the *Akagi*, the world's largest aircraft carrier, the *Kaga*, and the *Sōryū* to great piles of scrap, wreathed in flames and clouds of black smoke: they and all the aircraft on their decks were rendered useless. Only one carrier was left—the *Hiryū*—and from its deck an attack squadron took off in pursuit of the *Yorktown*, severely damaging it.

The battle raged until late afternoon. Admiral Spruance's bombing squadron caught the remaining *Hiryū* and made quick work of it before the sun went down. After Rear Admiral Yamaguchi had ordered all hands to abandon ship, he and Kaku Tomeo, the ship's captain, climbed onto the bridge of the sinking ship. Crewmen who were about to jump from the decks into the sea below heard Yamaguchi say to Kaku: "Well, now . . . a little moon-viewing, perhaps?"

In the Battle of Midway Japan lost four carriers, all the warplanes based on them, and a large number of elite pilots. America lost only one carrier. Admiral Yamamoto's main-force fleet hurried to reach the battle area, but by then the American navy had withdrawn far out of reach. The Battle of Midway had ended in an overwhelming U.S. victory, thanks to the split-second decision of Admiral Spruance. The hitherto undefeated Japanese navy had been dealt a severe blow; and now, for the first time in seven months of war, good fortune was with America.

The news of this, the first real American victory in the war, greatly restored the self-confidence of the American people. Imperial Headquarters, for its part, announced a "Japanese victory at Midway" and did its best to hide from the Japanese people the truth of this grievous blow to the nation's war effort.

Ever since April 1942 the Japanese navy's air squadron, which had advanced as far as Rabaul on New Britain Island and Lae at the eastern end of New Guinea, had been almost continually engaged with the enemy at Port Moresby. The Japanese had already occupied the north coast of New Guinea, and the next target of attack was this important city on the coast opposite Australia.

Zero fighter squadrons had been brought up as far as Lae, displaying once again their matchless strength. By the beginning of August, the Sasai Squadron had shot down nearly three hundred enemy planes; and Lieutenant Sasai Jun'ichi and Sergeant Sakai Saburō, vying for the position of top ace, had each brought down over fifty planes.

Nevertheless, the supply of allied planes to Port Moresby via the South Pacific continued without letup. If the Japanese eased up on their air attacks for a single day, the next day they would find themselves under attack from the allies. The American bombers came suddenly, flying very low, and without any defending fighters—American morale was high.

On the Japanese side, there was virtually no possibility of replenishing men or equipment; and plane after plane was lost as the air battles continued. The fatigue of a war of attrition began to be apparent.

On the morning of August 7, Sergeant Sakai and the rest turned out as usual at the Rabaul air base in preparation for an attack mission. But that day's mission was abruptly cancelled. The Americans had landed at Guadalcanal, which was to be the new target. A clamor arose from the airmen: "Guadalcanal? Where's that?" "Bring a chart!"

Guadalcanal was a one hundred-fifty-kilometer-long, fifty-kilometer-wide island near the eastern end of the Solomons group, some one thousand kilometers southeast of Rabaul. It was an inhospitable place, covered with dense tropical jungle and steep mountains. On its north central coast there was a level area where the Japanese navy had begun to construct a forward air base, using two thousand laborers with picks and shovels. Now Major General Vandegrift's First Marine Division had launched a surprise attack and landing timed, seemingly, to coincide with completion of the air base. It was the U.S. forces' first major offensive in the Pacific theater.

America's top planners, engaged in preparation for a North African landing as part of their strategy for the European theater, had no plans for a Pacific offensive. However, Admiral Nimitz at Pearl Harbor and General MacArthur in Melbourne—the two front-line supreme commanders—strongly urged that the U.S. take advantage of its victory at Midway and attack the Solomons. If these could be taken, the Japanese threat to Australia would be greatly reduced. In addition, the door would be open for an attack on Rabaul, to the northwest, and on Truk, the Japanese navy's most vital Pacific base, still farther north. This proposal was accepted. There followed the usual struggle between army and navy for leadership of the campaign, but in the end it was decided that the first stage at any rate would be under the control of Nimitz and the navy.

Eighteen Zeros, including Sakai's, and twenty-seven attack planes raced from Rabaul to the distant target at Guadalcanal. It was the first time, not only for the pilots themselves but in aviation history as a whole, that fighters had flown over a thousand kilometers to do battle. Well trained and seasoned in many previous battles, they flew and fought very skillfully. Engaging eighty enemy planes, including the latest Grumman F4F fighters, they shot down half of them.

No sooner had the coastline of Guadalcanal been sighted than Sakai saw a flotilla of transport ships covering the sea off the Americans' projected landing area. At that moment, he was assailed by an indefinable sense of doom. Countless ships moved back and forth between the flotilla and the coast, trailing white wakes behind them. In the bustling activity of those ships, stretched like a bridge across the sea, Sakai felt he had glimpsed the reality of the massive forces that he and his fellows were up against.

The attempts at bombing the transports failed almost entirely. Sakai himself had shot down one American fighter when, mistaking a formation of eight bombers for fighters, he closed in, only to be hit by machine-gun fire from the tail of the enemy plane. He managed to shoot down two of the bombers but took three more hits himself. His windshield was shattered and a bullet went through his right eye. Struggling to remain conscious, he flew back to Rabaul and arrived near dark, after a four-and-one-half-hour flight that used up his last drop of fuel. Having made his report to Lieutenant Sasai, who had rushed to meet the damaged plane, Sakai fainted.

The troops of the First Marine Division, who landed and routed the Japanese construction detachment and the small garrison detachment, did not underestimate the enemy, as had been the case with the American army in the Philippines. A pamphlet entitled "Know Your Enemy," which had been handed out to them on the troop transport, declared: "Mr. Moto [the Japanese soldier] is the world's greatest jungle fighter. He can swim under water for several miles while inhaling air through a reed; he can steal through the jungle noiselessly barefoot or in rubber-soled shoes. Tough and cunning, he can walk farther than us, eat less food, and put up with much more . . ." The marines learned to fear the enemy's attack: "The Jap's no ordinary man," they said, "he's a wolf-man."

On the other hand, Japanese Imperial Headquarters could not believe that this was the beginning of a genuine counterattack by the American army. They had estimated that this would take place during the latter part of the following year at the earliest. Thus the nine hundred soldiers of the Ichiki Detachment, who had been intended for the capture of Midway, were sent to drive out the Americans in what was thought would be an easy victory. Simultaneously, from the base on Rabaul, repeated naval air strikes were carried out against the U.S.

The remains of the Ichiki Detachment after U.S. tank units passed over it.

escort fleet and the base units that were promptly brought up to meet them.

In the area around Guadalcanal, there were numerous naval battles. Admiral Yamamoto regarded the landing of the American army as a good opportunity. As long as the American force remained, naval forces also had to maintain a presence nearby in order to replenish supplies and protect the troops. Now, Yamamoto hoped, was the chance to take revenge for Midway at Guadalcanal. On August 9, the Mikawa Squadron, consisting of six cruisers, carried out a night attack, sinking one Australian and three U.S. cruisers. On August 24, in a naval battle in broad daylight, a task force consisting of two aircraft carriers as its main force, led by Rear Admiral Frank J. Fletcher, fought a large Japanese task force including six carriers of the Nagumo Fleet. It sank one aircraft carrier, while the Japanese side was only able to land three shells on the *Enterprise*.

Meanwhile, an infantry detachment led by Colonel Ichiki Kiyono, an experienced officer who had been in command at the time of the

Marco Polo Bridge Incident, landed on Guadalcanal. On August 18, they set off through the jungle to reconnoiter enemy territory. As for the U.S. First Marine Division, they were suffering from low morale, but tried nevertheless to construct a defensive position. The supporting fleet on the open sea had left quickly for fear of an attack by the Japanese task force. The landing of supplies had been abandoned midway. Bulldozers and even shovels were in short supply. The troops had their rations reduced and tried to fill their empty stomachs with rice and canned food abandoned by the Japanese army.

In the early hours of August 21, the Japanese army launched its traditional night attack. The U.S. marines responded by firing all their weapons into the darkness. The Japanese soldiers attacked again and again, heedless of their comrades falling all about them. When the night was over, the Japanese corpses lay in heaps in front of the U.S. position. Major General Alexander Vandegrift ordered a sortie with light armor and received air support from an air corps detachment. The Japanese forces were almost totally destroyed, and Colonel Ichiki killed himself with a pistol after burning the colors that had been given them by the Emperor. The U.S. tanks rolled on heedless over his corpse and everything else. This was only the beginning of the gruesome battle of Guadalcanal, which was to go on for yet another half year.

Imperial Headquarters was not surprised by the total destruction of the Ichiki Detachment; failure was almost inevitable for such a small force. It was next decided that the 35th Brigade, under the command of Major General Kawaguchi, should be sent to Guadalcanal. Kawaguchi was the officer who had struggled vainly to save the life of Chief Justice José Abad Santos in the Philippines.

The transfer of the Kawaguchi Detachment was carried out by a destroyer together with some smaller ships that sailed among the islands. In the process the military value of the air base—the "Unsinkable Aircraft Carrier"—was vividly demonstrated. The transport of the Japanese troops without adequate air protection led to severe losses from U.S. air attacks. Two-thirds of the Japanese ships were sunk, and, although four thousand troops made it to shore at the end of the island, only three pieces of artillery were landed, while most of the ammunition and rations were lost at sea. Even so, the Kawaguchi Detachment started its advance, hacking a way through the jungle with hatchets and swords, scaling cliffs, and crossing gorges in order to attack the U.S. air base from the rear. Along the way they encountered the remnants of the Ichiki Detachment. They were so much skin and bone, with a heavy growth of beard, clothes torn, and boots falling to pieces; some had no footwear at all. They bowed repeatedly and asked for food. Regimental commander Oka Akinosuke, shocked, took pity on them and gave them some of the precious rice that his own troops were carrying. The troops of the Kawaguchi Detachment could not have guessed then that this group of wretched beggars was an image of themselves tomorrow.

After a difficult ten-day march through the jungle, the hand-to-hand night attack that the Kawaguchi Detachment made on September 13 failed. The Japanese troops dashed forward as their comrades fell around them in a hail of bullets. There were some marines who panicked, but their commanding officers urged them on, kicking them, thrusting weapons into their hands, firing their own pistols, and throwing hand grenades as they countered the attack. One unit of the Japanese forces broke through enemy lines and approached close to the tents of Vandegrift's headquarters. But in the end the attack was thrown back by heavy fire from the U.S. forces. The Japanese army withdrew into the jungle, having lost five hundred men in this single battle.

Although they had with great effort thrown back the enemy, the U.S. marines hardly felt like rejoicing over their victory. They had been cut off from supplies for over a month and were fighting on just two meals a day. With fewer than sixty aircraft left at the air base, control of the seas around the Solomons had become shaky. The aircraft carrier *Saratoga*, which had just been put into action, was severely damaged and the *Wasp* sunk by submarine torpedoes. Major General Vandegrift felt that the chances of the U.S. marines holding Guadalcanal were virtually nil.

As a result of the defeat of the Kawaguchi Detachment, Imperial Headquarters for the first time realized the seriousness of the situation. The navy was angered by its heavy losses, especially with respect to aircraft. The production of aircraft was not proceeding according to schedule, and the reinforcements necessary to make up the full complement of squadrons were not forthcoming. Furthermore, a shortage of fuel for the operation of the fleet was imminent. Navy General Staff, suddenly changing its attitude, wished to abandon Guadalcanal; but since it had initiated the battle itself, it hesitated to propose cessation of operations to Imperial Headquarters, lest it lose face.

Around this time, the army and navy began to clash over the allocation of oil, and animosity between the two reached a peak. The army argued that since Midway naval operations had been handled very badly and accused the navy of wasting oil—including oil that should have been used for production.

On the army's side, the preoccupation with Guadalcanal was not the result of cool military judgment. The proud Japanese army, having experienced its first major defeat on land, was determined to take back Guadalcanal in order to recover its prestige. But even within the army there were many who opposed this decision. Lieutenant Colonel Tsuji, a staff officer of Imperial Headquarters, suggested that Guadalcanal could be regained and air superiority restored by transferring the Manchurian Army Air Force to the southern zone. But Lieutenant Colonel Kumon Arifumi, an air staff officer of Imperial Headquarters, was opposed to risking a decisive battle, with probable heavy losses, in such a remote area. At the same time he feared that the Russians would invade Manchuria if it was vacated.

Tsuji, as usual, railed arrogantly at Kumon: "Will you be satisfied if your precious air force is kept intact, even though the Japanese army has been totally destroyed?"

"As long as I live," Kumon answered firmly, "I will not let the air force be wasted in a poorly fought battle."

At the beginning of October, the Second Army Division arrived safely on Guadalcanal from Rabaul, protected by naval forces assigned to the task by Admiral Yamamoto. Commander Hyakutake Harukichi, who was among the first to land, was stunned to see the enemy aircrafts' domination of the air, as well as the wretched state of the remnants of the Kawaguchi Detachment. There was no precedent for such a miserable situation in the annals of the Japanese army. He immediately sent a telegram to Rabaul stating: "The Kawaguchi Detachment is facing starvation. The transport of personnel should be stopped. Food and the ammunition necessary for control of the air base should be sent immediately."

Meanwhile, the U.S. First Marine Division had been brought up to full strength with replacements and abundant food, ammunition, trucks, fuel, and other materials. The perimeter of the air base was firmly built up with trenches, barbed wire, microphone equipment for night attacks, and a dense barrage of fire.

On October 13, Major General Vandegrift, happy with his fresh reinforcements and abundant ammunition and artillery, invited the officers of the 164th Infantry Regiment to lunch. No sooner had they picked up their forks than an artillery barrage began to rain down. The officers jumped hurriedly into a nearby dugout. After some time, the marine artillery was able to silence this barrage from the Hyakutake artillery.

That night heavy shells from Japanese battleships on the open sea landed in the American camp. The rain of shells turned the airfield into a sea of fire and blew up half the American planes. The deafening noise and earth-splitting tremors caused by the battleship artillery were more terrifying than anything the marines had ever experienced. Once again they were assailed by doubts of their ability to hold the position.

The Japanese forces, under the command of Lieutenant General Maruyama Masao of the Second Division, once more started to hack a way forward through the jungle. On the way Major General Kawaguchi, who was in command of the right flank, happened to come across Lieutenant Colonel Tsuji, who had come to Guadalcanal to supervise the conduct of the war. Kawaguchi had not forgotten the incident in the Philippines, but it seemed a trivial thing now. Feeling that this was a good chance to inform the army high-ups of the realities of the battle, he described his own experiences and stressed that an attack without artillery support was bound to result in miserable failure. Tsuji nodded seriously and said he would pass this on to Lieutenant General Maruyama.

The all-out attack was begun on October 24 and followed the usual pattern of a night attack. Kawaguchi, who had discovered strong enemy positions on his assigned front, proposed by telephone a one-day delay to permit further preparations and troop movements, but Maruyama reprimanded him harshly and relieved him of command on the spot. Maruyama had thought him a coward; but in the event the night attack followed the usual pattern. The Japanese army attacked furiously again on the following night, only to suffer great losses in the intense gunfire. When dawn came, the reinforced U.S. fighter planes flew overhead as though the sky belonged to them.

On the sea as well, a bloody struggle was in progress. On October 26, a naval task force including two aircraft carriers under the command of Rear Admiral Thomas Kinkaid engaged a Japanese task force with four aircraft carriers under the command of Vice Admiral Kondō Nobutake, and the aircraft carrier *Hornet* was sunk. The Japanese navy exaggerated the outcome (since Midway, naval leadership had been interpreting reports from the front in a rather wishful way) and announced a major victory to the Japanese public. This made the army high command, already depressed over successive defeats, even more frustrated.

November came, and Japanese and American ships continued frequent clashes. As a result of several open sea battles the U.S. lost two cruisers and five destroyers, while the Japanese lost two battleships and five destroyers. From then on, however, the Japanese fleet made no further sorties into the sea around Guadalcanal; domestic oil supplies had started to give out on account of the great number of sorties that had already been carried out.

Control of the air over Guadalcanal stayed with the Americans. The Japanese army sent the Thirty-eighth Division, which had been active in the capture of Hong Kong, to the island; but it was subjected to air attacks, and those troops that it managed to land were virtually without supplies. The navy brought supplies a little at a time, using destroyers and submarines in the dark of night, but there were great losses: supplies and rations were landed with difficulty on the rugged terrain only to be discovered by the enemy from the air and destroyed. For the soldiers who had landed, the main battle was against starvation and sickness. Almost all of the twenty-eight thousand troops were infected with malaria or dysentery due to starvation and the extremely insanitary conditions of life in the jungle. Soldiers who were unable to walk were given guard duty. Those who could just move on crutches were sent out in search of food and put in charge of preparing meals. (The Japanese army maintained its usual practice of cooking rice for the soldiers on the battlefield, despite the inconvenience and danger.) Those who were able to walk were sent out as scouts or joined in surprise raids.

Lieutenant Wakabayashi, who had served with distinction in the capture of Hong Kong, participated in the battle for Guadalcanal as a company commander and played an active role here as well. As leader of a raiding unit, he often slipped behind the enemy lines under cover of darkness, noiselessly attacked the enemy sentries, and stole foodstuff to take back to camp. His company was entrenched on Mount Austen, the highest peak on the island, in charge of its defense. The U.S. army's artillery fire grew heavier with every passing day, and gradually the besiegers' net began to tighten. More and more men were lost. In the diary Wakabayashi faithfully kept until just before he died, he wrote:

"December 20. The rice that we have been stretching as far as possible has finally given out, and the soldiers are forced to eat tree leaves before they go into battle. An extraordinary effort is required to gather even these leaves.

> "Praying for their welfare,
> I pass the pale, battle-weary faces
> of the sleeping soldiers."

Another poem ran:

> "Despite the elderly warrant officer's warning
> That the soldiers are exhausted,
> I give the order: Two sentry-parties!"

The elderly warrant officer in question was a very difficult man and had a reputation throughout the regiment as a nuisance. But when Wakabayashi was appointed as company commander, the warrant officer showed him the greatest respect and became, to everyone's surprise, a model NCO. When Wakabayashi died from a head wound, this same man walked toward the enemy lines, saying he had no more desire to live, and was quickly shot down.

On November 8, 1942, General Imamura received orders to transfer from Java to a new position as army commander of the Rabaul area. He was recalled to Tokyo to receive his orders at Imperial Headquarters; then, after an audience with the Emperor, he flew to Truk Island to meet with Admiral Yamamoto. Imamura had once served as a military attaché in England; and later, as a young officer, he had often played bridge with Yamamoto. Both men went on to fill important posts in the

army and navy and often had occasion to meet on official busines
they never had any difficulty working together.

The two were delighted to meet again at the Command Head
quarters on Truk. Imamura said he thought his bridge record had bee
a bit better than the admiral's, while Yamamoto's recollection was jus
the opposite: the two exchanged wry smiles, but either way they ha
no time for bridge now. After supper, Yamamoto looked Imamura i
the face and said:

"There's no point in trying to hide things from one another at th
stage. At the beginning of the war, it was true that one navy Zero wa
the equal of ten U.S. planes. But we lost many fine pilots at Midway
and those losses have not been made up. If it were one to one we coul
still win, but the enemy already has three times as many planes as w
do, and the gap is increasing."

"Are the U.S. pilots well trained at present?" Imamura broke in.

"They are," Yamamoto went on. "The real battle now is a compet
tion between Japanese discipline and American scientific technology
Whenever we replace our losses with new recruits, the level of con
petence goes down. Meanwhile the other side has introduced new, im
proved planes and more systematically trained pilots. So there's less c
a gap between the two sides now. Our emphasis on intensive trainin
and discipline isn't wrong, but we should have made sure it was accom
panied by scientific and technological improvements as well. As on
connected with the naval air force, I feel a strong sense of responsibi
ity for our failure in that regard."

Imamura noticed that Yamamoto's face had a grave look; but h
never dreamed that the admiral would be killed in action within half
year.

Imperial Headquarters finally learned the real situation on Guadalcan
from Lieutenant Colonel Tsuji and others who had actually been there
At the end of December, after numerous meetings, it finally decided t
order a withdrawal from the island. Carrying out a withdrawal in th
face of clear enemy superiority is far more difficult than launching a
offensive. The navy, fearing heavy losses, had been unenthusiast
about supplying ships; but on Admiral Yamamoto's decision, the with
drawal operations were in fact all carried out by naval destroyers.

The U.S. army had already begun a general attack. The Japanese with hardly any able-bodied soldiers left, seemed clearly doomed to be overrun and annihilated. But the Yano Battalion, which had been dispatched to serve as a rear guard, fought well enough to make the Americans think that elite reinforcements had arrived and was able to hold the Americans back for a while. The Oka Regiment on Mount Austen was completely wiped out, with the exception of one second lieutenant who broke through the enemy lines with the colors wrapped around his waist and made it to the evacuation point on the coast. The withdrawal was carried out in an orderly way. When the American forces advancing from both the east and the south met at Cape Espeance on February 9, they realized that the Japanese army had already left.

The struggle for Guadalcanal was over. American losses included twenty-four warships, one thousand six hundred dead, and five thousand wounded. Japan lost twenty-four warships, nine hundred planes, and over two thousand pilots. Japanese losses on land numbered eight thousand killed in battle and eleven thousand dead of starvation, dysentery, and malaria.

8

The Fall of
the Tōjō Cabinet

On May 21, 1943, the news of Admiral Yamamoto's death in actio
dealt the Japanese people a profound, indescribable shock. Despit
Imperial Headquarters' frequent announcements of victories, the
began to feel a vague uneasiness about the progress of the war and, fo
the first time, a clear sense of foreboding for the future. On the day c
the state funeral, more than two hundred thousand mourners lined th
streets along which the coffin slowly passed on its way to Hibiy
Park, the site of the funeral. A military band played "I've Given M
Life" and the crowds wept to the mournful tune.

Yamamoto had been killed more than a month before this. U.S
forces were then gradually regaining the Solomons and the north
shore bases on New Guinea, and Japanese reinforcements were bein
sent to the bottom of the sea in what promised to be a secon
Guadalcanal. It had become abundantly clear that without comman
of the air there could be no hope for victory. Yamamoto was plannin
a decisive air battle and, wishing to command it personally, on April
proceeded from Truk to Rabaul.

Four aircraft carriers with 160 planes on board and 140 aircraft c
the air-force-base unit participated in the operation. The joint forc
that had taken part in the attack on Pearl Harbor had had 350 plane
aboard its carriers alone; in the decisive air battle of the Philippine
400 ground-based planes had been used. By comparison, the suprem
commander of the Combined Fleet had a rather pitiful force at his di
posal for this campaign. Newly organized air force units were trainin
in Singapore but had not reached combat readiness yet. Yamamoto d
cided to risk everything and throw in all the air strength the Japanes

Joint funeral service for troops killed on Attu. The mourners carry white boxes, ostensibly containing the ashes of the dead but in fact empty.

navy could muster. Reports telling of large amounts of enemy shipping sunk and numerous aircraft shot down were continually arriving at Yamamoto's command post. Believing them himself, he relayed them to the Emperor. The Emperor, who had been greatly disturbed by the decline in Japan's situation since Midway, was delighted and bestowed a special commendation on Yamamoto. In fact, the losses of the American forces were light compared with those of the Japanese side, which suffered far greater losses, even in fighter planes. This was not so much the fault of Yamamoto's judgment as of errors by inadequately trained pilots.

As Yamamoto confided to General Imamura at the Truk command post, not only had the American air forces increased their numbers but the efficiency of their aircraft and the skill of their pilots had improved remarkably. Fighter planes, such as the P-38 Lightning, which flew at altitudes inaccessible to the Zero fighter; the P-40 Warhawk, which excelled in steep-dive speed; and the Grumman F6F Hellcat and F4U Corsair, which could match the Zero in any respect, had begun to appear on the battlefield. Moreover, the protective plates lately installed on American planes made penetration by the Zero's machine guns difficult. By contrast, Japanese machines—including the Zero—were inadequately armored, and once hit would immediately go down in flames. Not only was this handicap left unremedied but the combat skills of fresh pilots were declining steadily.

Hoping to boost the morale of their subordinates, Admiral Yamamoto and Vice Admiral Ugaki Matome boarded two separate planes at 8 A.M. on April 18 in Rabaul and headed for Ballale on the front line. In the meantime, the U.S. navy's front line received a top-secret message from Secretary of the Navy Frank Knox in Washington. Based on intelligence obtained by cracking the Japanese code, it conveyed an order to shoot down Yamamoto. A squadron of fourteen planes led by Major John Mitchell took off from its base on Guadalcanal to lie in wait on Yamamoto's course. The admiral's plane, almost as though by previous arrangement, reached the island of Bougainville exactly on schedule. Captain Thomas G. Lanphier, lying in wait at low altitude in a twin-fuselage P-38, attacked the first plane head-on. The escorting squadron of Japanese fighters was flying high and, taken by surprise, could not intervene in time. The next moment, Yamamoto's plane burst into flames and plummeted into the jungle. When the commanding officer of a Japanese road-construction unit stationed on the island arrived at the site of the crash, he found Yamamoto dead. The admiral was sitting in his seat, his body pierced by two bullets and his hand clutching his sword.

Bad news was reaching Japan from the northern Pacific as well. On May 7, under cover of a protective barrage from Rear Admiral Thomas Kinkaid's task force, eleven thousand men of the Seventh Division landed on the island of Attu in the Aleutians. It was defended by three thousand men under Colonel Yamazaki Yasuyo. The Japanese soon gave up fighting on the beaches and retreated into the mountains. The U.S. army, finding the going unexpectedly hard on account of the dogged resistance of the Japanese troops and the severe cold, asked for reinforcements. Admiral Kinkaid was furious.

Nevertheless, the Japanese army was isolated, fighting a battle in which reinforcements could not be counted upon. On hearing of the American landing, Imperial Headquarters promptly decided to abandon the Aleutians, fearful of another battle of attrition like that on Guadalcanal. Yamazaki's soldiers were gradually surrounded. Continuous bombardment caused a great many casualties, and the unit was finally reduced to 150 men. On the evening of May 29 they launched an all-out banzai attack and were annihilated. On this battlefield only 29 POWs were taken, the Japanese having almost literally fought to the last man. The U.S. had 500 dead, with 1,000 wounded and about 1,500 men out of action on account of frostbite.

Taken aback by these unforeseen losses, the U.S. army sent thirty thousand of its own troops and five thousand Canadians on arctic-survival training, mobilized ninety warships, and set out to capture the neighboring deserted island of Kiska. After six weeks of bombardment, when the American troops made a somewhat timid landing, all they found was three puppies. The six thousand Japanese defenders had already left the island, vanishing into the fog on waiting destroyers.

The bad news from Attu was at once made public in Japan. Until then, fearing that the nation's morale might be affected, Imperial Headquarters had published nothing but news of victory and had strictly concealed all losses; now it realized that the time had come to tell people the truth in order to stir them to further efforts. In a voice filled with deep sorrow NHK's announcer read the gallant last message of the commander of the Yamazaki unit: "There may have been other ways out, but I am unwilling to let warriors die a dishonorable death. To the attack, then, together with the spirits of the great departed!"

The fact that Japanese soldiers seldom surrendered to the enemy is often attributed to the traditions of the samurai era, but this is not correct. Most military men throughout the world feel the same: surrender is dishonorable. Yet in fact the Japanese samurai of old surrendered quite frequently, nor was there any traditional feeling of shame involved. Even during the Russo-Japanese War, Japanese soldiers who became POWs—there were not many, it is true—expected quite naturally to be treated according to international conventions. It was only in the Shōwa era (1926–), when the spirit of nationalism began to be fostered, that the belief that it was shameful to be taken alive really sank into the nation's mind. During the Shanghai Incident in 1932, Major Kuga Noboru was seriously injured and, while unconscious, was taken prisoner by the Chinese army. Treated well in the hospital, he was subsequently repatriated, but was so ashamed of having been a captive that he went back to the former battlefield and committed suicide there. This event received overwhelming news coverage and created a new standard of the "model soldier." As the war with China dragged on, this spirit was encouraged still more until it permeated the entire population.

Once taken prisoner, a Japanese could no longer return to his old home; no one but his mother and father would be happy that he had returned alive, and sometimes even the parents and family, swayed by the other villagers' scorn, would start wondering why he had not died a "glorious death." It was not necessarily "for the Emperor" that the Japanese soldier fought to the last, but, rather, because of such rules of the community. What he wished most of all to avoid was shame for the family; the Emperor's name was no more than a convenient symbol used for that purpose.

In the Japanese army not only officers but enlisted men were taught not to become prisoners, to fight to the death; and most of them practiced what they were taught. They also believed, by and large, what rumor told them: if they were captured, the barbaric U.S. soldiers would torture them to death. Such rumors were hardly true in their entirety, yet there was a grain of truth in them. The World War I air hero Charles A. Lindbergh witnessed many cases or heard many accounts of American atrocities, and wrote in his diary: "In fact, I am not sure that our record in this respect stands so very much higher than the Japs'."

Though he had been a staunch opponent of war, once the war started Lindbergh yearned for an opportunity to serve again in the air force. His political opponent, President Roosevelt, exerted all the influence he could to prevent the fulfillment of his wishes, and it was not until May 1944 that, thanks to the navy's good will, he was able to participate in active service on the pretext of aviation research.

By that time, the Americans had advanced almost to the easternmost tip of New Guinea's north shore. Lindbergh saw action in the air, shooting down at least one Zero fighter himself. What disturbed him more than any combat, however, was the corruption of the soldiers' moral sense. Wherever he went on the front, the officers made him welcome, but he also heard the men talking about atrocities as something perfectly ordinary and natural. The soldiers treated the Japanese as "lower than animals," stripping everything from the enemy's dead, searching their pockets for souvenirs, and even slicing off ears and drying them or amassing collections of gold teeth. Greenish skulls were often seized by inspectors when the soldiers returned home. Prisoners were not welcome, either. Exhausted Japanese prisoners were promptly delivered to headquarters only when rewards were being offered for securing "personnel for interrogation," but otherwise most were "disposed of," usually by cutting their throats. The corpses were thrown into a hole dug by a bulldozer, and no grave markers were erected. The soldiers' explanation was "we're just paying them back for what they did to us." Lindbergh did not deny the soldiers' bloodthirstiness—he knew well it was a part of war. But their entire lack of recognition of anything worthy of respect in the enemy—this greatly saddened the hero of World War I. He expressed these feelings in his journal: "We claim to be fighting for civilization, but the more I see of this war in the Pacific, the less right I think we have to claim to be civilized."

At a liaison conference between Imperial Headquarters and the government held on November 27 the previous year—before the Japanese army had given up ideas of retaking Guadalcanal—Prime Minister Tōjō's expression was exceptionally gloomy. Placing documents concerning Japanese war-supplies production on the table, he said, "If things continue in this way, Japan will go broke."

The problem was shipping. At the beginning of the war Japan's total gross tonnage was 6.3 million tons, of which the army and the navy requisitioned 3.9 million tons for their operations. To sustain industry on the home front, a minimum of 3 million tons was absolutely essential, and the government had planned that requisitioned ships would gradually be returned by the army and the navy as the first round of campaigns came to an end. However, from Midway to Guadalcanal, a second round of operations unfolded without pause. Not only did shipping not return to private hands, but losses in battle exceeded the tonnage of newly built and captured ships and interfered with the conduct of many operations. Thus, while Japan was able to obtain oil and other raw materials, it could not transport enough of them back home, and production of steel and aluminium, indispensable for making warships, planes, and other armaments, was severely hampered. In a country poor in natural resources—this poverty was the reason that the Western powers' economic blockade had driven Japan to war—industry could not function without shipping. Despite this, the army and navy demanded still further requisitions by the government for their operations. Tōjō cut these demands drastically and issued a stern warning: shipping must be returned to civilian hands as soon as possible, or production would collapse and Japan would lose the ability to carry on the war. In December, when Army General Staff Headquarters learned that the government had officially confirmed this policy, it was highly indignant.

Major General Tanaka Shin'ichi, the division chief of Operations, became spokesman for the opposition. He summoned Major General Satō Kenryō of the War Ministry and pressed strongly for change, using the customary browbeating phrases: "His Imperial Majesty has ordered the recapture of Guadalcanal Island. How dare the government make decisions that obstruct this operation!" Satō, who was Tōjō's assistant in the War Ministry, tried to defend the prime minister's views. The two generals became involved in a heated argument, witnessed by the officers of General Staff Headquarters who had gathered around them. Tanaka lost his temper and impulsively punched the other in the face. Satō kept calm but gave as good as he got. The bystanders pulled them apart and Satō left, but Tanaka's temper did not subside. Although it was already past 10 P.M., he went to the official residence of the war minister, where he saw Vice-Minister Kimura Heitarō and obstinately expounded his own ideas to him until three in the morning.

When daylight came, the dispute was resumed. Tanaka and the vice-chief of the general staff marched uninvited into the office of Prime Minister and War Minister Tōjō. Tōjō was flanked by Vice-Minister Kimura and Major General Satō. Facing them, Tanaka stubbornly reiterated his argument, urging Tōjō to reconsider. Tōjō, however, was obdurate. It was not that he failed to realize the importance of the operation at hand, but that the burden of responsibility for running the nation lay too heavily on his shoulders; torn between the long-term claims of industry and the immediate claims of military operations, he had resolved that production should come first.

Tanaka flew into a rage again. Jumping up from his chair, he barked: "What does the Minister think he's doing? If you do this, the war is lost. You idiot!"

Tōjō stood up as well, and, glaring at his opponent, shouted, "Why, you . . . !" The two men eyed each other for a long while, until both realized that their emotions were running too high and they sat down. But a chill had fallen on the room; the atmosphere made it impossible to continue the meeting, and Tanaka and the other man withdrew.

The next morning Tōjō requested an interview with Chief of the General Staff Sugiyama and proposed Tanaka's transfer on grounds of insulting a superior officer. Tanaka was promptly sent to the south, but, as a sop to the general staff, an increase was made in the number of ships the government agreed to requisition—a typically Japanese solution.

In opening hostilities, Japan had made two fatal mistakes in its overall plan for war-supplies production. One concerned shipbuilding; the government not only failed to perceive its importance, but was also too optimistic in estimating losses. Americans, it considered, would lack the endurance for prolonged periods of underwater duty, and submarine activities would thus be insignificant. Events proved that this was nothing but wishful thinking.

Nineteen forty-three came, and the shipping situation failed to improve in the least. From around the time that the two generals fell to blows, the government concentrated earnest efforts on building new ships, and production rose markedly. Yet this failed to make up for all the losses. By autumn of that year, total tonnage of civilian shipping—cargo ships and oil tankers—had fallen to one-third of the minimum required, i.e., to one million tons. These were frightening figures in their implications for future industrial production.

The second major mistake concerned the production of aircraft. Just as Admiral Yamamoto did not, in a sense, fully grasp the importance of air power until the debacle of Midway, the Japanese government, too, was guilty of serious oversight in this respect. When war broke out in 1941, Japan was producing 5,000 planes yearly. In the following year it did not produce more than 8,000. Yet the 1943 figure was 16,000, which shows that increased production was not impossible; the conclusion becomes inevitable that those responsible for the war had simply been resting on their laurels. In the same years, America turned out 17,000, 45,000, and 81,000 planes, expanding its production dramatically. The lag in Japan's production in 1942 created a decisive gap between Japanese and American air power. Moreover, as mentioned earlier, Japan was not able to develop a manual for the speedy training of large numbers of pilots (which relates to the fact that Japan was also unable to develop an easily flyable fighter), and as a result the new aircraft resulting from increased production were lost in huge numbers together with their unskilled pilots.

The gap between the two navies gradually became equally clear. The navies of the two countries were both determined first of all to build aircraft carriers, but it was only a matter of time before America, with its overwhelming industrial power and its vast shipbuilding capacity, gained superiority. By the autumn of 1943, the U.S.S. *Essex*, carrying one hundred planes, and five other carriers of the same class, together with five vessels newly remodeled as carriers with thirty-five planes each were added to the American Pacific Fleet. By contrast, the Japanese navy was not able to add a single genuine aircraft carrier to its naval arsenal until 1944. The mobility and air superiority given the Americans by their carriers meant that they could launch concentrated attacks anywhere in the Pacific, choosing their own battleground.

Their first assault was directed against the island of Tarawa, lying just below the equator to the south of the Marshall Islands, which were under Japanese mandate. The island of Tarawa was a kind of fortress with an airfield, so the U.S. task force first shelled and bombed it for a week with naval guns and airplanes, then landed the Second Marine Division. Desperate fighting followed on the beaches, and the battle was over in four days. To occupy the island, the Americans had to pay a steep price: 1,000 dead and 2,000 wounded. The 5,000 Japanese defenders, except for 150 men taken prisoner, all fell in battle. Throughout those four days, the Japanese troops were hoping for a counterattack by the Japanese Combined Fleet. But the Japanese navy had suffered such heavy losses—mainly warships and combat planes—in the air battle around Bougainville Island that it had no reserve strength enabling it to regroup swiftly to meet an enemy attack.

The new year of 1944 came, and in January the U.S. army, after the most painstaking preparations, launched an attack on the Marshall Islands, occupying two atolls, Kwajalein and Mejuro. Then on February 17 the task force of Admiral Marc Mitscher launched an air raid on the Truk base. This was the control base of the Japanese Combined Fleet and was called "Japan's Pearl Harbor" by the Americans. But the Combined Fleet had already withdrawn a week before, heading for home under the flagship *Musashi*. It was no more than a shadow of its former self, with no carriers—these were being refurbished at home—and had no choice but to escape from the battlefield.

At 4 A.M., Mitscher's first assault wave of seventy planes hit the Truk base in a surprise attack, knocking it out. There were three hundred planes on the base, but less than half of those were active; most of the pilots were away from base, having been taken off alert stations. Many of them were with women when the raid came. The few planes that managed to take off were shot down like flies, and the rest were demolished on the ground. The raids came in nine waves, and even after they ended the Truk base continued to burn all the day. The next day Mitscher's unit meticulously wiped out the vessels left lying at anchor, and, along with many other ships, sank thirty-four of the treasured transports. Admiral Nimitz commented, "We have repaid part of the Pearl Harbor debt."

By pure chance, the vice-chief of the Army General Staff, Hata Hikosaburō, and Section Chief of Operations Hattori Takushirō (a superior of Lieutenant Colonel Tsuji) happened to be on Truk, on their way to Rabaul. Witnessing with their own eyes the miserable plight of the navy, battered mercilessly and unable to lift a finger in return, they could only exchange mute glances. They gave up their trip to Rabaul and hurriedly returned home.

In early November 1943, as the Second Marine Division was completing preparations for landing at Tarawa, an important political conference was held in Tokyo.

In August of that year, Japan had granted independence to Burma, and in October, to the Philippines. The Japanese government needed to show people both at home and abroad that its wartime slogans about the liberation of Asia were not just empty talk. At the Tokyo conference—referred to as the Greater East Asian Conference—leaders of Manchukuo, the Nanking government, Thailand, the Philippines, and Burma met. Indonesia's independence had not yet been acknowledged and Sukarno did not attend. Administration of the Indonesian occupation had gone exceptionally well, and since Sumatra and Borneo were also rich in oil resources, the Japanese government wanted to keep the area under its direct rule as long as possible. Independence for Burma and the Philippines, on the other hand, was given priority, mainly as a demonstration against England and America. Chandra Bose, head of the newly established provisional government of Free India in Singapore, was allowed to participate in the meeting for the same reason.

There was a feeling that it was actually a little late for a meeting of this kind. With Mussolini's overthrow, Italy had already ceased active participation in the war, and the German army had been retreating ever since the defeat at Stalingrad. Japan too was gradually reducing its defense perimeter in the Pacific. Dark clouds had descended on Japan's chances for victory, and the heads of governments assembled in Tokyo felt a touch of anxiety about the future. The fact that Thailand sent Prince Wan Waithayakon instead of its prime minister—that it was merely going through the motions—can be seen as a reflection of this situation. The Thais' attitude was also a show of pride, indicating that Thailand, which was not offered its freedom by Japan, did not wish to be treated as another "puppet state."

In retrospect, the Greater East Asian Conference now seems little more than a wartime sideshow. But the very fact that the leaders of several Asian countries that were emerging from long colonial rule by Europe were gathered in one room opened an important new epoch in world history.

The president of the Philippines, José Laurel, suggested as much in a fiery speech. "There is no country in the world," he said, "that can deny or delay the right of one billion Asians to freedom from oppression. God Almighty will not forsake Japan, nor will He forsake the people of Greater Asia."

The speech of Burma's prime minister, Ba Maw, was no less passionate. "For many years in Burma I have in my own way pursued a dream for Asia. My Asian blood has long called out to other Asians. And today I have the feeling that through this speech the voice of Asia is summoning together her children. It is the call of our Asian blood. In the past, it was unthinkable that Asians should meet with each other as we have met here today. The impossible has happened. The way that it happened surpasses the boldest dreams and fantasies of the boldest men in our midst."

Yet the most passionate speech was delivered by none other than Bose. The people gathered there—except for the Japanese—had no reason to continue the war, but Bose believed that to do so was essential for India's liberation. "India has no choice but to wage an uncompromising struggle against British imperialism. Even if other nations can consider a compromise with Britain, to the Indian people, at least, this is out of the question. To compromise with Britain would mean a compromise with the slave system itself, a system with which we are determined henceforth to make absolutely no compromises."

"I don't know," Bose went on, "how many soldiers of our National Army will survive in the coming war. But this is not a problem to us. Whether we as individuals live or die, whether we come through the war to see India's freedom or not is less important than India's freedom itself."

During the two or three days the conference lasted, Prime Minister Tōjō seemed happy, presiding over the meetings with a broad, almost paternal smile, satisfied to see one of the war's objectives about to be realized. So serious was his "Asian fever" that the cool officers who sought to use everything as a means of pursuing the war exchanged ironical whispers: "The boss is going a little soft in the head, isn't he."

A proclamation demanding "a new order of live and let live, based on justice, mutual independence, sovereignty and respect for tradition, as well as economic development in the spirit of mutual benefit, and the abolition of all racial discrimination" was unanimously adopted by the conference.

Two weeks later, China's leader Chiang Kai-shek met President Roosevelt and Prime Minister Churchill for the first time in Cairo. He left satisfied, with a promise from Roosevelt to give aid to China. The two Allied leaders then flew on to Tehran for their meeting with Stalin. The three great men had begun close bargaining on how to bring the war to a close with the maximum benefit for their respective countries. At these meetings Roosevelt's position was that of the "rich uncle": on all of the world's battle fronts, more help from America was expected. Each country was hoping to bring the war to an end soon with America's help. In order to make sure of American aid, Stalin announced that when Russia had subdued the Germans, it would be able to send reinforcements to Siberia and open a joint front. The Russo-Japanese Neutrality Pact, this implied, was a scrap of paper that could be torn up at any time. The representatives of Britain and America returned to Cairo, where they decided to give top priority to the landing operation that was to take place on the coast of Normandy in late spring the following year; they also decided to cancel an offensive in the Bay of Bengal that they had promised to Chiang.

At this time, the fortunes of war were shifting in the north of Burma. Here too command of the air had gradually passed into Allied hands. Lieutenant General Joseph Stilwell, who had taken command as American commander of the army group in the China, Burma, and India area, was threatening northern Burma. The Japanese army on the other hand was planning an invasion of India under army commander Lieutenant General Mutaguchi Ren'ya. At the Greater East Asian Conference, Bose had approached Tōjō and expressed the desire that the provisional government should have its own territory. Tōjō generously replied that he would give them the Andaman and Nikobar Islands. Bose, however, hoped for territory on the continent, linked by land with India. And when he learned that the Japanese army had plans for an invasion of India, he pledged to cooperate in them and urged their realization with great enthusiasm. Tōjō gave the operation his approval, after consulting Mutaguchi's views. Mutaguchi had had a

Chiang Kai-shek, Roosevelt, and Churchill meet for the first time in Cairo. Madame Chiang is seen on the right.

hand as a regimental commander in the Marco Polo Bridge Incident, which marked the beginning of the Sino-Japanese conflict, and was fond of saying, "I must see through to the end the war that I started." Three divisions strong, Mutaguchi's army crossed the Chindwin River in mid-March—the dry season—negotiated the steep Arakan Range, and began its advance on the city of Imphal. The soldiers loaded their ammunition and twenty days' rations on oxen and elephants, marching along the mountain paths behind the animals.

The first thrust of the Japanese army was so swift that even the British supreme commander, Lord Louis Mountbatten, had to admit it put his forces at a disadvantage. But without command of the air, the Japanese offensive was soon to end in failure. In a total of 760 airlifts the British army transported great numbers of troops, cannon, jeeps—mules, even—into Imphal to reinforce its positions there. The Japanese army had aimed at a "lightning operation," but as the furious fighting dragged on it began to be plagued by shortages of food and ammunition.

The rainy season came. The Japanese forces had encircled the enemy, but their supply lines were cut and they could do little more than crouch in flooded trenches, endure the furious bombardment, and grimly defend their positions. The commander of the Thirty-first Division, Lieutenant General Satō Kōtoku advised Army Headquarters time and again that the only alternatives were more ammunition and food supplies or retreat, but Mutaguchi persistently ordered them to the attack. When Satō finally received a message from his subordinate regimental commander saying, "Rather than die of starvation, we are carrying out a final assault on the assumption that we shall all be killed in battle," he gave the order to retreat on his own initiative. Having thus saved the lives of the ten thousand remaining troops, he was relieved of his command on the field. The other two divisions were given strict orders to carry on their attacks, but they no longer had the strength. Thus the order came for the whole army to retreat, and the Japanese forces, pelted by rain and leaning on sticks, retraced the same mountain paths through the rocky bluffs to where they had come from. Here and there by the roadside, wounded soldiers lay where they had collapsed. In their wounds, eye sockets, and nostrils, the maggots were already wriggling. The British army was close behind and enemy airplanes were screaming overhead. This road of retreat where so many Japanese soldiers died like flies came to be called the "Highway of Bleached Bones." In this operation the Japanese army lost thirty thousand men either to fighting or to starvation. It was a tragedy that surpassed even Guadalcanal.

Around the time that the Truk base was raided in the Pacific and Mutaguchi's troops launched their offensive in Burma, back in Tokyo Chief of the Army General Staff Sugiyama and Chief of the Navy General Staff Nagano both resigned. The position of chief of general staff was promptly filled by Tōjō, while Admiral Shimada took that of the chief of navy general staff, in addition to his post as navy minister. Tōjō had thus taken upon himself the three vital functions of prime minister, war minister, and chief of general staff. This was totally unprecedented and Sugiyama of course had objected vehemently.

On hearing what Tōjō proposed, he said, dumbfounded, "That's going to make you another Hitler, surely?"

To which Tōjō retorted, "Unlike Corporal Hitler, I'm not illiterate in military matters!"

Tōjō was by now thoroughly disgusted with the divorce between the running of the war and the political world—with the inefficiency, in short, of the whole governmental system. Just as the arbitrary acts of the military had continually interfered with Japanese government in earlier years, so, even after the opening of hostilities against Britain and America, the prime minister's power did not extend to the basic planning of operations. Both the army and the navy made their plans as they wished, then forced them ready-made upon the government. Moreover, by now Japan was suffering a series of defeats, and there was no foreseeable way out of the situation. If this continued, defeat would be inevitable. Tōjō was convinced that nothing really mattered but final victory, even if it meant his facing the charge of being a dictator—which was, after all, only a question of personal reputation. Compared with Tōjō's obstinate character, Sugiyama, though one of the army's senior leaders, was a type who worked by relying on his adjutants and skillfully coordinating their opinions. It was quite clear which of the two would survive a head-on confrontation.

The unsatisfying progress of the war had done considerable harm to Tōjō's reputation as the man ultimately responsible. Konoe Fumimaro would have considered stepping down, but Tōjō strode forward unafraid to collect all major functions in his own hands. The Empire was, in fact, in the midst of an all-consuming war, and Tōjō's rationale had some basis. But his step also caused anxiety and ill-feeling on the part of Japan's senior statesmen, who had so far kept quiet.

On June 6, 1944, zero-hour for the Allied D-day operation in Normandy came. On the same day in the Pacific, a huge fleet of 775 vessels, including a core of 8 giant aircraft carriers, weighed anchor at its base on the Mejuro and Eniwetok atolls in the Marshalls and set out for the island of Saipan under the command of Admiral Spruance. This armada was almost twice the size of the Japanese task force that had once sailed toward Midway.

The U.S. landing operation on Saipan, carried out by the Second and Fourth Marine Divisions and the Twenty-seventh Infantry Division, started before dawn on June 15. Commander Saitō of the Japanese army's Forty-third Division, who had been appointed just one and a half months before, had little confidence in the defenses of the island. The main force had arrived too late to be familiar with the place, and no overall plan had been established, much less firm defensive positions.

The decisive battle at sea took place on the nineteenth and twentieth of June. Under the command of Vice Admiral Ozawa Jisaburō, a Japanese navy task force with a core of 9 aircraft carriers challenged the American task force cruising in the waters off Saipan. The Japanese side spotted the enemy first and initiated the assault by launching a first wave of 250 planes. Yet the advantage of a head start was severely diminished by the remarkable advance of American technology during the war years. Thanks to its well-developed radar, the American army was able to intercept the attack 240 kilometers away. A wave of 450 fighters promptly soared into the air to wait impatiently for the enemy.

The American Hellcat fighters knocked down the attacking planes with great dispatch. It was such an easy air battle for the American pilots that they referred to it ever after as the "Great Marianas Turkey Shoot." Even those Japanese planes that managed to break through the wave of fighters and reach the U.S. fleet were held off by enemy flak. The VT fuses developed by the American displayed their efficiency. Almost all the approaching Japanese planes were hit and plunged helplessly into the ocean in a spray of mist. Altogether, the Japanese lost two hundred planes including those of the second assault unit. Their gains amounted to a mere twenty enemy planes downed and a few scratches inflicted on the U.S. warships.

The next day, the American fleet gave chase and at 4 P.M. finally found its adversary. If it attacked then, its planes would be returning after dark and losses due to landing misses could be expected; yet the commander of the task force, Admiral Mitscher, firmly ordered an attack. A large formation of two hundred planes assaulted Ozawa's force and was met by seventy fighters. The torpedo planes that also closed in on the Japanese fleet were destroyed by salvos from the ships' main batteries, turned down to water level. Twenty planes were shot down and eighty more were lost somewhere in the ocean, having run out of fuel, but the Japanese also suffered great losses; their task force had lost three aircraft carriers in the two days' fighting, while the pride of Japan's army—its air force—along with the pilots it had taken a year to train, was all but wiped out.

Apart from the thirty thousand defending soldiers, there were about four thousand native islanders and twenty thousand Japanese civilians on Saipan. The daughter of one of those immigrants from Japan, an eighteen-year-old girl by the name of Sugano Shizuko, was employed by a trading company at the time. The air raids on the island that interrupted her peaceful life started on June 11. Wave after wave of enemy planes filled the sky like clouds for days on end, leaving army and navy installations destroyed in their wake. At dawn on the fourteenth, the enemy fleet started to bombard the land. That evening, Shizuko took refuge in the hills, among a procession of stretchers carrying wounded and aged soldiers.

The enemy began to land. From the hilltop, she could see countless boats being spawned by the warships and leaving a white wake behind them as they approached the shore. At the same time, a barrage of artillery fire came from the groves on shore. Then Japanese tanks appeared on the main street of Garapan town—by now a burned-out waste—and advanced against the enemy. Involuntarily, Shizuko cried out, "Brother!"

Only a month or so before, her elder brother's tank unit had arrived on the island from Manchuria; now it was fighting before her very eyes. The Japanese fire was accurate, and before long many enemy landing craft had overturned, spilling their occupants into the water. At that point, the fleet offshore, which until then had waited in silence, blazed with white light. The thunder of guns and exploding shells filled heaven and earth. Airplanes wheeled and circled in the air; black smoke veiled the Japanese posts along the shoreline—till finally they fell silent. The tanks lay on their sides, ruined hulks.

Shizuko struggled along to the Mount Donnay field hospital, where she volunteered and was given special permission to work as a nurse. From then on she labored without sleep, dressing the wounds of a stream of injured soldiers, assisting in surgical operations, and carrying drinking water. Since she knew the topography of the area well, she tied some twenty flasks around her body and fetched fresh water from the source in order to give it to the wounded. But the hospital was discovered by enemy planes and strafed mercilessly from the air. When the planes left, the bodies of freshly bandaged soldiers were all bloodied again.

Shizuko asked the commander, "Why don't you put up a Red Cross flag and let the enemy know that this is a field hospital?"

The commander stood for a while with folded arms, groping for an answer. Then he blurted out, "Nurse—war has nothing to do with human pity or compassion."

The order for a general attack came to the field hospital as to everywhere else. All who could stand received arms. Those who could not move were given a bag of rusks, one can of food each, and one hand grenade for every eight men. With the grenades they were to dispatch not the advancing enemy but, when the time came, themselves. The patients were unmoved—they had given up vain hopes of friendly forces coming to save them and knew that the war was lost. Rather than linger on in a maggot-infested body, they seemed, rather, to long for the next world.

As the unit marched forward in the moonlight, Shizuko heard a series of grenade explosions to the rear. Simultaneously, she heard voices, some crying out the names of children and wives, others calling "goodbye, mother." She went limp and would have collapsed on the spot had it not been for the firm arm of the commander, who supported her.

The unit arrived too late to join the general attack. Shizuko, who had lost her companions, strayed down the road back to the field hospital. The unit had returned also. When the commander saw her, he started scolding her:

"Why didn't you run away? You're a civilian! It's still not too late."

Leaflets urging them to surrender had been dropped here too. But Shizuko rejected it all. Her brother had died in battle, her parents were most probably dead as well, and living on all alone made no sense.

"That won't do. Here—start walking to the west holding up a white handkerchief," the commander told her sternly.

This was at daybreak on July 5. By now signs of the approaching enemy were seen everywhere. A whistling GI, holding a submachine gun at the ready, would jump out of the jungle and call out something unintelligible—apparently a "Japanese" command to surrender. Here and there grenade explosions could be heard. The commander pointed his pistol at his throat and pulled the trigger. Shizuko pulled out the safety pin of her hand grenade and threw herself on a rock she had placed ready.

When she came to, she was lying in a bed at the American field hospital. A sudden rumor spread that the Japanese army had WACs.

With this last all-out attack on the evening of July 8—an "attack" of wounded soldiers that was more like a procession of ghosts—the Japanese forces ceased to exist. Four thousand civilians who were driven to the northern tip of the island threw themselves off the cliffs into the sea. American destroyers gathered there urged them with loudspeakers to surrender, but the words were drowned out by explosions, and the people, at the limits of exhaustion after three weeks of flight, did not hear them. Parents jumped into the ocean holding their children high in their arms. Girls tumbled down in pairs, holding hands. The sound of bursting hand grenades was coming from everywhere. The Americans stood aghast at this hellish scene. Now and again a child would come running by; the Americans would catch it in their arms, and give it a drink of water from their flasks. Many of the GIs had tears in their eyes.

The fall of Saipan was not announced to the nation for some time. However, although an overseas dominion, the island was but a stone's throw from Japan proper, with many Japanese residents; when it became a battlefield, people's anxiety was naturally aroused. The elder statesmen, led by Prince Konoe, held a secret meeting at which they considered retiring Tōjō.

Konoe foresaw that the war would most likely end in defeat. His view was that it would be best to put the whole responsibility for the war on Tōjō, and that the latter should not be replaced, yet eventually he went along with the opinion of the other elder statesmen. To remove Tōjō, who was now at the peak of his power and had not, moreover, lost his nerve, was a difficult task. It was Marquis Kido, the man who had recommended Tōjō in the first place, who was given the task of belling the cat.

He requested of Tōjō that the cabinet be reorganized, and recommended that the posts of war minister and chief of general staff be separated once more. Tōjō agreed and set about reforming his cabinet in good faith. But the whole thing was a political trick of the senior statesmen: the candidates asked to join the cabinet had an agreement with them and declined to take office, while Minister of Commerce and Industry Kishi Nobusuke, refusing to submit his resignation, helped corner Tōjō from the inside. Thus Tōjō found himself surrounded by enemies and gave up the attempt to form a government.

In accordance with custom, Marquis Kido consulted Tōjō concerning his successor as prime minister. Tōjō's reply was brief and ironic: "You threw me out, you should know better than I."

Although the senior statesmen fully agreed that Tōjō was no longer competent, none of them had any idea who would make a worthy successor. After a long argument, they came up with former Army General Koiso Kuniaki, governor general of Korea, and former Admiral Yonai Mitsumasa, who had once organized a cabinet, and asked the two men to cooperate in forming a government. But both had been too long away from the center of government, and especially from wartime leadership, and it remained doubtful whether they could take swift, efficient, and forceful measures to reverse the tide of defeat and lead the nation to victory.

9

The Coming of the Kamikaze

On October 20, 1944, two hundred thousand American troops began landing on the island of Leyte in the Philippines, amid a raging storm. Until then the Joint Chiefs of Staff had paid little attention to the Philippines, favoring a strategy that would take U.S. forces straight to the Japanese mainland following a direct assault on Taiwan. However, both Admiral Nimitz at the front and General MacArthur thought this plan too dangerous. MacArthur, especially, maintained that the recapture of the Philippines and the liberation of its people was America's national duty. In July of that year President Roosevelt, who had come to Hawaii on his fourth-term presidential campaign tour, invited the two commanders and Admiral William Halsey to dinner. When the president asked MacArthur about his views on future strategy, the general proceeded to lecture them about their duty to initiate an offensive against the Philippines, allowing no interruption until Roosevelt finally bade them good night. All three commanders on the front, nevertheless, did share the view that an attack must be launched on the Philippines, and the Joint Chiefs of Staff approved a plan to carry out a landing at Leyte on December 20.

In the meantime, the American army occupied the Pacific islands of Tinian and Guam and in early September seized the island of Morotai, a steppingstone to the Philippines. A powerful task force under the command of Admiral Halsey began raids on air bases in the Philippines. The quality of Japanese radar still being poor, most of the U.S. air raids were successful, with only slight losses on the American side. In protest against these continuous raids, President José Laurel issued a declaration of war against the Americans. Rather than have his country "liberated" by the Americans, he had hoped the storm of war would bypass it altogether, but this seemed too much to hope for.

Around this time, a lieutenant junior grade happened to be shot down over Leyte and after being sheltered by local inhabitants was returned to his ship, the *Hornet*. The intelligence on Japanese defense installations that he brought with him showed they were practically nonexistent. When Admiral Halsey lighted on the report among the huge bundle of messages on his desk, he had a strange intuition that this could shorten the war by months, and moved up the date of attack on the Philippines by a large margin. His advice was accepted by the Joint Chiefs of Staff.

At the same time, his staff officers were pondering what they called their "nasty plan"—a stratagem to deceive the Japanese. Halsey's fleet first made a great show of shelling and bombing the islands south of Japan, then launched air raids on Taiwan. The Japanese army fell for the trick completely. The naval air units that were waiting fully prepared for a decisive battle in the Philippines—which both the government and Imperial Headquarters saw as their last chance of victory— were sent one after another to engage the task force in Taiwanese waters. On October 16 Imperial Headquarters broadcast, to the strains of a stirring military march, news of a major victory: eleven enemy aircraft carriers sunk, six badly damaged. In Tokyo and Osaka, rallies were held to celebrate this rare victory. NHK's foreign broadcasts announced that Mitscher's task force had been annihilated. But this again was nothing but self-deception based on a compound of exaggerated estimates by immature pilots. In fact, the U.S. navy did not lose a single carrier; two cruisers were seriously damaged—that was all. The Japanese navy's air squadrons went into battle with 1,000 planes and lost 500, with only 250 of the remaining aircraft capable of action. At precisely this point, General MacArthur's massive army began landing in the bay of Leyte.

As he set foot on the island, the general announced in characteristic style: "People of the Philippines, I have returned. By the grace of Almighty God our forces stand again on Philippine soil . . ."

Around the same time, Vice Chief of General Staff Hata and Section Chief of Operations Hattori came to Manila from Tokyo to confer with Terauchi Hisaichi, supreme commander of Army Group South. The two officers from army headquarters believed that the

Americans were committing a grave error in landing in the Philippines in spite of having lost the mainstay of their fleet, and demanded that a force be transferred immediately to Leyte in order to drive the enemy back into the sea in one all-out effort. Terauchi agreed. The Japanese navy, having by now conducted an inquiry, had realized that the "major victory" had to be downgraded substantially, but it did not relay this information to the army.

Two weeks before, the army had appointed General Yamashita supreme commander of defense forces in the Philippines. Yamashita was the general who earlier in the war had taken Singapore, earning himself the nickname Tiger of Malaya. He had not seen eye to eye with Tōjō and had been obliged to serve in Manchuria for some time, but as the anticipated final battle drew nearer, he was hastily summoned to the front line. He was assisted by Lieutenant General Mutō, the man who had once given a taste of defeat to the celebrated Ishihara of the general staff. Ishihara had been at the center of things, shaping the army's policies, ever since the time of the Manchurian Incident. The two men still thought that the main force defending the Philippines should be concentrated on the island of Luzon, as specified by previous plans; a hasty transfer of combat units to Leyte would only result in confusion and invite heavy losses at the hands of the enemy air force. They argued with great fervor with the staff officers from General Staff Headquarters and with Terauchi and his staff, the discussion growing so heated that their voices carried far beyond the room. Yet Terauchi, who had already received an Imperial Headquarters' order, bluntly rejected their proposals with a cold "that's an order." As Yamashita and Mutō stepped onto the porch of the Supreme Command building, their eyes met for a moment and they both burst out laughing, apparently for no reason. They stood together watching the moon, both fully aware that there could be no hope of victory in the coming battle. Even if they had to die, they had thought at least to take some of the enemy with them and by detaining the enemy as long as possible to give the main islands a chance to complete preparations for a last stand; now even that was impossible. Feeling at this point that there was no outlet for their resentment, the two generals instead chose to laugh it away, thus achieving a certain peace of mind and accepting their fate like soldiers.

The battered Japanese fleet desperately sought some opportunity to

outsmart the Americans. The coming fight would be essentially a land battle, but the navy must still give its full cooperation. Ozawa's fleet, including four aircraft carriers with only one hundred planes altogether, would serve as a decoy and lure the enemy task force to the north. Meanwhile, the main fleet consisting of seven battleships under the command of Vice Admiral Kurita Takeo would arrive on the field, sailing from the Brunei base in Borneo via the San Bernardino Strait north of Leyte. Pouncing upon the transport fleet, crowded together in the bay of Leyte, it would destroy it with its superior fire power. Such was the plan prepared by the Japanese navy.

Meanwhile, the newly appointed commander of the navy's air squadrons, Lieutenant General Ōnishi Takijirō, summoned five officers for an important meeting at Clark Field, on the outskirts of

Manila. Ōnishi, the naval officer who had prepared for Yamamoto the draft plan for the attack on Pearl Harbor, explained: "The battle of the Philippines is a decisive engagement, a matter of life or death for Japan. To ensure the success of the raid by Kurita's fleet it is essential, even if we don't manage to sink the enemy's aircraft carriers, to render their flight decks inoperable for at least one week. To accomplish that," he continued, "I can see no other way but to put 250-kilogram bombs on Zero fighters and ram them into the ships."

Defense of the American task force by fighter planes and the ships' own protective blanket of antiaircraft fire were by now all but perfect; almost all Japanese bombing and torpedo attacks were ending in failure, their planes crashing futilely into the sea. If one had to die anyway—Ōnishi reasoned—was it not preferable to resign oneself from the beginning and carry out a successful attack by ramming one's plane into the enemy vessels? Before leaving Tokyo, Ōnishi revealed his plan to Navy Minister Yonai and discussed it with him. "I understand your reasoning," replied Yonai. "But you can't *order* such a measure. If the crew members want to do it of their own free will—well, I suppose you can't stop them."

The second in command of Air Unit 201 at Clark Field, a veteran lieutenant colonel by the name of Tamai Asaichi, after consulting all the officers at the base, expressed approval of Ōnishi's "special attack plan." Then he summoned to his room twenty-three pilot-trainees he had personally trained, and explained the plan to them in the dim lamplight. As their instructor, he had a warm, almost parental relationship with the young airmen. Most of these youngsters still preferred sweets to sakè, but their eyes shone brightly as they listened to their superior's words. Without a moment's hesitation, all of them agreed. Tamai's greatest worry was who to select as leader of the mission, but his choice finally fell on Captain Seki Yukio, a graduate of the Naval Academy. The captain listened to Tamai's briefing with great attention, then, putting his elbows on the table, sat for a long while with his chin in his hands. His silence made Tamai wonder what could be going through the man's mind. The captain had been married only a few months earlier. Moreover, he had the confidence of a veteran combat pilot who could place a bomb dead on target on an enemy ship without resorting to body crash (he said as much to a friend, in fact, before going on his mission). Yet he must have understood the vital necessity of this plan and the need for some one—preferably a veteran like himself—to take the lead, for at last he replied, smoothing back his hair: "Please—let me take this mission."

This is how the first assault unit of twenty-four kamikaze (literally "divine wind") planes was organized. The name derived from an incident in the thirteenth century, when a Mongolian fleet that had come to attack Japan was annihilated by a "god-sent" typhoon.

From the moment it left port, Kurita's fleet was hounded by submarines and attacked many times from the air, losing one ship after another; even the mighty battleship *Musashi* went down in the Sibuyan Sea. Yet despite all, the fleet somehow managed to keep going, and on the evening of October 24 passed through the dangerous straits into the Pacific. Ozawa's decoy fleet also succeeded in drawing out Halsey's fleet and although it had lost all its carriers, the capital ships still maintained their combat readiness. The next day, early in the morning, a lookout on Kurita's flagship, the *Yamato*, spotted an enemy carrier only thirty-seven kilometers away. He could even see aircraft taking off and landing on its deck. The young officers danced for joy at this stroke of good luck; some even had tears of happiness in their eyes. The big guns opened fire, hurling shells weighing 1.5 metric tons each at the enemy. One of them landed right on target on the carrier's deck. This was the first time in the Pacific War that the world's largest battleship directly bombarded an enemy vessel. But the encounter with the enemy was so sudden that both fleets had trouble maintaining formation; in addition, scattered squalls over the ocean often made the ships lose sight of each other. The American fleet did its best to get away while its destroyers fought back with torpedoes. On the American side, the outcome of the fighting was one escort carrier lost and two almost shot to pieces before they shook off Kurita's attack.

At this point, three Japanese planes appeared, and two of them came diving down at the escort carriers *Santee* and *Suwannee*. In the teeth of furious antiaircraft fire, the two kamikaze struck their targets in quick succession. Flames and black smoke engulfed the carriers, but thanks to excellent firefighting equipment they succeeded in putting out the fires and carrying out emergency repairs within about two hours. Three hours later, five more kamikaze planes escorted by four fighters appeared in the sky above the fleet. The first plane, piloted by Captain Seki, was badly damaged by machine-gun fire and trailing

The battleship Missouri *at the moment of being struck by a kamikaze plane off Okinawa on April 16, 1945.*

black smoke. Even so, he crashed it onto the deck of the *St. Lo*, an escort carrier, where it made a great somersault and plunged into the ocean. Its bomb, however, pierced the deck and exploded inside the hangars. The fuel caught fire immediately, causing bombs to detonate, and the whole ship blew up, breaking in two and sinking immediately. Two more kamikaze planes hit their target—the deck of the escort carrier *Kalinin Bay*—but it narrowly escaped destruction. Thus the first handful of kamikaze had achieved results matching those of the entire Combined Fleet.

Kurita's fleet had by now reached a point only twenty-one nautical miles from Leyte Bay. For some reason, however, Admiral Kurita suddenly changed course and started retreating toward the San Bernardino Strait. Since the fleet's wireless equipment was of very limited capacity, he was totally in the dark about the overall state of the fighting. He concluded that the landing craft in Leyte Bay had already unloaded their troops and that it would be of little use to sink empty ships. In fact, eighty transport vessels were still in the midst of landing operations; had Kurita's fleet struck them then and there, chaos would have been created among the landing American units. But Admiral Kurita, true to Japanese naval tradition, scorned "piddling chores" of this kind—no matter that he was under orders from Imperial Headquarters—and, hoping for another combat encounter with enemy carriers, sailed due north, retracing his steps. The deep desire in every navy man's heart was destruction of the hated aircraft carriers, not participation in the army's campaigns or the sinking of helpless transports. Thus Kurita's fleet, to its great subsequent regret, missed its opportunity by the thinnest of margins.

The army's power was being whittled down by continuous air raids, but the two hundred remaining planes of its air force carried out daily missions above Leyte Bay, bombing and strafing the enemy's landing craft and disembarking units. Although they had some success, American defenses were by now so strong that the air unit was being thinned out with alarming rapidity.

It was in spring the same year that Army Headquarters began considering kamikaze attacks. Many people, however, had negative views on putting the kamikaze technique into practice, and it was not until the American landing on Leyte on October 20 that the first Special Army Attack Units were organized at Hokota airfield. One day before, when the British fleet came to launch an attack off Sumatra in support of the U.S. army, several fighter planes of the army air unit that took it on had, in fact, rammed the enemy vessels. Lieutenant Abè Nobuhiro and two other pilots crashed their fighters into enemy destroyers, sinking two and starting a major fire on one of the carriers. Kamikaze units, organized in Japan and sent off with many prayers and tears by flag-waving crowds, advanced to the Philippine base on October 26, but did not see real action until November 7. Even after setting out on their mission, they failed to find the enemy fleet until the twelfth, when they struck at the American transports and their escort ships in the bay of Leyte.

Bitter fighting against overwhelming American forces continued on

Even teenage girls were mobilized to work in the munitions factories.

Leyte. The Japanese army managed to land one division of reinforcements from the island of Luzon and was waiting for another, but this fell easy prey to American planes and the whole fleet of transports was sunk. The American pilots hunted down the soldiers swimming about in the ocean and strafed them with machine guns; soon the ocean was red with the blood of ten thousand men. Only three years before, when the Japanese navy sank the *Prince of Wales* and the *Repulse* off Malaya, it refrained from attacking the destroyer that came to rescue the British sailors, allowing it to get away unharmed. The next day the officer who went out on reconnaissance dropped a wreath of flowers on the site of the previous day's battle. By now, however, the spirit of chivalry—or bushido—had vanished from the battlefield.

To build just as many planes as possible was the overriding aim of the Japanese people at home. From around December the previous year, studies at Japanese universities had all but come to a halt, and all able-bodied students had joined the army or the navy. High school boys and girls, mobilized to work in munitions factories, were busy producing weapons, particularly airplanes. A thin trickle of these planes was reaching the Philippines, but frequently the workmanship was so poor and the pilots' skills were so variable that many aircraft crashed on account of engine trouble or had to make emergency landings. Day and night, American fighters were constantly patrolling the Bashi Channel, which separates Taiwan and the Philippines, shooting down planes in great numbers. Japanese pilots would refer to the area as the "River Styx."

Fresh Special Attack Units were being organized in Japan and sent to the front line, while others were formed on the spot. Between October 24 and November 29 the army and navy launched about one hundred kamikaze missions, and more than forty American ships were rammed; of these, five sank and about sixteen carriers suffered damage. The Japanese air force as a whole had changed its style of attack—the kamikaze units were now its backbone. Harassed by their frequent assaults, Halsey's crews developed a kind of "kamikaze neurosis," rushing out to intercept even a single Japanese plane that appeared in the sky. The result was deadening fatigue: during medical checkups on October 30 aboard the U.S.S. *Wasp*, a large aircraft carrier, all but thirty crew members were diagnosed as "in need of sick leave due to overwork."

At the outset, membership in the kamikaze units was voluntary, and many Japanese youngsters willingly joined them, suppressing their personal agonies. But once the kamikaze attacks developed into a "system," the atmosphere in the air units made it virtually impossible to avoid volunteering. The Supreme Command now ordered kamikaze attacks wherever and whenever they were needed. Why, though, did the young men at that time so willingly give up their lives? A letter written to his fiancée by Takushima Norimitsu, a twenty-four-year-old student from Keio University and a navy pilot, throws some light on his psychology. He fought first in the Philippines and later died in combat off the coast of Japan. Here is what he wrote:

"I'll put it bluntly. I do love you. But at this moment, something more important than you has come to occupy my heart—the country that gives a home to such gentle girls as you. Yesterday I was deeply moved by the sweetness of some children who bowed to us pilots from afar, across the rice fields, even though they could not recognize our faces in the tranquil dusk. If I said that what I felt then was far stronger than my love for you, would you be angry? No—you'd surely understand my feelings. Really, I feel I could give up my life without regret for the sake of such lovable children. I'm too egoistic to believe in any religion. So please try to understand that I couldn't go on living unless I had such strong emotions as a motivation for my actions. I want to cherish that precious something in my heart as I die."

When the U.S. forces landed on Leyte, the Filipino armed-guerrilla movement numbered barely eight thousand men. The difficulties of the Japanese army on Leyte gave them encouragement, and as they gained confidence in an American victory the partisans grew daily more active. On December 15, the Americans besieged the island of Mindoro. After the new year, on January 9, they directed a furious artillery barrage at Luzon, then landed in Lingayen Gulf—where the Japanese army had once attacked. From there the Americans started their rapid push toward Manila. The Japanese forces moved their supreme command to Baguio, digging in in the mountains and preparing for an endurance contest. With them were the Filipinos of the Makapilis group (Patriotic Society of the northern Provinces), led by General Artemio Ricarte.*

On January 18, Lieutenant General Kuribayashi Tadamichi, commanding officer of the defense forces on Iwo Jima, sent the following letter to his son and daughter:

"I have no idea how many years this war will last. It's getting fiercer all the time and there's no guarantee that Tokyo and other cities won't become a wasteland. In fact, parts of cities like London and Berlin have already been razed. There are no prospects for you two in the future and I feel sorry for you; yet all of Japan is in the same situation and I can only say be brave and hold out."

Bombing raids on the Japanese home islands had in fact already started in November of the previous year, when American B-29s were stationed in Saipan. The ultra-long-range Superfortress, a masterpiece of American technology and industrial power, had an effective range of 3,500 kilometers and could carry four tons of bombs; it cruised at an altitude of 9,000 meters, out of reach of antiaircraft guns and reasonably safe from interception by fighters. To accomplish effec-

*General Ricarte was frequently sent to jail because of his anti-American independence movement. Since 1915 he had lived in exile in Japan and only returned to the Philippines with the advancing Japanese army. He became leader of a pro-Japanese political party.

tively their "scorched earth" strategy upon the Japanese main islands
the U.S. Joint Chiefs of Staff were hoping to seize Iwo Jima, which la
exactly halfway between Saipan and Tokyo. With this island, the
would be able to attach escort fighters—P-51 Mustangs—to the bombe
squadrons, and also to rescue some of the crews from the fairl
numerous forced landings.

By the end of January, Iwo Jima was under heavy artillery bom
bardment and suffering daily air raids. Defense units forced to repa
the damage had no time to spare, but Commander Kuribayashi sent
last letter to his wife:

"The war will most likely drag on indefinitely, becoming fiercer a
the time—you must bear that in mind whatever you do. There are a
many as 150 B-29s ready to bomb Japan proper at the Saipan base; b
April there'll be 250, and by the end of the year perhaps 500. Tha
means that the raids will become correspondingly more intense, and
if the island where I am now is taken, the number of enemy bombe
will increase further and the raids will be terrible. If the worst come
the enemy may land on the coast of Chiba and attack Tokyo. Th
campaign in the Philippines seems to be gradually going against u
and the enemy will soon be upon us here. We are all ready to mee
whatever comes. Don't have any notions about my coming bac
alive: be resigned."

On February 16 and 17, carrier-based air squadrons of the U.S
task force carried out a series of raids on air bases and aircraft fac
tories in the vicinity of Tokyo. Those raids paved the way for th
American offensive at Iwo Jima. On February 19, seventy-five thou
sand men of the Third, Fourth, and Fifth Marine divisions arrived o
the coast of the island. The commander in chief of the landing troop
marine General Holland Smith, was reading his Bible aboard the com
mand ship *Eldorado*. Several weeks before, he had sent a letter to h
superiors, maintaining that the capture of Iwo Jima was not worth th
deaths and suffering of so many of his soldiers. But now he had an ord
to take the island—"within five days," moreover. "Within five day
may be impossible," he thought, "but it shouldn't take too long even s
It's far smaller than Saipan and the terrain isn't complex."

At 3:20 on the morning of February 19, steak was served for breal
fast to the marine corps, as tradition decreed. Then the first assau
wave of fifteen thousand men boarded five hundred landing cra

while the battleships and escort cruisers opened up a furious cannonade. When the naval guns fell silent, a formation of one hundred airplanes took off from the carriers and covered the entire island with a carpet of rockets and napalm bombs. Then, when the planes left, the naval cannonade started all over again. The tiny island disappeared in clouds of black smoke and whirling sand and dust, until it seemed that nothing beneath them could survive.

Yet this awesome barrage did not harm the defenders at all. General Kuribayashi, who had served in the United States and knew well the enemy's real power, rejected the strategy of "annihilation at the water's edge" favored so far by both army and navy. From the beginning he set his encampments at the foot of the mountain, digging underground tunnels where the soldiers could hide and, if the enemy approached, spray him with oblique and flanking fire or charge in a bayonet attack. To his soldiers he gave the following instructions:

"We will fell the enemy with the deadly accuracy of our fire. Clutching dynamite to our breasts, we will throw ourselves against the enemy tanks and smash them to pieces. We will volunteer to charge into the heart of the enemy ranks, wiping them all out. And even if only one of us is left, he will become a guerrilla and continue to harass the enemy."

This was probably the best defensive strategy he could adopt under the circumstances: his troops were ordered to fight a vastly superior enemy without the least chance of supplies or assistance by either sea or air.

From the landing craft that approached the shore in a flood, amphibious vehicles rolled out first and crawled up the beaches. In the first thirty minutes, there was no fire at all from the Japanese side. It was so quiet that one of the marines muttered, "Let's hope the Japs have cleared out"—only to get a bullet through the head. Without warning, a fierce hail of rifle and machine-gun fire swept over the Americans. Mortar shells rained down on their heads. Before nightfall, five hundred of the landing marines were dead, and they had advanced no more than a thousand meters from the beach even at the points of deepest penetration. The marine commanders had thought that the decisive battle would be fought during the first night. But the usual all-out banzai attack by Japanese troops never came. Instead, shells came pouring on the marines, crouched in the narrow hollows, and one exploded their ammunition dump. When dawn broke on this hellish nightmare, the beach was strewn with dead bodies.

On the second day after the landing, in a light drizzle, the attack on Mount Suribachi was launched. The island of Iwo Jima is shaped like a tadpole, and the main camp was located near its head, while the 167-meter Mount Suribachi loomed over its tail. Under a protective barrage from their destroyers, the marines set about eliminating the cave strongholds one by one, using flame throwers and powerful explosives. By noon, they had advanced seventy-five meters. In the afternoon, covered by tanks, they took another two hundred meters. Here and there, there was hand-to-hand fighting. The raising of the Stars and Stripes atop Mount Suribachi took place three days later, on the morning of February 23. The mountain had been worked over from foot to peak, transforming it into a bleak wasteland. Lieutenant Colonel Chandler Johnson of the 28th Marine Regiment dispatched First Lieutenant Harold Schrier as a messenger and said, handing him the Stars and Stripes, "Raise this flag on the top of the mountain." The lieutenant assembled forty marines and at 10:15 reached the crater at the mountaintop. His scouts found a discarded steel pipe, about six meters long, and attached the flag to it, driving it into the soft earth. The unfurled flag could be seen clearly from both land and sea. "The big shots will want to have that flag. But it belongs to all of us. Go and find another one somewhere and replace it," said Lieutenant Colonel Johnson to a corporal.

The corporal fetched a flag from one of the LST landing craft on the beach—a large ship's flag, twice as big as the original. A photographer named Joe Rosenthal arrived at the top of Mount Suribachi just as the marines were replacing the old flag. It was this second raising of the flag that Rosenthal captured in his famous photograph. This unique picture instantly captured the imagination of America from coast to coast, and the names of the six marines who helped raise the flag became as famous as those of movie stars. The six men all came from different parts of the union—some from the East, others from the South or the West—and were of varied ethnic backgrounds, from Anglo-Saxon to American Indian, East European to French Canadian; they genuinely represented America, and the picture thus was truly "America's victory."

But the fighting at Mount Suribachi was nothing more than an opening skirmish in the taking of Iwo Jima. By the evening of February 24 the marines had sustained seventy-eight hundred casualties, yet had seized no more than one-third of the island. As they advanced toward the tadpole's head, the Americans' losses swelled day by day, and it took well over another month before organized resistance by the Japanese ceased altogether. Twenty-three thousand marines were killed or wounded in the fighting at Iwo Jima. Of the six soldiers who had raised the Stars and Stripes, three fell in battle. On the Japanese side, twenty-one thousand men were killed in action.

Late in the afternoon of March 9, while the marines were inching their way toward the main encampment at Iwo Jima, three hundred B-29s loaded with two thousand tons of incendiary bombs took off from their base at Saipan on one of their lethal raids. They attacked Tokyo, flying at the low altitude of three thousand meters, and showered the whole downtown area with bombs, causing an unprecedented con-flagration. A tragedy as terrible as—or worse than—General Kuri-bayashi had predicted thus befell the residents of Tokyo. A sea of fire, fanned by winds of twenty meters per second, engulfed them—mainly women, children, and the elderly—and the Sumida River overflowed with corpses. There were eighty thousand dead, and as many as one million people lost their houses in the fire. It was the greatest recorded conflagration in the entire history of mankind. Two B-29s were damaged but managed an emergency landing at the Iwo Jima airfield, already in American hands. Of fourteen Flying Fortresses that crashed into the ocean, the crews of five were rescued. The incendiary bomb-ings by the B-29s continued. On the twelfth they struck Nagoya, on the thirteenth Osaka, and so on until all major Japanese cities had been razed to the ground. The wholesale massacre of the civilian population had begun.

Around the time that Kuribayashi's defense force at Iwo Jima, dying of thirst and running out of ammunition, launched its last banzai charge, U.S. Task Force 58 under Vice Admiral Marc Mitscher was about to weigh anchor and sail north from its temporary shelter at Ulithi in the Pacific. This massive task force, with a core of ten large and six light carriers, was to begin the softening up for an offensive at Okinawa. Beginning on March 18, all air bases in western Japan were subjected to continuous bombing by carrier-based aircraft. Admiral Ugaki's naval air squadron responded by throwing its entire remaining force into a counterattack against the task force. As usual, the Japanese navy concluded that the enemy had suffered heavy losses and had retreated to safe harbors in the Pacific; in fact, the task force showed up virtually unscathed off Okinawa.

Beginning on the morning of March 23, military installations on Okinawa were bombed with great thoroughness. Its four airfields were the first to be wrapped in heavy black smoke, then Naha port was completely demolished. Without a single aircraft to send up against the enemy, the Japanese could only crouch in their caves and trenches, watching the great host of enemy planes flying wherever they pleased. From time to time an antiaircraft battery would return fire, but the enemy's response was so violent that it would fall silent immediately. At 6 P.M. sharp, as if returning home from work, the tide of enemy planes would retreat, and on the ground the funeral pyres of the dead were lit, the smoke drifting about until late at night. The next day too, and the day after that, the carrier-based air squadrons renewed the attack as soon as day broke and continued with great precision until nightfall. The afternoon of the second day, a deep rumbling in the ground—a sound penetrating the very marrow of the soldiers' bones—was added to the bombing: the big naval guns had opened fire.

On March 26 the Americans stormed and occupied the Kerama Islands off Naha. On these islands, the Japanese had hidden 250 of their Special Naval Attack craft. The Japanese army was preparing to pounce upon the enemy fleet from the rear with its kamikaze boats, but the Americans had routed and seized its bases before it could complete preparations for the attack. Thus the only way of counterattacking the U.S. task force was from the air, with kamikaze pilots. Squadrons of planes had been leaving the home islands, heading for the south like migrating birds, and a total of 2,500 aircraft were now ready to crash into the enemy fleet. The terror of their ramming assaults caused panic among the ships' crews and as many as 187 vessels were damaged. But the damage was not fatal, and only 13 of these ships sank. On April 4, the last Combined Fleet, under Admiral Ito Seiichi aboard the *Yamato*, sailed from the Inland Sea. It had just enough fuel for a one-way voyage, and its task—at best—was to run aground on the Okinawa coast and shell the landing Americans with its guns—a gallant if ill-advised final sally.

On April 1, Okinawa lay under a bright, cloudless sky. The Americans, who for many days had been raking the area with a nonstop naval cannonade, now began landing opposite the Kadena airfield, screened by a huge fleet of more than a thousand ships. The landing units consisted of three marine divisions and four infantry divisions, 180,000 men in all. Having taken to heart the lesson learned in the fighting on Iwo Jima, they started digging shelters on the beach as soon as they landed—but only a few scattered rifle shots met them. Four divisions strong, the men advanced steadily in line and soon took the Kadena airfield. Evening came and still no resistance whatsoever from the Japanese army. It was like some grim April-Fools' joke.

Even on the second day the island remained quiet, with no trace of human presence. The front line had already moved three kilometers inland, yet the Americans encountered no enemy encampments. The following day reconnaissance-unit jeeps crossed the island, reached the opposite shore, and reported, "No sign of the enemy." The commander of the First Marine Division, Major General Pedro A. del Valle, was surrounded by war correspondents.

"No," he said, "I have no idea why we were allowed to land so easily. I don't know where the Japanese troops are and I don't know what their intentions are. The Japanese commander is either a total idiot or a strategic genius."

Until summer the previous year, Okinawa had been left practically without defense. Imperial Headquarters thought it sufficient to send air force battalions to the island, where they would wage a decisive aerial battle. But the overall progress of the war in the Pacific finally made them realize its crucial importance. Between July and August, three divisions were dispatched, and fifteen-centimeter howitzers, as well as two hundred cannon, were unloaded without mishap. From the very beginning, shore defenses were abandoned and solid cave bunkers constructed in the hilly inland area. Imperial Headquarters was not particularly pleased with the plan to abandon the defense of the airfield, and ordered a change of strategy many times, but staff officer Yawara Hiromichi, who was responsible for the operation, was adamant.

On April 5, American units made their first contact with the enemy line of encampments and had a taste of unexpectedly tough resistance. Not one of the American units was able to advance more than three hundred meters. First American guns blasted away the cover of trees on the hill, then the infantry approached step by step, covered by scores of advancing tanks. But the Japanese had a skillful way of countering these attacks. During the bombardment they would sit quietly in their caves, but as soon as it stopped they would occupy their gun emplacements and shower the enemy with oblique fire and stop the infantry's advance. The advancing tanks were met by mercilessly accurate fire from antitank cannon hidden in camouflaged shelters only a hundred meters away. As the tanks tried desperately to change direction, soldiers would spring out of their hiding holes like locusts and throw mines at them. In one of the camps, the Americans lost as many as twenty-two tanks out of thirty. The Americans would repeat the artillery barrage, then send their infantry again. When they finally seized one of the hills, shells from trench mortars, pinpointing the spot, started raining down from the sky. The Japanese first line was manned by veterans of the Sixty-second Division who had gained their fighting experience in China. They were filled with a burning determination to win. Though even they grumbled at the toughness of the battle, they fought on like tigers. For fifty days the two armies were locked in a struggle for, literally, every inch of the ground. Particularly around the town of Shuri (near Naha), a gruelling offensive was followed by a no less gruelling defensive battle. It was not unusual for one hillock to change hands many times. When the Japanese army lost a hill, they would dig in halfway up the opposite one and hold out there; then at night they would storm the first hill and retake the position. Although they were inflicting heavy casualties on the enemy, repulsing his attacks was taking its toll on the Japanese side, and, as the days passed, a pallor of exhaustion came over the soldiers' faces.

Admiral Itō's Combined Fleet had been shadowed by submarines from the day it left the home islands. When Vice Admiral Mitscher received the report, he promptly sent Task Force 58 northward. Thirty minutes after the Japanese escort fighters had returned to their bases on the main islands, at 12:30 on April 7, the battleship *Yamato* was attacked by Mitscher's four hundred planes. The *Yamato* turned all of its two hundred high-angle guns, as well as its machine guns, to the sky, and the escort vessels all followed suit. But the destroyers and the cruisers were sunk one after another, or rendered unmaneuverable, and the *Yamato* itself, damaged by twenty mines, had to reduce speed to fifteen knots. At about 1:20 P.M., a second wave of over a hundred planes assaulted the fleet, and the *Yamato* was hit by twenty torpedoes and left listing at an angle of thirty-five degrees. Admiral Itō ordered the whole crew to abandon ship, and quietly withdrew to his cabin. Captain Ariga Kōsaku tied himself to the compass to await death beneath the waves.

At noon on May 9 there came a great salvo from every gun of every kind on the American side. The ships at sea joined in too, in a great thunder of cannon. Then, for a moment, silence fell over the battlefield, and not a single missile came flying at the Japanese. The Americans were busy embracing and slapping each other on the back, overjoyed at the news of the German surrender that had just arrived. On the Japanese side, the news spread by word of mouth from the communications unit, putting a dark weight of desperation into the hearts of officers and men.

At last, the American forces began moving against the town of Shuri. Suicide units of junior high school boys were organized and ordered to defend the old capital of Okinawa. With the sleeves of their baggy uniforms tucked up and clutching explosives, they threw themselves at charging tanks. On May 28, Shuri fell. Captain Julian Dusenbury, who led the forward unit, was not expecting such a stroke of good luck and did not have a flag with him. However, being of southern descent, he always kept a family heirloom—a Confederate flag from the Civil War—in his steel helmet. Thus it came about that General Lee's old flag was unfurled on the gates of Shuri.

The Japanese army, given respite by the torrential rains of the rainy season that had set in just a week earlier, began its retreat to the south, looking for a position to make its last stand. Stumbling along muddy roads throughout the night, a mixed lot of soldiers and civilian refugees headed south. Military formation had already broken down, and very few soldiers now had proper arms. There were even some who had lost their trousers, and the wounded hobbled along leaning on sticks. Whenever a flare lit the night sky, they would rush for shelter in the dark. The civilians, with a few household essentials on their backs or on carrying poles, instinctively followed the lead of the group. By this time every youngster had joined the fighting, and the crowd of refugees consisted solely of old people, infants, and women.

Charging American tanks rode mercilessly over Japanese soldiers—"they would never surrender, anyhow." There was no hospital care, not even a scrap of bandage available for the wounded. Those with serious injuries either committed suicide voluntarily or were forced to do so. In early June the sky cleared, but this only made the "hunting" livelier for the Americans. American infantry was pressing upon the Japanese rear, and at the island's southern extremity the muzzles of their fleet's guns lay in wait beneath the cliffs. Many of those who tried to retrace their steps north were felled by American bullets. The Americans were demolishing one by one the shelters where soldiers and civilians were hiding. Those dugouts that did not respond to the call for surrender got a load of explosives. Even teenage nurses of the medical corps were killed in this way. The Japanese army had lost fifty thousand men by the end of May, and in the last three weeks lost another sixty thousand. At least the same number of civilians accompanied them into death before the curtain finally fell on the last land battle in the Pacific.

10

Day of Defeat

Shortly after American forces landed in Okinawa, Prime Minister Koiso Kuniaki, his confidence in his own management of the war destroyed after a mere eight months, relinquished the reins of government. On the way back to his private residence after formally handing over his duties to his successor, he was accompanied by no one apart from his chauffeur, Karasawa Kōzaburō. The latter had served fourteen prime ministers in all, beginning with Tanaka Giichi, who had formed his government in 1927, and including Konoe and Tōjō. As Koiso alighted from his car, he turned to this faithful driver and said, almost as though to himself, "There were all kinds of things I should have done, but I didn't do a single one. Not one . . ." Then he formally thanked Karasawa for his long service and disappeared into the gloom of the entrance hall, which was pitch-dark on account of the blackout.

The man proposed as his successor was former Admiral Suzuki Kantarō. Suzuki was seventy-nine, and it was many years since he had played any part in public affairs. He was one of the senior statesmen who had been attacked by rebel troops in Tokyo on that snowy, bloody morning of February 26, 1936. Hit by several bullets, he had barely escaped with his life; if his wife had not tried to stop the soldier who made to deliver the coup de grâce, and if Captain Andō Teruzō, the man's commander—who had met Suzuki personally and respected him as a man—had not agreed, he would have been dead long since.

Requested by the Emperor to form a government, Suzuki at first firmly refused. He had lived, he said, faithful to the Emperor Meiji's precept that a military man should play no part in politics, and he had no political opinions whatsoever.

"That is how I imagined you would reply," said the Emperor. "But no one else will do at this crucial juncture. I hope you will agree, however much it may be against your will."

It was most unusual for the Emperor to make a request in this fashion.

"I don't hear well, either . . ." said Suzuki, still hesitant. "It wouldn't matter if you were blind or deaf," replied His Majesty. "We need *you*."

One of the strongest advocates of Suzuki as the next prime minister was Marquis Kido, who had become the Emperor's closest confidant following the death of Saionji. He was the chief figure in the group of Japanese leaders that felt strongly that the time had come to end the war as soon as possible. The Emperor himself was in complete agreement. It would have been dangerous, however, to broach the subject publicly and unequivocally. The army, still bent on pursuing the war, would almost certainly object, and a false move might lead to the government's downfall, or even a coup d'état.

Nobody gave Suzuki any hint of the course that the state was supposed to take henceforth. Thus, as he set about forming a cabinet, he was under the firm impression that the war was to be continued. As candidate for foreign minister, he summoned Tōgō Shigenori—who as foreign minister in the Tōjō government had made earnest last-ditch efforts to salvage the U.S.-Japanese negotiations. Tōgō assumed that the new government would naturally aim at ending the war, and he sounded out Suzuki on this score.

"We shall have to think about that when the time comes," replied Suzuki, who was out of touch with what was going on. "I imagine the war will go on for another two or three years at least yet."

Dismayed, Tōgō countered by arguing that a peace agreement was a matter of the utmost urgency. Unless this was understood, he could not accept the post of foreign minister. Suzuki listened intently, then said, "That's fine, on the lines you suggest."

Kido staked everything on Suzuki's combination of apparent aimlessness and extreme flexibility. Now that the Emperor was firmly set on peace—Kido hoped and calculated—the loyal Suzuki would sooner or later waken to the fact, seize a suitable opportunity to win over the army and navy, and personally steer his government safely into harbor.

As the situation in Okinawa deteriorated, the army had begun to call for a final battle on the main Japanese islands. Even the army, of course, was aware that the situation was hopeless, yet despite this—or rather, precisely because of it—it hoped at least once to inflict grave losses on the American forces by doing battle with them on Japanese soil, where their supply lines would be stretched to the utmost, and thereby to achieve an honorable peace settlement. America was loudly insisting on Japan's unconditional surrender, and it was the idea of giving in unconditionally that was intolerable to the army. It hoped to salvage at least a minimum of Japan's honor by obtaining a guarantee that the Emperor's position would not be compromised; it was an article of faith that Japan would no longer be Japan should the Emperor lose his position.

On taking over the premiership, Suzuki publicly announced the government's determination to carry the battle onto Japanese soil and urged the nation to gird its loins. Yet the old man was also a realist; the day after he took office, he summoned Chief Cabinet Secretary Sakomizu Hisatsune and directed him to make an immediate survey of the nation's resources. The first essential, he pointed out, was to find out for certain whether Japan really was capable, as the army insisted, of carrying on the struggle further. The report on the survey was presented as a top-secret document in early June. Yearly production of iron and steel was a mere third of the yearly target of three million tons. Less than half the target figure of one thousand planes per month were being turned out—and this figure was likely to drop to zero by the following April on account of the shortage of aluminum. Stocks of petroleum were running out and vessels of the Imperial Navy were mixing soybean oil with the heavy oil they used. Damage from air raids was far greater than had been expected, and if the B-29s continued active at the present rate, all Japan's cities with populations of thirty thousand or more would have been razed by the end of September. Overseas, Berlin had fallen and Nazi Germany had collapsed. The Soviet Union was sending forces to the Far East and would be in a position to launch an invasion of Manchuria by September.

Foreign Minister Tōgō was in favor of direct peace negotiations with the United States; however, the opposition of the army was too strong for this. So Tōgō, rather reluctantly, decided to pursue the next best alternative and ask the Soviet Union, with whom Japan had a treaty of neutrality, to act as intermediary in arranging a settlement. In April of that year, the Soviet Union had informed Japan that it was not going to renew the Russo-Japanese Neutrality Pact. Relations between the two countries, thus, were distinctly chilly, but the treaty itself was valid until March of the following year. The Soviet replies to Japan's request gave neither a clear yes nor a clear no, and contacts dragged on indecisively day after day. Growing impatient, Tōgō decided to appoint Prince Konoe Fumimaro as special envoy to go to Moscow and hold talks directly with Stalin. Konoe hesitated, but when the Emperor himself repeated the appointment, he recalled how the Emperor, at the time of the signing of the Tripartite Pact, had had a presentiment of Japan's future defeat and had asked him to "share the burden" with him, and with some diffidence he undertook the difficult mission. However, the Soviet reply to Japan's request that it receive the special envoy was as equivocal as ever. Japan's leaders were unaware of the deals that had been made in February of that year, when Roosevelt, Churchill, and Stalin had conferred at the Crimean resort of Yalta. In fact, Stalin had made a firm commitment to enter the war against Japan, in return for which the Soviet Union had demanded possession of Sakhalin and the Kurils and the lease from China of the Manchurian railways and Port Arthur. President Roosevelt, who at that time did not know that the Japanese forces in Manchuria had almost all been switched to the south and were little better than an army of scarecrows, welcomed Soviet participation in the war as a means of reducing, however slightly, the amount of blood that must be spilled by American youth in order to lay low the Japanese Empire.

On July 17 a conference of three Allied leaders—Churchill, Stalin, and Truman (who had succeeded Roosevelt as president upon the latter's death)—began in Potsdam, Germany. Truman had already held a series of conferences in Washington concerning American policy in Europe following the end of the war and methods of bringing hostilities in the Pacific to a conclusion. He also knew that an atomic bomb was shortly to be tested in New Mexico, but this did not deter him from requesting Soviet entry into the war.

Another method of getting Japan to surrender was also considered. First brought up by acting Secretary of State Joseph C. Grew—a former ambassador to Japan—it involved making a declaration that unconditional surrender did not mean an end to the Emperor system. Truman

On May 29, 1945, over five hundred B-29s unloaded 3,200 tons of explosives and incendiaries on Yokohama, reducing one-third of the city to ashes.

showed interest in this suggestion, and the opinion of the army and navy was sought. In the end, the idea was obliged to give way before the view that it would be an excessive concession on America's part. John J. McCloy, assistant secretary of war, who was convinced that only a madman would insist to the other side that it submit unconditionally, worked busily to obtain support for it, but without success. In the same way, his proposal that the atomic bomb should not be used immediately but that Japan should be warned of its impending use was dismissed on the grounds that it was not wise to refer to a weapon that was still at the experimental stage.

Ways of getting Japan to surrender and the question of how to deal with it after the end of the war were also discussed at Potsdam. Stalin revealed to Truman—who in fact had long been aware of everything, thanks to Operation Magic—the undercover Japanese request that the Soviet Union should put out peace feelers for it. The Soviet Union, he promised, would put off its reply on some pretext, such as that the Japanese messages were too vague; either way, the Soviet Union was going to enter the war.

Five days later, the report of the successful atomic test on July 16 reached Potsdam. Excited by the acquisition of a superweapon of such fearful power, Truman considered that all problems had thereby been solved and that Soviet aid would probably no longer be necessary. He confided the secret of the atomic bomb to Churchill, and the two men agreed that it should be used in order to bring the war to an end. Opposition to its use on moral grounds still persisted within the American army and navy—Dwight D. Eisenhower was a typical case—but an order to drop the bomb was promptly sent from Potsdam to the newly appointed commander of the strategic air forces, Lieutenant General Carl A. Spaatz.

The Potsdam Declaration was published on July 26 in the names of Truman, Churchill, and Chiang Kai-shek. Within the Japanese government, it was Foreign Minister Tōgō who insisted most strongly that Japan should agree to its terms; he had taken note of the fact that they could be interpreted as implying something other than unconditional surrender. The fact that Stalin was not among the signatories of the declaration also gave him grounds to suppose that the Soviet Union, faithful to the neutrality pact, had mediated on Japan's behalf. The terms laid down in the declaration—the limiting of Japanese territory to the four main islands, the restriction of the functions of the Japanese government, occupation, disarmament, and the punishment of war criminals among them—were extremely harsh, and there was plenty of food for doubt and uneasiness; yet, as Tōgō saw it, to let this opportunity to begin negotiations go by would be even more fatal. Nevertheless the opposition of the military was as implacable as ever. Suzuki put forward a compromise proposal, whereby the press was to report the declaration without any comment whatsoever, thereby giving a signal that Japan was paying heed to it.

The morning editions of the twenty-eighth, however—despite the government's attempts to impose restraints—carried headlines referring to a "plot by the three powers" and dismissing the call for unconditional surrender as "preposterous." Hastily, Suzuki personally called a press conference at which he stated that the attitude of the Japanese government toward the Potsdam Declaration was one of "*mokusatsu*." As Suzuki intended it, this word was the equivalent of the English "no comment," but in Japanese broadcasts directed overseas it turned out as "ignore," and the *New York Times* of July 30 carried a headline announcing that Japan had rejected the Allies' final call for it to surrender. Thus President Truman lost any chance of checking use of the atomic bomb at the last moment. The Japanese government, in short, still expecting that the Soviet Union would mediate on its behalf, had attached insufficient importance to its own response to the Potsdam Declaration.

At 3 A.M. on August 6, the *Enola Gay* took off from the base on the island of Tinian carrying the first atomic bomb ever to be dropped on mankind, and at some time past 8 A.M. arrived in the sky over Hiroshima. The bomb, suspended from a parachute, exploded at a point 600 meters above ground level. It was 8:15, at which time the city's clocks stopped forever. A single bomb wiped out an entire city. Thirteen square kilometers of the city center were seared by its terrifying blast, heat, and radiation; at least two hundred thousand citizens either were killed instantly or died after days—in some cases, months—of suffering. As the plane in which Dr. Nishina Yoshio—an atomic physicist who flew to Hiroshima at Japanese army orders—arrived in the sky over Hiroshima, one glance was enough to tell him that it could only have been an atomic bomb.

His judgment was confirmed by foreign broadcasts. On the afternoon of August 8, on receiving formal notification from Dr. Nishina that the weapon dropped on Hiroshima had unquestionably been an atomic bomb, Prime Minister Suzuki realized that the war must be brought to a rapid conclusion and directed Cabinet Secretary Sakomizu to summon a meeting of the Supreme Council for the Conduct of the War for the following day. In Moscow in the meantime, Ambassador Satō Naotake, after much waiting, finally gained an interview with Foreign Commissar Vyacheslav Molotov at 11 P.M. on the eighth (Japan time). Satō was about to tell the other man how the Japanese government felt when Molotov stopped him and informed him instead that from the next day—August 9—the Soviet government would consider itself at war with Japan.

Startled, Satō complained that this would represent a betrayal by the Soviet Union of its treaty. Molotov countered by citing Soviet duty toward the Allies. The exchange was, of course, pointless. In the end, Satō requested permission to send a cable home to Japan. Molotov agreed amiably enough, but when Satō got back to the embassy, he found all the telephone lines cut and the building surrounded by police. Confined to the embassy, he had no means of contacting Tokyo. The Japanese government did not hear of the Soviet declaration of war against Japan until 1 A.M. on the ninth, when it picked up a broadcast from San Francisco. By then, Soviet forces had already crossed the Manchurian border at three points, in the northwest, north, and east, and were pouring into the country like an avalanche.

At 5 A.M., unable to wait for dawn, Sakomizu hastened to Suzuki's private residence, where he found Foreign Minister Tōgō already present. When he joined them, Suzuki merely remarked laconically, "Well, it's finally happened."

Confronted with the atomic bomb and the Soviet incursion, Suzuki clearly perceived that the only course left open to Japan was to accept the Potsdam Declaration. At the meeting of the Supreme Council for the Conduct of the War, which began at 10:30 A.M., no conclusion was reached, on account of successive objections raised by the army and navy. At a cabinet meeting held in the afternoon, ministers were more or less unanimous in agreeing to acceptance of the declaration, but War Minister Anami Korechika refused to budge in his absolute opposition.

In the meantime, news came of the atomic bombing of Nagasaki, but he remained adamant. The rules of the Japanese government provided that unanimous approval by the cabinet must be followed by approval by the Emperor. Ten P.M. came, and still the discord was unresolved. Finally, Suzuki decided to go to the Palace and request an Imperial Conference at which the Emperor would give his personal decision.

The conference room, in an underground shelter of the Imperial Palace, was almost unbearably hot and humid. The Imperial Conference began at midnight on August 9; copies of "Plan A" and "Plan B" had already been laid out on the table. Plan A accepted the declaration "on the understanding that it does not comprise a demand for any change in the legal position of the Emperor," while Plan B added two further reservations—that occupation should be as restricted as possible in scope and that the disarming of Japan and the trial of war criminals should be carried out by the Japanese themselves.

When the Emperor appeared, the marks of distress were plain on his face, and his hair was disheveled, several strands hanging down over his forehead. On Suzuki's instructions, Sakomizu first read aloud the entire text of the Potsdam Declaration. As he read, Sakomizu could not hold back the tears, and his voice choked; he barely got through to the end. Next, Tōgō got to his feet and explained systematically and unemotionally why Japan would be obliged to agree to the declaration unconditionally—in other words, in accordance with Plan A. The next man called on to speak was War Minister Anami.

"It should not be impossible to take on the enemy and deliver him a serious blow on Japanese soil," he declared. "The opportunity to conclude the war would occur then. If," he added, "it were possible to terminate the war according to Plan B, I myself would also agree."

Chief of General Staff Umezu Yoshijirō and Chief of Navy General Staff Toyoda Soemu expressed more or less the same views as Anami, while Navy Minister Yonai and President of the Privy Council Hiranuma Kiichirō agreed with the foreign minister. Not counting Prime Minister Suzuki, the chairman, the opinions of those present were split evenly, three against three.

"We have spent a long time in debate," Suzuki said, "but have finally failed to reach any conclusion. However, we cannot afford to lose a moment." And, contrary to the expectations of those present, he gave no personal opinion but went on: "Therefore—without any precedent and with the utmost distress—I would respectfully submit that His Imperial Majesty give the final judgment."

Suzuki was moving to take his place before the Emperor when Anami, shocked, hissed, "Prime Minister!" in a low voice. Anami was under strong pressure from officers in the army, who were pinning their hopes on him. It was laid down that no supreme matter of state policy could be determined without the agreement of the war minister, and they were determined to take advantage of this system in order to continue the war until there was some guarantee that Japan's honor would be salvaged. Anami's involuntary exclamation had indicated his realization that things were proceeding according to an unscheduled scenario.

Ignoring the voice—or possibly not hearing it—Suzuki went up to the Emperor, bowed deeply, and asked him to speak. The Emperor nodded and told him to return to his seat. Suzuki put a hand to his ear as though he had not caught what was said, so the Emperor motioned him to his seat with his hand. Understanding, Suzuki returned to his place, whereupon the Emperor, leaning forward slightly, said in a firm voice:

"My opinion is the same as that of the foreign minister."

The words had an electrifying effect on those present. The silence seemed to spread and deepen. Before long, the sound of stifled sobs arose from among the assembled men. At that moment, defeat—a defeat such as Japan had never suffered before in all its history—had become certain, and the fact struck home to each man present with a particular poignancy. The Emperor's hand moved—at first, he seemed to be rubbing the rim of his spectacles with a white-gloved thumb, but soon he was frankly wiping away the tears that coursed down his cheeks. After a while he said, as though the words were being wrung from him, "To make things clear, I will tell you my reasons."

First, he pointed out how, all through the war, the predictions of the army and navy had invariably proved wrong.

"The army and navy reported just now that they could mount a decisive battle on the main islands and that they had confidence in their ability to do so, but here again I feel extremely worried. What the chief of General Staff says is seriously at variance with the reports of my aides-de-camp. In fact, almost no defenses are ready. According to what I hear, not all the troops have guns, even. What would happen if we embarked on a decisive battle in such a state of affairs? The Japanese people would surely be virtually wiped out. It is my duty to hand on to our descendants this land that we have inherited from our forebears. Now that things have reached this pass, the only hope, I feel, is to see that as many Japanese as possible survive so that they can rise again in the future and rebuild the nation. Nor would it be a good thing for the peoples of the world that the war should continue any further."

"I understand very well," he went on, "that for the army and navy the idea of disarmament and occupation is intolerable. I, too, detest the idea that those who have served me loyally might be executed as war criminals. However, I recall the distress of the Emperor Meiji at the time of the Triple Intervention and believe that what has to be borne must be borne with patience. I have decided that this war should be ended."

The Emperor's words brought the conference to its conclusion. After he had left, those present confined themselves mostly to discussions of procedure and to signing the necessary documents. It is said that by the end of his solitary uphill struggle Tōgō's hair had turned quite white. As they began to move toward the exit to the shelter, Chief of the Military Affairs Bureau Yoshizumi Masao, who had been standing by, suddenly stepped into Suzuki's path and declared menacingly, "Prime Minister—you've broken the rules!"

To Yoshizumi, the unprecedented course that events had suddenly taken was totally unexpected, and he felt indignantly that the prime minister had deceived him. Stepping between the two men, Anami pushed Yoshizumi aside. "That's enough, Yoshizumi," he warned him.

At 7:30 on the morning of the tenth, Anami summoned over fifty influential officers to the conference room in the basement of the War Ministry and told them that an Imperial Conference held in the course of the preceding night had decided to accept the terms of the Potsdam Declaration. Pandemonium broke out. Anami held up a hand to silence them. "It is His Majesty's will," he said. "How we act from now on will depend on the enemy's answer. Whether we have peace or war, advance or retreat, the army must act as one man, with perfect unity, in accordance with strict military discipline."

"You spoke of 'advance or retreat,' Mr. Minister," demanded one major accusingly. "Does that mean you are seriously considering retreat?"

Anami slapped the side of his boot with the whip he was holding and raising his voice declared, "Anyone who isn't satisfied can start by killing me!"

On the afternoon of August 13, Major Koga Hidemasa, a staff officer of the Imperial Guard, turned up without warning at the home of former Prime Minister Tōjō. He was Tōjō's son-in-law, and his wife and children were living in the house. It was his wife Makie's birthday. The major spent a few minutes with his wife, greeted his father-in-law, who had a visitor at the time, then left hurriedly. As he parted from his wife, he said something vaguely disturbing: "I'm going back to my home in the country very soon. So listen—you're to go on living your life with your head up. You must go straight ahead, without shrinking, however rough the going gets."

The officers at the War Ministry and General Staff Headquarters had not yet given up hope of having things their way but were working out a plan whereby—if the nature of the Allies' reply made it necessary—they would use military force to isolate the "peace faction" in the Suzuki cabinet, the faction that was leading Japan toward surrender, and carry through a coup d'état. Lieutenant Colonel Shiizaki Jirō and Major Hatanaka Kenji, the most positive advocates of this plan, visited the Imperial Guard and tried to win Major Koga to their side. The cooperation of the Imperial Guard was absolutely essential to the success of a plan of this nature. Koga promised to work with them; it would, in fact, have been extremely difficult for a junior officer, asked point-blank whether he could stand by and let Japan surrender, with no attempt to join battle on the main islands and under highly dishonorable conditions into the bargain, to counter with a definite assertion that Japan ought to surrender.

The Allies' formal reply to Japan's inquiry reached the government late at night on the twelfth. It contained the sentence "the authority of the Emperor and the Japanese government to rule the state shall be subject to the Supreme Commander of the Allied Powers." The Foreign Ministry, hoping to soften public opinion, translated the phrase "subject to" as "*seigenka*," "under the control of," whereas the War and

Navy Ministries interpreted it as meaning "enslaved to." Chief of General Staff Umezu and Chief of Navy General Staff Toyoda visited the Palace together and submitted to the Emperor their view that to accept the Potsdam Declaration would be dangerous. The middle-ranking officers also began to move again. The sudden visit that Koga—who was staying at the Imperial Guard Command working every day—had paid to his wife had been due to his recognition that, once embarked on such a plan as this, one must, whether successful or not, be prepared to give up one's life. His reference to his "home in the country" had, in fact, signified the family grave there.

The cabinet meeting that began on the morning of August 13, at which the final decision was due to be made on whether or not to accept the Allies' terms as they stood, once again lapsed into confusion. The majority were leaning toward acceptance, but the opponents of surrender, led by the war minister, continued to resist. Chief Cabinet Secretary Sakomizu noticed, however, that a subtle change was taking place in Anami's attitude. As the cabinet meeting dragged wearily on, Anami called Sakomizu into another room and, in his presence, called Chief of the Military Affairs Bureau Yoshizumi at the War Ministry.

"The cabinet meeting is beginning to go as we hoped," he said, "so don't move but wait till I come back. If you have any doubts, Sakomizu is here."

His hearer seemed to have rung off satisfied. Sakomizu had the impression that Anami was desperately striving to keep the army, which was inclining toward a coup d'état, in check.

The cabinet meeting failed to reach any conclusion, so that once more Suzuki was obliged to resort to an Imperial Conference to break the deadlock.

The second Imperial Conference began at 10:30 A.M. on the fourteenth in the same hot, humid underground conference room as before. The Emperor made it clear that his resolve to accept the Allies' reply had not changed. "I understand the people's desire to give up their lives in a fight to the end for the sake of the country," he said. "But my role now is to save as many people's lives as possible. Of course, it may not be possible to place complete trust in the Allies' approaches, but the important thing is the nation's resolve and its faith. Assuming that the way still lies open, not to Japan's destruction but to its continued survival, then there is hope, probably, for future recovery. I, too, realize that the path will be long and steep. I, too, will strive together with the people. My heart is heavy when I think of those who died or were injured in battle, of their families, and of the life facing those whose homes have been destroyed. At this point, it does not matter what happens to me. I will do anything I can. I am sure that the people, unaware of the true state of affairs, will be greatly disturbed by this development, but I am ready to broadcast to them at any time if necessary. I am sure, too, that the war and navy ministers will have a hard time placating their officers and men, but I am willing to go anywhere to persuade them directly."

Suzuki stood up and apologized to His Majesty. "I feel it unpardonable," he said, "that our own failures should have obliged us to trouble Your Majesty so often for a verdict. But," he added, "Your Majesty's words have made Japan's course clear. That being so, it is our desire to tackle the restoration of Japan under Your Majesty's rule."

Back at the prime minister's official residence, the principal cabinet ministers joined in a simple meal of whale meat and bread. A draft of the imperial edict ending the war was ready there; after the meal, they had still to debate it and sign the final version. Exhausted by physical and mental strain, most of them could scarcely get the food down. Suzuki alone showed the same healthy appetite as ever. Despite his age and the bewildering succession of heavy tasks presented by the past few days, he had not once shown any obvious signs of fatigue. He slept briefly but deeply and ate well. At the meeting, he scarcely spoke at all yet performed his duties one by one as though everything had been laid down from the outset. War Minister Anami, on the other hand, had been dogged at every turn by the officers. Even during this meeting, he was called out of the room by Lieutenant Colonel Takeshita Masahiko, his son-in-law. In the privacy of another room the latter proposed to him that, as his last card, he should either refuse to sign the imperial edict, or resign. For a moment, Anami looked perplexed, but the next moment recovered himself, smiled, and said, "Even if I resign, it won't change Japan's course by now!"

Moves to bring the war to an end went ahead steadily. Late in the evening of the fourteenth, the signing of the imperial edict by members of the cabinet was completed. Informed by telephone, Tōgō—who had already returned to the Foreign Ministry—gave instructions to the chief of the communications section to send out immediately the formal reply to the Allies. Scarcely had he done so when, without warning, Anami put in an appearance, wearing white gloves and with a military sword at his side. He bowed punctiliously, then apologized for the fact that ever since the question of ending the war had come up he had represented the army in putting forward warlike views, causing no little trouble to Tōgō. Then he added:

"I had a look at the Foreign Ministry's draft reply a while ago. I must thank you for incorporating all the suggestions that I made."

The main text of the draft reply represented, of course, Plan A of the Imperial Conference, just as it stood, whereas the army minister's views—in short, the contents of Plan B—were appended as "desirable conditions."

"If I had known this," Anami concluded, "I would never have opposed the reply so adamantly."

"Even during the conference," said Tōgō with a wry smile, remembering the fierce controversies of the past few days, "I'm sure I told you that our reply and the 'desirable conditions' were two different things and that we would append the latter as representing our hopes."

Anami bowed correctly once more and took his leave. Tōgō stood for a while looking vacant, watching him go. Anami had one more visit to make. At the prime minister's official residence, Suzuki and Chief Cabinet Secretary Sakomizu were sitting facing each other in silence when Anami came in with a murmured apology. Facing the prime minister, he repeated more or less what he had said to the foreign minister.

"I understand how you feel; it was all motivated by concern for your country," said Suzuki. "However,"—and this was typical of an elderly man who had lived through the Meiji era—"the Emperor's position will be preserved, I am sure—because His Majesty is so assiduous in paying his respects to his ancestors."

"I am convinced of that, too. I am convinced that His Majesty and the nation will join together in bringing about Japan's recovery."

The war minister left. When Sakomizu, who had seen him as far as the entrance, returned to the room, Suzuki remarked laconically: "Anami came to take his leave, didn't he."

Late that night, after a few cups of sakè shared alone with Lieutenant Colonel Takeshita, his son-in-law, at the war minister's official residence, he killed himself by committing ritual disembowelment. He was aware that, as one of those responsible for leading the glorious army into defeat, his sacrifice was demanded at this juncture. The news of the war minister's suicide was reported to the officers and men of the Japanese forces at home in Japan, then in turn to those stationed in the continental Asian and Pacific zones, having a sobering effect on their normally hot-blooded reactions and preparing the ground psychologically for acceptance of Japan's defeat.

Late on the same evening, equipment was transported from the Japan Broadcasting Corporation (NHK) to the Imperial Palace ready to record the Emperor personally reading the text of the imperial edict ending the war. The broadcast of the recording to the nation was due to take place at noon the next day, August 15. At this point, however, plans for a rebellion aimed at preventing the ending of the war were still taking gradual shape. General Tanaka Seiichi, commander of the Eastern Army, and Lieutenant General Mori Takeshi, commander of the Imperial Guard Division, were still receiving waves of visits from radical officers demanding that Japan fight to the bitter end. Within the Imperial Guard Division, young officers of the First and Second Regiments under the leadership of Major Koga were getting together and planning first to occupy the Imperial Palace then to spread the rebellion to the whole army.

It was divisional commander Mori who held the key to the plan's success. Something of a martinet, Mori had already sent away unsatisfied several groups of officers and was engaged in deep discussion with his brother-in-law Lieutenant Colonel Shiraishi Michinori, who happened to be visiting him, when, at one in the morning, two newcomers arrived. They were Lieutenant Colonel Ida Masataka and Major Shiizaki of the War Ministry, who demanded earnestly and persistently that the commander take resolute action to prevent the end of the war. So fiery was Ida's eloquence in particular that Mori found his feelings beginning to be swayed.

"Right. I see your point," he said. "You have moved me, too. As a member of the Japanese nation, I will visit Meiji Shrine and consider once more, in the divine presence, what it is best that I should do. However," he added, "it is also important to know the chief of staff's views. You must talk to him about it too."

Ida was content with having made some impression, at least, on the general's mind; even should the reply be no, he had done what he had to. When he got up to go, there were already another two visitors in the room. They were Major Hatanaka and another officer, a captain. Giving Hatanaka a meaningful smile, Ida went off alone into the chief of staff's office next door. Scarcely had he exchanged a few words with the chief of staff, however, when from the next room there came the sound of shots. Rushing back, he found Major Hatanaka standing there vacantly, a pistol in his hand. The other man, the captain, had his sword unsheathed and was splashed with the blood of his victim. On the floor, the general and Lieutenant Colonel Shiraishi lay side by side.

"There was no time left!" cried Hatanaka, almost in tears.

The general, Hatanaka had believed, had concurred with Ida's smiled signal. Thus a misunderstanding had developed between him and the general, and the general, a formidable man, had bawled him out. As a result, the younger officers, feeling desperately that time was running out, had had resort to the pistol and the sword.

Rushing in, staff officer Koga was momentarily shaken. But he did not go back on his commitment. A spurious divisional command was transmitted over the phone by Koga to the regiments. The Imperial Palace was occupied by the Second Regiment of the Imperial Guard, which was on guard there that day, and cut off from the outside world. From that moment, however, Ida had determined to disassociate himself from the plan. He reported the true state of affairs to the Eastern Army, then hastened by car to the Palace, where he set about arguing with Major Hatanaka, who was now commander of the rebel forces.

"It's not possible to win over the Guard by murdering the divisional commander," he said. "The rebellion has already failed. Get your troops out by dawn. If only you do so, the whole affair will be dismissed as a midsummer night's dream."

Though utterly dejected, Hatanaka was still reluctant to give up. He wanted time to appeal to the army as a whole—he had found out that the recording for the Emperor's broadcast had already been made and that the record was being kept at the Imperial Household Ministry. He ordered his men to search the Imperial Household Ministry, but they failed to find it. The structure of the building was extremely complex, and nobody realized that the all-important object was tucked away in a small, innocent-looking safe in a simply constructed closet used for storing the chamberlains' bedding. The chamberlains themselves, who were being confined to the ministry, kept silent, nor were they subjected to any indignity in their interrogation.

The summer night was gradually drawing to an end. Chief Secretary Sakomizu, who had spent the night at the prime minister's official residence, had leapt out of bed at the sound of machine-gun fire. Having personally experienced the February 26 Incident at the same official residence when he was secretary to the prime minister, his first feeling was one of relief at having sent the prime minister home to his private residence that night. The rebels were forty soldiers led by Captain Sasaki Takeo, commander of the Yokohama garrison. He had tried to persuade his unit that they should assassinate leading figures in the government and overthrow the Japanese "Badoglio" government, but the commanders of the companies had refused to a man, and a mere thirty soldiers had responded to his call. So he had harangued some students of the Yokohama Industrial College with whom he was already acquainted, and ten of them joined his band. They got on a truck and made, first of all, for the prime minister's official residence. Sakomizu, who had realized the danger he was in, left things to Satō Asao, head of the General Affairs Section, and made his escape via a secret underground passage leading to an emergency exit. Sasaki and his followers splashed gasoline about the residence and set fire to it, then set off for Suzuki's private residence. The prime minister, who had been immediately warned by phone, similarly escaped via an emergency exit and, with no definite destination, made off into the streets of Tokyo in a car driven by Karasawa. Finding him gone, the terrorists set fire to his home and left.

Unable to wait for the dawn, General Tanaka, commander of the Eastern Army, had himself driven to the headquarters of the Imperial Guard in a car flying his general's pennant. On the parade ground of the First Regiment of the Guard, which was situated next to the headquarters, the unit, having received an emergency muster, was drawn up ready to set off for the Palace. Tanaka promptly ordered them to disband. Next, ahead of everyone else, he marched into the headquarters of the Imperial Guard, roundly berated Major Ishihara Teikichi, another staff officer who had supported the rebellion, and had him arrested. He also called the commander of the Second Regiment—then at the Palace—over the phone and ordered him to come to meet him at the Palace gate. Finally, he informed the regiment commander of the truth of the situation and had the unit return to its normal stations.

The building in which the Emperor was living had thick steel doors, and no sound from the outside world reached the interior. However, Chamberlain Mitsui Yasuya had decided that it would be better to rouse the Emperor in case rebel troops should force their way in; he informed the Emperor that the Palace had been occupied.

"A coup d'état?" inquired the Emperor. Mitsui informed him that the troops were searching for the recording and that the chamberlains were being confined at the Imperial Household Ministry. "I will go out," said the Emperor. "Assemble the troops in the garden. I will talk to them personally."

But there was no need. At that moment General Tanaka, having pacified the rebel force, was hurrying to meet the Emperor and report to him on the incident. The sun was already rising red in the eastern sky.

At 7:21 A.M., the radio made the first announcement that the Emperor would broadcast to the nation at noon. To ensure that it was missed by no one, the same announcement was repeated many times at intervals throughout the morning. Thus when the broadcast finally began, most of the nation, still unsuspecting, was seated formally in front of its radios, awaiting His Majesty's word. Following the broadcast, Koga committed harakiri in front of the coffin of the Imperial Guard commander. Lieutenant Colonel Shiizaki and Major Hatanaka, the two officers who had continued resistance to the end, shot themselves with their pistols in the plaza before the Imperial Palace.

Two days later, the Suzuki cabinet submitted its resignation. Suzuki himself, to avoid the danger of assassination, remained in hiding with his chauffeur, at the home of a friend in the suburbs, for another week or so. During that period, he warned Karasawa, "The Japanese must never become servile. Wait and see—in ten years' time I'm sure that a better Japan will have emerged out of the war. Not that I shall be here to see it myself . . ."

To this faithful chauffeur, he gave a piece of brush-written calligraphy in his own hand. The four characters he wrote read "the sky is limitless, the sea boundless."

It was on the afternoon of August 24, after completely quelling a number of minor revolts, that General Tanaka shot himself through the heart with his pistol at the army command. The number of military men and civilians who committed suicide out of a sense of responsibility for Japan's defeat—including also Vice Admiral Ōnishi, founder of the navy's Kamikaze units—is estimated to have reached 600. Of their own free will, they had formed the last rank in the army of 2,750,000 Japanese who had died in the war since the outbreak of the China Incident. As General Tanaka committed suicide, the advance unit of America's occupation forces under the command of General MacArthur, which had already flown to Okinawa from Manila, was eyeing the weather, waiting for a fierce typhoon to pass.

11

Occupation:
Light and Shadow

On the afternoon of August 30, 1945, General Douglas MacArthur arrived at Atsugi airfield as Supreme Commander for the Allied Powers in the occupation of Japan. Emerging from his personal plane *Bataan* with his corncob pipe clenched between his teeth and carrying no weapon of any kind, he paused momentarily at the top of the steps and gazed slowly about him, beneath a barrage of flashbulbs of the Japanese and American press. His first words as he shook hands with Eighth Army Commander Robert Eichelberger, who had arrived earlier and had come to meet him, were: "It's a long way from Melbourne to Tokyo, but this seems to be the end of the road."

At the time, some seven million Japanese troops were deployed throughout an area extending from China through Southeast Asia and the Pacific zone, with two and a half million of them on Japan's main islands alone. The advance party of Americans that had reached Atsugi airfield forty-eight hours before MacArthur's arrival had been strictly on its guard, fearing that the Japanese military might yet launch a banzai attack against them. In fact, not a single shot was heard save one fired by an American soldier over-excited by the tension. MacArthur first drove straight to the New Grand Hotel in Yokohama, where he was served a late lunch. He took a mouthful of the meal—mackerel and cod, with a salad of vinegared cucumber—and laid his fork down again.

Yokohama was a waste of rubble. MacArthur did not go to Tokyo until nine days later, during which period the signing of the instruments of Japan's surrender had taken place on board the *Missouri*, but there too almost everything had been completely leveled by fire—

shops and private homes alike, from the low-lying commercial areas near the bay to the residential areas on the surrounding higher land. The inhabitants grubbed among the ruins, living in improvised shelters patched together with pieces of board and scorched corrugated iron. In these shelters, scarcely recognizable as human dwellings, the Japanese were managing somehow to keep out the elements, to eat, to sleep, and to work. In places, the rubble had been cleared away and vegetables and sweet potatoes planted. "Tokyo," commented MacArthur, giving his first impression, "no longer has the capability to produce a single gun." He established his headquarters in what had been the Daiichi Insurance offices in the Marunouchi business district, many of whose Western-style buildings had escaped destruction. The building over which the Stars and Stripes now flew so proudly was a well-situated—even imposing—structure separated from the Imperial Palace grounds by a moat, and with walls faced with Italian marble.

If the Occupation forces had so wished, they could have placed Japan under military rule. They had, in fact, prepared military scrip, and some of it was actually put into use. When Foreign Minister Shigemitsu heard of this, he hurried to SCAP headquarters in alarm. MacArthur—whose desire it was to have Japan ruled by the Japanese government, with himself as a supreme authority in the background—accepted Shigemitsu's plea at once. And Japan—unlike Germany—escaped both partition and the loss of its own government.

There were a number of pressing tasks facing the Occupation. The first was to dismantle the vast apparatus of the Japanese armed forces and to get their members home. In Japan proper these operations went ahead without resistance and at an astonishing speed. Despite all the confusion and actual bloodshed that had been necessary before the war could be brought to an end, once the Japanese military man was convinced that no one would blame him for laying down his arms, he laid them down with alacrity. Next, the Occupation forces busily set about arresting the figures they considered to be important war criminals. Neither MacArthur himself nor Brigadier General Eliot Thorpe, who was commanded to carry out the task, had any idea of who, apart from Tōjō, the important people in Japan were. Either way, the first priority—as they saw it—was to seek out Tōjō and put him under arrest.

The wary Tōjō, foreseeing that this would happen, had had his doctor show him the precise position of his heart and had marked the

The Emperor visits MacArthur at the American embassy on September 27, 1945.

spot with Chinese ink. When the American military police arrived, they found the doors locked. Tōjō, who had been talking with a reporter through the window, suddenly retired to an inner room and shot himself. The bullet went part of the way into his heart, but a doctor was summoned immediately, and prompt action by the American military together with the resources of modern medicine saved his life. Tōjō's abortive suicide was greeted with scorn by the average Japanese and dealt a decisive blow to the reputation not only of the Japanese army but of the former ruling class as a whole. Next, former members of the Tōjō government and General Honma, who had fought the Americans in the Philippines, were arrested and sent to jail.

The Emperor first met General MacArthur on September 27. When the latter received information that the Emperor hoped to have an interview with him, he was delighted, since he had been concerned as to how the Emperor would react to the Occupation. It was arranged that the meeting should take place at the American embassy. The Emperor accompanied only by an interpreter, arrived in a single car. Initial greetings over, the Emperor said, in effect: "The question of who was responsible for the war is being debated in various quarters, but the person ultimately responsible for both political and military affairs in Japan during the war was myself. I leave it to your judgment as to how I should be treated. What I want now is to request your aid in relieving the distress of the Japanese people, who are on the verge of starvation. To that end, you may dispose of the property of the imperial family as you think fit."

This selfless speech made an enormous impression on the general who had privately assumed that the Emperor was coming to plead for his life. He was wrong; the Emperor's attitude accorded well with the image cherished by MacArthur—who prided himself on his knowledge of the East and of Japan in particular—of the "ideal monarch." It was also doubtless exhilarating for the general, as victor, that the Emperor should use such humble language toward himself.

The question of how to treat the position of the Emperor after the war was an important one that had been under study by the U.S. government ever since 1942. The majority opinion was inclined to favor making use of the Emperor, since this—it was believed—would make it easier to rule Japan. This pragmatic American approach was working in the Emperor's favor, but opinion was still strong among the

Allies—for instance, the English and the Russians—in favor of exe-
cuting the Emperor as the chief war criminal of all. However, the first
impression made on MacArthur by the Emperor was to prove decisive. The general made up his mind that this "supreme gentleman"
should be used to ensure the success of his own rule of Japan; all that
remained was to work out theoretical reasons to justify this course.

The meeting of the Emperor and MacArthur had a great effect on
the Japanese public also. That the Emperor should voluntarily go to
visit another—rather than summon him to the Palace—was unprecedented in itself, but more astonishing still was the photograph of the
meeting. The general, much taller to begin with, looked dignified and
relaxed; the Emperor in his frock coat stood beside him, short-statured
and somewhat stooping, his hands dangling at his sides. To most of
the Japanese who saw the photograph in the newspapers, it brought
home as little else could the fact of Japan's defeat.

The occupation of Japan, in which U.S. forces played the chief role
(although both British and Australian forces also took some part,
MacArthur as supreme commander exerted tight control over the
whole), had both its lights and its shadows. The positive side was represented by the various reforms carried out in order to effect the
democratization of Japan. General Headquarters (GHQ) staff included
a large number of well-meaning New Dealers who saw in this Asian
nation, crushed and powerless as a result of defeat, a chance to try out
the reforms they had not been able to carry through in America. The
Occupation troops, too, contrary to the fears of the Japanese public,
were relatively well-behaved. From their own experiences in wartime,
the Japanese had a vague idea of how an occupation force might be expected to behave—and feared an orgy of rape and looting. In the
event, however, such incidents were extremely rare. There were a few,
of course, who behaved badly—and Occupation authorities prohibited reporting of such incidents—but on the whole the Occupation
went through in a mild and friendly atmosphere seldom before seen in
history. The Japanese of the time, sunk in the depths of economic
distress and existing in a kind of spiritual vacuum, tended if anything
to look with admiration at the American troops as, well-fed and energetic, they gaily drove their jeeps about their daily tasks.

The negative side of the Occupation arose from the basic facts of
defeat and occupation as such. Just as he acted swiftly to disarm the

Japanese forces physically, so MacArthur also hastened to deprive the Japanese as a whole of their spiritual defenses. It was necessary, he felt, to pass judgment on Japan's former leaders as an example to the nation and to drag into the light of day the atrocities committed by the Japanese army, so as to break the—as he saw it—unfounded pride of the Japanese people. The majority of Japanese, long deprived of any chance to learn the true facts, were appalled as Occupation authorities read the long list of misdeeds committed by Japan's forces. And they concluded that where the war was concerned everything had been Japan's fault; or, if they came across something about which they remained unconvinced, accepted it resignedly as an inevitable concomitant of defeat.

The Japanese harbored almost no resentment toward the Americans, even where the dropping of the atomic bomb was concerned. The Occupation forces who moved into Hiroshima used bulldozers to level an army cemetery that stood on an eminence called Hijiyama, leaving untouched only the graves of Westerners who had died of disease in Japan. In its stead, they set up an Atomic Bomb Casualty Commission institute, the aim of which was to study the effects of the atomic bomb on the human body. Here, victims of the bombing came every month to give blood specimens but were given no treatment whatsoever. Yet even this caused no resentment, though there were some who lodged complaints at the institute. On the memorial set up at what had been the center of the blast, an inscription read: "Rest in peace; we shall not repeat the same mistake." At first, the "we" was taken as applying primarily to the Japanese themselves, then, as time went by, as applying to mankind as a whole. There were also some who complained that it was odd to talk of a Japanese "mistake" where the atomic bomb was concerned, but even they were not seriously angered at the idea. The Japanese are used to the Buddhist idea that one should forget what is past and done with; it was peculiarly characteristic of the Japanese people, moreover, that most of them should have viewed the atomic bomb as a kind of natural disaster akin to an earthquake or a typhoon.

The Occupation authorities were extraordinarily sensitive about the atomic bomb and banned all reporting concerning its effects. The *Bells of Nagasaki*, an account of his fight against radiation disease by a certain Dr. Nagai Takashi, a victim of the Nagasaki bombing, was only permitted to be published in the same volume with an exaggerated American account of the Bataan Death March. The book, which became a best seller, was thus arranged so that the same Japanese who shed tears over the horrors of the bomb should also be given the impression that these were a natural punishment for the misdeeds of the Japanese themselves.

The war-crimes trials were particularly effective in breaking the pride of the Japanese and casting a pall over the nation. The first such trial was that of General Yamashita, who had surrendered in the Philippines. Yamashita had taken up his post two weeks prior to the landing of American forces in Leyte and had conducted a hopeless defense as his command lines were progressively disrupted by the superior American forces. Now he was being put before an American military tribunal in Manila, accused of responsibility for all the actions—and it is indisputable that these included a large number of atrocities that violated the rules of war—of his subordinates in the field. To the Japanese he was a hero, the Tiger of Malaya who had commanded the force that occupied Singapore earlier in the war, and to start straightway by charging him with crimes and bringing opprobrium on his head would, MacArthur seems to have believed, accord well with the aims of the Occupation. He pushed the trial through at breakneck speed, in an Alice-in-Wonderland atmosphere in which verdict came first and proofs second. The foregone conclusion was that Yamashita should die on the gallows.

The next target chosen by MacArthur was General Honma, who had defeated him in the Philippines. In precisely the same way as with Yamashita, his death was certain even before the trial began. His wife, Fujiko, who appeared in the Manila courtroom as a witness for the defense, arousing much sympathy among those present, was later to give her impressions of the trial: "The trial was nothing but an acting out of revenge motives. The ostensible charge was atrocities against prisoners of war, but the real aim was revenge against Honma, the man responsible for the only blot on General MacArthur's brilliant war record."

Next, on a much larger scale, came the Tokyo Trials, at which Japan's former leaders were arraigned. The International Military Tribunal for the Far East was made up of judges and prosecutors from the Allied nations, and thus was not subject to MacArthur's personal wishes to the same degree as the Manila trials. Nevertheless, the trials were still subject to his supervision, and he exerted as much influence as he could on everything from the composition of the court to details of its schedule. His chief concerns were to have the Emperor removed from the list of war criminals and to impress on the Japanese, as soon as possible, their defeat and their guilt. For him, speed was of the essence; true fairness was a secondary consideration.

The chief concern of most Japanese in the postwar period was how to avoid starvation. As a result of its defeat, Japan had lost 44 percent of its territories and had simultaneously been cut off from such traditional spheres of economic influence as Manchuria and China. Moreover, the Japanese were obliged to receive into the narrow confines of their four main islands seven million compatriots returning home from various parts of Asia. Economist Inaba Hidezō, who established an economic research institute at the time to collect and analyze information relating to the wartime and postwar periods, reached the following conclusions, roughly summarized, concerning the state of affairs in Japan at the time.

The raids that had begun in 1944 had dealt a destructive blow to all factories, communications, and transport facilities. Cotton-spinning equipment, for example, had been reduced to less than 15 percent of the figure for 1941, and raw materials had become almost impossible to obtain. It was the same with almost all installations producing everyday essentials, such as textiles, fertilizers, cement, pulp, and paper. The iron and steel, machinery, and chemical industries, which had been diverted to military production during the war, were in the same plight; moreover, they had been informed by the Allies that any remaining facilities with more than a certain production capacity were either to be destroyed or to be handed over to foreign countries by way of reparations (this last measure was not, in fact, put into practice save for facilities in Manchuria, which, without exception, were taken over by the Soviet Union).

The energy industry was likewise on its last legs, and power failures were a daily occurrence. The petroleum industry had been ordered to cease operations, and for domestic supplies of power Japan was obliged to rely on hydroelectricity and coal, both of which were in short supply. The mining of coal, which during the war had depended on Korean labor, had been paralyzed by the repatriation or desertion of those Korean workers. Thus by November 1945, production indices in the mining and manufacturing industries had dropped to a mere 10.4 percent of the 1935—36 level.

Inflation, in the meantime, was rampant, while in autumn 1945 there was an unprecedentedly poor harvest of rice, Japan's staple food—a result of shortages of manpower, fertilizers, agricultural implements, and everything else. Foodstuffs had been subject to an overall rationing system since wartime days, but defeat and the weakening of governmental authority made rations ever later in arriving, and city dwellers were increasingly obliged to shoulder rucksacks and go to forage around the farming villages in the hope of being able to buy black-market provisions.

This was the Japan in which GHQ's social reforms were carried through with such boldness. On February 4, 1946, Major General Courtney Whitney assembled in his office the members of the Government Section, of which he was chief, and, once the doors were firmly closed, told them:

"From now on, the Government Section will act as council for the establishment of a new Japanese Constitution. General MacArthur has entrusted our section with this historic task."

MacArthur was in a hurry to replace the Meiji Constitution with a more democratic one. However, in order not to give the impression that the Occupation was imposing it on Japan, he had at first entrusted the task to the Japanese side. A number of drafts were presented, but none of them were essentially very different from the old constitution. Lieutenant Colonel Milo E. Rowell, a lawyer working in the Government Section, came to the following conclusion: "The Japanese are like bamboo in a storm. When a strong wind blows, the bamboo bows its head, but it returns to normal once the wind is past. The Westerner tries to put up an iron wall to stop it. It is no use engaging in abstract talk with a people whose way of thinking is so fundamentally different from ours. The only course is to draw up a concrete draft of a constitution so as to show them what we mean."

MacArthur, therefore, directed the Government Section to draw up a draft to be based on three principles: (1) the Emperor was to be hereditary head of state, but sovereignty was to reside with the people; (2) Japan was to renounce war and the possession of arms; (3) aristocratic and other privileges were to be abolished. A committee of three members of the section—Colonel Charles L. Kades, Lieutenant Colonel Rowell, and Commander Alfred R. Hussey—together with a female secretary, worked at the task almost literally day and night. During the day, they continued their discussion even at mealtimes, munching sandwiches in the snack bar on the top floor, then worked till nearly dawn, when they had a shower and an hour's nap at their lodgings before returning to work again. Obsessed with an enthusiasm to rewrite Japanese history, they completed the draft in five days. MacArthur's approval was obtained, then the draft was presented without ceremony to the Japanese government.

The Japanese, on first perusal, were astonished at the scale of the reforms proposed. The most important sections were those dealing with the Emperor's position and the renunciation of war and weapons. Whitney recommended that the Japanese government accept the draft as it stood as quickly as possible, pointing out that pressure was mounting among the Allied powers to have the Emperor tried as a war criminal. The prime minister of the day was Shidehara, who as foreign minister at the time of the Manchurian Incident had been caught between the opposing claims of the Japanese army and American Secretary of State Stimson. To Shidehara's mind, a state that had renounced all armaments was almost unthinkable, but, on learning that this was one of MacArthur's idealistic obsessions, he gave up any idea of opposition. It was necessary to give the impression, on the surface at least, that the constitution had originated with the Japanese themselves, and the Occupation authorities naturally gave instructions to that effect. Shidehara accordingly agreed to stand in for MacArthur as father of the idealistic articles. The "ideal Constitution" was supported by a broad section of the Japanese, prostrated as they were by the war; and several years later it was to prove a source of trouble to the American government when, reversing its own policies, it began to demand that Japan rearm itself.

Of all the reforms carried out by the Occupation, the only one initiated by the Japanese themselves was the agricultural land reforms.

The necessity for these had already been mooted before the war by both government and intellectuals. Twenty-five percent of the Japanese population of seventy million was engaged in agriculture at that time, and one-half the total area of land under cultivation was worked by tenant farmers. Matsumura Kenzō, agriculture minister in the Shidehara cabinet, had long championed policies designed to create a larger proportion of owner-farmers, and he believed that Japan's defeat in the war made the necessity for such policies still more urgent. Reform, he believed, would help prevent an intensification of the farmers' movement and also encourage farmers to increase production. He drew up a highly progressive plan for reforms, which met with considerable opposition both within the government and in the Diet and in the course of debate was deprived of much of its effectiveness. Thus MacArthur himself was to step in once more.

From the American Department of Agriculture, MacArthur summoned Wolf I. Ladejinsky, whose name he had come to know when working as military adviser in the Philippines. At that time, Ladejinsky had suggested to the Philippine government that the guerrillas would surrender immediately if only the government offered to give them two hectares of land for each rifle they turned in. The plan, of course, was rejected, but it had served to engrave its originator's name on MacArthur's mind. MacArthur's own father, military governor of the Philippines, had been one of those who dreamed, without success, of agricultural reform in that nation.

Thus Ladejinsky was given a chance in Japan to carry into practice that unrealized dream from the past. A plan still bolder than Matsumura's was drafted, and a total of two million hectares of land—80 percent of the total worked by tenant farmers in Japan—was set free. MacArthur showed a particular interest in this reform, and kept a careful eye on its progress. It is said that on one occasion, when Charles L. Kades, vice-chief of the Government Section, brought a report and gave it to the general, the latter glanced through it, then looked up at a photograph of his father hanging on the wall and exclaimed proudly:

"Well, Pop—don't you think I'm doing well?"

Of all the reforms carried out by the Occupation, the land reforms had the most important influence in laying the foundations of postwar

Japanese society. The farmers who received the land, instead of join-ing hands with the Communist party in reviling the conservative gov-ernment, became some of the conservatives' most loyal supporters.

The first postwar general election, in which all adult Japanese—women included—participated, took place in April of the year following that in which the Occupation began. The emancipation of women was another reform enthusiastically supported by MacArthur, to whom it seemed that to raise the position of women—who were naturally reluctant to see their husbands and sons go off to battle—was one way of preventing a resurgence of militarism. As a result of the election, the Liberal party led by Hatoyama Ichirō emerged as the strongest party (though it did not obtain an absolute majority), and it was natu-rally assumed that Hatoyama would form a government. In 1931 Hatoyama, a politician born and bred, had been appointed minister of education at the age of forty-eight. As the power of the military gradually increased, his background as a party politician had put him at a disadvantage; few Japanese now doubted that he would become prime minister, and he himself, full of confidence, set about forming a cabinet. Quite without warning, however, an edict purging Hatoyama from political life was issued by GHQ.

The Occupation authorities had issued an order prohibiting all former military men and all politicians who had cooperated with the military from taking any type of public office, and the list was grow-ing day by day. This measure was believed to be essential to the de-militarization and democratization of Japan. Even so, the purge of Hatoyama came as a shock to Japanese society: if men such as he were to be purged, then the only politicians left to qualify would, surely, be the Communist party members who had languished in jail during the war. The true reason for Hatoyama's purge is still not clear even to-day; some say it was an essay he had published criticizing America for using the atomic bomb, while another theory claims that his anti-Communist pronouncements had offended the Soviet Union, one of the Allies. Whatever the true cause, the Liberal party was obliged to fix on a successor in a hurry. The man who surfaced as a result was Yoshida Shigeru.

Yoshida had been in the Foreign Ministry for many years and had held posts in England and China. A faithful disciple of Shidehara, he saw cooperation with England and America as the first essential of Japanese foreign policy. As a result he too, like Hatoyama, had found himself at a disadvantage during the war years; toward the end of the Tōjō government's rule, he was actually arrested and detained for having plotted the downfall of the government. He was thus among the most suitable leaders for the new age and had occupied the post of foreign minister in the Shidehara government. Yet personally he had little ambition to become a statesman and refused the job on the grounds that he had no experience in handling party affairs. Eventually, however, the talks between him and Hatoyama reached agreement; Hatoyama was to assist him from behind the scenes with party affairs, while Yoshida himself was to concentrate on the premiership until such time as the other man should be restored to political life. In this way, Yoshida was to fill the post of prime minister for a total of seven years and two months—interrupted only by the brief coalition government formed by the Socialist and Democratic parties that held office from May 1947 to October 1948—and to steer Japan through the most difficult years of the postwar period.

A son-in-law of Count Makino, who had been one of Japan's plenipotentiaries at the Paris Conference, Yoshida was a typical conservative, and aristocratic in his tastes. On almost every point, whether it be the new constitution or the dissolution of the zaibatsu, he was opposed to the progressive policies of the Occupation, and in each case was to compromise in the end. The one goal that he pursued consistently throughout was the earliest possible restoration of international trust in Japan and its return to international society.

As prime minister, Yoshida maintained close and constant contact with MacArthur, paying him unofficial visits—surreptitiously, via the rear entrance to GHQ—at least once a month. Since official visits tended to attract the attention of the press, both men preferred to keep their meetings secret. MacArthur bothered the press with his unpredictability, while Yoshida had an extreme dislike of journalists (on one occasion, he even threw a glass of water over a cameraman). In this respect, the two men resembled each other; yet MacArthur looked on Yoshida as too conservative and incompetent to be of use in realizing his own ideals, while the latter saw the general as a man ruled by the whim of the moment.

Yoshida always brought with him a large number of problems that needed solving. First among them was the need to feed the hungry nation, to which end the reconstruction of industries was necessary, together with the removal of the restrictions placed on them and help from the Occupation authorities. The secretary who accompanied him could always tell at a glance, by Yoshida's expression when he emerged from GHQ, whether his talk with MacArthur had gone well or not. Usually, the larger part of the allotted hour was spent in lengthy, untiring expositions by the general of his own ideals. The prime minister would nod and cluck approvingly, then, when he judged that the general was in a sufficiently good mood, would trot out his own urgent request. If it was granted, he would emerge from the back entrance wreathed in smiles; when it was refused, he would come out with a sour expression. On one occasion, the secretary asked him whatever MacArthur could find to talk about for so long. "I don't understand his English all that well," replied Yoshida with a mischievous smile.

While Japan's wartime leaders were rapidly following each other into jail, the leaders of the Communist party were being released. Party secretary Tokuda Kyūichi, regaining his freedom for the first time in eighteen years, immediately became popular among the public on account of his cheerful personality and the eloquence with which he lambasted authority in every shape and form, from the Emperor on down. Nosaka Sanzō, who was returned to Japan by Mao Tse-tung in 1946, likewise received a warm welcome from a large part of the public. On May Day the same year, a crowd under their leadership swarmed into the plaza before the Imperial Palace with placards bearing the following legend:

"The Emperor's position has been preserved: 'My belly is full,' saith His Majesty, 'My people may starve to death.'"

Horrified, the government hastily prepared to charge them with lese majesty but failed to receive GHQ approval in the attempt.

The only targets ignored in Tokuda's otherwise blanket condemnation of authority were MacArthur and the Occupation forces themselves. The Japan Communist party had made up its mind that the Occupation forces were an army of liberation and was convinced that they trusted itself more than anyone else. The New Dealers among the Occupation authorities were, in fact, well disposed toward it, believing that it would prove useful in reforming Japan. The Americans were unfamiliar with the Communist party, while the Communist party, on its side, was unfamiliar with America. In China, too, the American government had demanded of Chiang Kai-shek, on pain of suspension of all American aid, that he achieve a reconciliation with the Communists and cooperate with them.

Many Japanese still retained their wariness of the Communist party, but the labor unions rapidly came under its potent influence. The Occupation authorities encouraged the formation of labor unions, which spread to places of work throughout Japan, increasing their membership till they became a major force in society. The workers had barely enough to eat, while enterprises whose production failed to rise were trying to put surplus employees out on the street. Strikes broke out here, there, and everywhere, and in February 1947 the unions, under Communist party leadership, finally planned a general strike aimed at driving out the Yoshida government. Their ultimate aims were the establishment of a "people's government" and revolution. Indirectly, MacArthur recommended that the strike be called off, but the unions, convinced that the Occupation was on their side, failed to take the hint. At the last moment, GHQ exercised its supreme authority and officially stopped the strike. From that time on, the illusion that the Occupation forces were an army of liberation for the revolution was shattered, and doubts about the Communist party's leadership developed even within the unions.

The period around the time of the planned strike saw the food shortage reach its peak. Occupation authorities had already alarmed the nation by publishing a forecast that "ten million Japanese would probably die of hunger," but in fact worst never came to worst. Occasionally there were victims among the bands of children, deprived of home and relatives by the raids, who haunted the stations and underground passages of the cities, yet their number was negligible compared with that of the troops who had died of starvation on Guadalcanal and other battle fronts. The Japanese as a whole, though suffering a certain degree of malnutrition, managed to survive. In their battle with hunger, the Japanese of those days were indebted to America in two senses. The first involved the humble sweet potato. This vegetable, originating in America, had reached Japan in the seventeenth century via Europe, and from then on its cultivation was encouraged by the

Tokugawa government as a means of preventing famine. During World War II, it was grown in large quantities as a raw material for alcohol to be mixed with gasoline used as plane fuel. It was to prove the salvation of the postwar Japanese; many was the family that survived for a whole month almost entirely on sweet potatoes.

The second debt to America arose from the fact that MacArthur, as the man with supreme responsibility for ruling Japan, believed it to be his duty not to let anyone starve under his rule and accordingly asked Washington for emergency imports of foodstuffs. As with most work involving the bureaucracy, the imports usually arrived in Japan six months to a year late, but they were of indisputable aid in easing the food situation in Japan.

Japanese children at the time weighed, on an average, a full 20 percent less than in prewar days. Brigadier General Crawford Sams of the Public Health and Welfare Section called on Prime Minister Yoshida and recommended to him the establishment of a school-lunch program. "If you put it into effect," he urged, "the height of schoolchildren will increase by one inch within a year."

Yoshida agreed to the program on the spot. Gazing at him as he nodded agreement, Sams noted that although Yoshida had physical breadth, his height was less than five feet. It was too late in the day to help Yoshida himself, but the marked improvement in the physique of young Japanese after the war was indubitably due to the milk in the school lunches first provided in January 1947 using aid materials supplied by the American LARA (Licensed Agencies for Relief in Asia).

In the second postwar general election, held in April 1947, the largest number of seats was won by the Socialist party. The party president, Katayama Tetsu, was appointed to form a government, and got together a coalition cabinet with the Democratic party. At this stage, MacArthur pinned great hopes on him and even went out of his way to send him a message of encouragement. Katayama was not just a socialist, but a Christian as well.

MacArthur cherished a particular ambition to convert the people of Japan to Christianity. The number of missionaries invited to Japan by the Occupation totaled 2,500, and everything, from housing to travel, was arranged for them by GHQ. Yet all these efforts produced surprisingly little in the way of results. The number of Protestants remained stable at 100,000, while the number of Catholics increased from 100,000 to 150,000—a virtually negligible change in terms of a population of close to 100 million. MacArthur himself, for some reason, was firmly convinced that 20 million Japanese had become Christians, and said so in public. Where he got his figures from remains a riddle.

The Katayama government collapsed after four months. The Democratic-Socialist coalition that followed it similarly lasted a mere four months. Both governments left the scene in haste having achieved precisely nothing apart from setting up the Economic Stabilization Board, which came into being under the Katayama government and played an important part in Japan's economic recovery. The board's first director was Wada Hiro-o.

Wada, an official of the Agriculture and Forestry Ministry who, like the economist Inaba mentioned above, had worked as survey officer at the government's Planning Board before the war, was subsequently suspected of Communist sympathies and spent a long time in jail. It was he who, restored to political life after the war, carried through the farm-land reforms as agriculture and forestry minister in the Yoshida cabinet. At the same time, he gave much thought to the recovery of the Japanese economy, for which purpose he brought together as many outstanding economists as possible, whether scholars, bureaucrats, or businessmen, in order to draw up a plan. Their conclusion was that the economy should be restored in a planned fashion, precedence being given above everything else to the iron and steel, coal, and fertilizer industries. As Wada saw it, a majority in the Diet was necessary if this plan was to be put into effect, so he proposed to Yoshida a coalition of the two largest parties, the Liberal party and the Socialist party. Yoshida was disposed to go along with him, and Wada worked behind the scenes to bring about the coalition. He failed, however, and lost the position of agriculture and forestry minister for his pains. Nevertheless, when the general election produced a Socialist government under Katayama Tetsu, Katayama, who was impressed by Wada's intellectual grasp, appointed him head of the Economic Stabilization Board. The idea of a planned economy was attractive to the Socialist party.

The new organization, thus, became the focal point of the government where economic policy was concerned, and the economists whom Wada had already gathered about him were appointed to man it. This marked the starting point of what was later to become known as "Japan, Inc." At that time, however, the economy was passing through its darkest days, and the men who had once been purged as fellow travelers got together with the men who had accumulated experience of a controlled economy during the war in order to tackle the problems of the new age.

The International Military Tribunal for the Far East, which in May 1946 had begun trying the so-called A-class war criminals, finally reached its verdicts at the end of 1948. In addition to ordinary war crimes, the defendants were also accused of "crimes against peace" and "crimes against humanity." The Pacific War was defined as a war of aggression resulting from a conspiracy by former Prime Minister Tōjō and twenty-seven other leaders, and the crimes they were charged with dated as far back as the Manchurian Incident. Those arraigned included generals, such as Itagaki, Doihara, and Mutō, who had been active ever since the time of the incident, former Foreign Minister Matsuoka, who had delivered the speech announcing Japan's secession from the League of Nations, and Marquis Kido, the Emperor's chief adviser and one of the men who had worked hardest for peace. They all sensed that the trials were being carried out not in the name of justice and civilization, as the Allies claimed, but in order to satisfy the revenge psychology. Most of them, therefore, submitted to the proceedings from the outset in a spirit of Oriental resignation. Lieutenant General Satō, the man who under the Tōjō government had come to blows with General Tanaka over the allotment of shipping, remarked humorously, "Fancy putting me in Class A . . . Personally, I'm delighted at the promotion, but I'm afraid the others will be put out."

Tōjō alone, by nature fond of arguing, intended at first to take up arms against the Allies in court by making clear all the facts and showing the reasons why Japan had been obliged to go to war. However, when Kido pointed out to him that this might well lead to involving the Emperor, he did some serious rethinking, as a result of which he determined, as far as possible, to assume sole ultimate responsibility himself. Thus his argument, while harsh in its indictment of Western aggression in the East before the war, became somewhat hazy when it came to explaining circumstances at home in Japan.

Some of the defendants protested the trials in other ways. Prince

Japan's former leaders in the dock at the Far East war-crimes trials.

Konoe, who still vividly remembered the earnest negotiations he had held with President Roosevelt in the attempt to maintain peace between Japan and America, had at first no idea that he would be included among the war criminals. Following the entry of U.S. forces into Japan, he had twice met with General MacArthur, who urged him to play a leading role in postwar Japan, and he had actually set about the task of revising the Constitution. In December that year, however, the order for his arrest had been put out by GHQ.

He was disgusted by the passive way in which Japan's highest officials allowed themselves to be herded into jail, and the night before he was due to present himself at Sugamo prison, after a gathering attended by a large number of friends, he went into the next room, took poison, and died. He had a deep sense of responsibility for the political errors that he had committed since the time of the China Incident, but his pride as a member of one of Japan's leading aristocratic families would not allow him to be tried for war crimes in a victors' court.

Just before he died, he told his son, "I shall be judged in a just court only when the world has regained its sanity."

Lieutenant General Ishihara, who with Itagaki had been responsible for the brilliant campaign in which Japan occupied Manchuria, had retired during the war and was sick in bed at his home in the country. He had publicly announced that he was a war criminal, yet he was not accused. Instead, he was called as a witness, and prosecutors and judges were specially sent to take his evidence. A large number of reporters, both Japanese and foreign, gathered to hear the exchanges.

"I have heard," said the prosecutor, "that your views were at odds with those of Tōjō . . ." Rumor had long said that disagreement with Tōjō was what had brought about Ishihara's retirement.

"No," declared Ishihara, to the great amusement of those present. "Tōjō is a man with no opinions and no philosophy. Having personally a few opinions of my own, I could not possibly disagree with a man who had none."

The men who had been dragged into court in Tokyo were all—he said—men who had quite simply gone along with the times, led astray by wishful thinking, and were not worth the enormous expense of an international trial. When the prosecutor agreed, he went on. "America is the victor now, one of the world's great powers. But to arrest such a worthless bunch and put them on trial will make it the laughingstock of history. Why don't you all give up the trials and go off home?"

The humor with which he skillfully interlarded his remarks caused frequent laughter among his listeners. His point—the futility of the trials—was clear. His reasoning was as follows: Japan had never had a dictatorial leader like Hitler, nor a political party like the Nazi party; moreover, the men who had been dragged before the court at the Tokyo trials were just individuals who, with Japan's defeat, had already lost their authority. The fact of defeat was in itself a sufficient lesson for the Japanese.

The verdicts in the Tokyo trials, still harsher than those handed down to the former German leaders at Nuremberg, surprised even chief prosecutor Joseph B. Keenan. Seven of the defendants were sentenced to death by hanging, and thirteen to life imprisonment. (Five others—including Araki, who had been war minister at the time of the May 15 Incident—were given sentences of varied lengths, while Matsuoka and one other died of illness during the trial and another was judged unfit to stand trial because of mental derangement.) Keenan found the sentence of death against former Prime Minister Hirota particularly difficult to accept. Perhaps the court required at least one civilian victim to replace Konoe; or possibly Hirota's insistence from the start that he had no need to defend himself—which caused his lawyers no end of trouble—had counted against him. The other six who received the death sentence were all military men. They included Tōjō himself, the General Satō who had welcomed his own "promotion," and the General Mutō who had laughed with General Yamashita as they gazed at the moon in Manila. A large part of the Japanese public heard the list of sentences of "death by hanging" over the radio, sitting in cold, drafty, makeshift dwellings.

The voting on the death sentences among the eleven judges is believed to have been seven to four in favor in the case of six of the defendants, and six to five in favor in the case of Hirota. Judge Radhabinod B. Pal of India presented the court with a lengthy document in which he justified his verdict of not guilty in all seven cases. Victory, he concluded, did not confer the right to judge the defeated, and there were no legal grounds whatsoever for the trials. He did not deny the political errors committed by Japan's leaders, nor their moral responsibility. But, he argued, it was dangerous for the judges to pronounce verdicts of guilty based on acceptance of fictitious stories, a hodgepodge of the prosecutors' own preconceptions and testimony of extremely doubtful veracity. It was illogical that the Soviet government, which had clearly violated an international treaty, together with representatives of the British and American governments, which had incited it to do so, should be in a position to judge Japan, which had violated no international treaty whatsoever. Moreover—he stressed— if anyone was going to be accused of the indiscriminate slaughter of civilians, then America too should be arraigned for the dropping of the atomic bomb. In short, he warned, to impose the death penalty on the defendants in what was supposed to be a court of justice would mean a step back of several centuries for human civilization.

At 00:00 hours on the morning of December 23, one month after the handing down of the verdicts, the death sentences on the seven men were carried out. During his stay in Sugamo prison, Tōjō is said to have reminisced to a fellow prisoner in the following fashion:

"The countries of the world struggle with each other in the names of justice and self-preservation. Yet, when one thinks about it, it all stems from human greed—which leads, in the end, to war. Two thousand years have passed since the Buddha in the East and Christ in the West appeared in the attempt to rid man of his greed and bring him salvation, but today the world is steadily moving toward its own destruction. That is the fact that politicians should dwell on before anything else."

"Did you feel like that already when you were prime minister?" inquired the fellow prisoner doubtfully.

"No," he replied with quiet thoughtfulness, "the truth of it has only dawned on me since I came here." The poem that he wrote for his wife, Katsuko, before his death read:

> From tomorrow
> I shall rest at peace
> In the presence of the Buddha
> With no need to fear
> The opinion of any man.

12

A Time for Recovery

On the morning of July 5, 1949, Shimoyama Sadanori, president of the Japanese National Railways (JNR), left his home in a shiny black Buick. He alighted from his car in front of the Mitsukoshi department store, telling his driver he would be gone only five minutes or so. He was never seen alive again. Late that night, his body was discovered, run over by a train, on the tracks of a JNR line.

This was the precursor of a series of disturbing incidents that were to occur in the course of that summer. The day before his death, Shimoyama had announced the firing of thirty-seven thousand JNR employees. On the following day, he had been due to announce the dismissal of a further ninety thousand. These measures had encountered fierce opposition from the union; there had been a series of strikes, and Shimoyama had spent many sleepless nights, so that the possibility of suicide could not be dismissed. However, in their autopsy report the doctors were cleanly divided as to whether he had been run over before or after death. If after death, it would mean that he had been killed by a person or persons unknown. And if so, then one of two culprits seemed likely: either Communist party members, or members of the Occupation forces hoping to place the blame on the Communists. Controversy raged throughout the nation concerning the true cause of his death.

The controversy was still continuing when the JNR authorities announced a second series of measures to dismiss some sixty thousand employees. Three days later, on July 15, an unmanned train that had been standing stationary in JNR's Mitaka Station on the outskirts of Tokyo suddenly ran out of control, burst through the buffers, and crashed into a private house, causing six deaths. Just prior to this bizarre incident, the union had been loudly proclaiming that if JNR were to continue personnel cuts without any attempt to improve its dilapidated equipment, some unforeseen accident would be probable. Several union members, including members of the Communist party, were arrested as suspects. A month later again, on a main line in northern Honshu, a train was derailed, overturning the locomotive and killing three engineers; it was found that someone had removed spikes from the rails. Once more, the investigating authorities cast suspicion on radical union members and arrested them.

The true causes of these incidents are still shrouded in mystery. The union members who were brought to trial were all eventually declared innocent on grounds of insufficient evidence, after several trials and retrials lasting in some cases more than ten years. In the case of the Mitaka incident, it was concluded that the culprit had acted independently and was not a Communist party member. The important thing, however, was that a large part of the public was convinced that the incidents were the work of the Communist party, a fact that reflected the general atmosphere of the period.

In May of the previous year, Colonel Charles L. Kades, one of the drafters of Japan's new constitution and a leading champion of the democratization of Japan, had been sent on a mission to Washington by the Occupation authorities. There he discovered that neither the government nor the generals at the Pentagon had any longer the slightest interest in Japan's democratization. By now, they were preoccupied with Soviet moves and the situation in China, where the Communist forces had gained the ascendancy. The so-called Cold War had begun on a global scale, and the U.S. leadership had determined that Japan should be used as a bastion against Communism in the Pacific. Colonel Kades went around trying to persuade the Washington highups that Japan's democratization was still necessary, but no one was ready to lend an ear to his views. He sent, accordingly, a letter of resignation to Tokyo and washed his hands of all further responsibility. It was late that year that Communist forces, without bloodshed, occupied the city of Peking.

Early in 1949, Joseph Dodge, president of the Detroit Bank, went to Japan at MacArthur's invitation. In the eyes of the American government, Japan was no longer a target for deliberate debilitation, but a country that should be encouraged to stand on its own feet just as soon as possible. The important task with which Dodge was entrusted was to rehabilitate the Japanese economy, which, while just beginning to turn the corner toward recovery, was still suffering from inflation and a serious deficit in its national finances. The big firms that during the war had been making planes, ships, and tanks and that had made a new start by manufacturing anything and everything that would sell—from frying pans and washbasins to bicycles and cigarette lighters—thus keeping themselves going and feeding as many employees as possible, were gradually beginning to carve out their own niches in peacetime industry. However, not a few of the all-important basic industries were barely managing to get by with the aid of government subsidies and special government orders.

Running his eye through the Japanese government's draft budget, Dodge went to work with a pruning knife, making drastic overall amendments. His policy was simplicity itself: to balance the budget. Among other things, the draft budget that he produced heavily slashed government expenditure on subsidies and the like, drastically increased taxes, and raised public-service charges—as much as 60 percent in the case of passenger fares.

"The absolutely essential tasks for Japan today," he said, "are to get industry standing on its own feet and to increase savings. For this reason, the public will still have to put up with austerities."

The Japanese government's economic experts were unanimous in opposing such a drastic switch in the economy—it might well, they claimed, deal a fatal shock to the patient just when it was showing signs of recovery. But Dodge, fired with zeal to act as physician to the Japanese economy, refused to allow the slightest amendment to his prescription. With the authority of the Occupation behind it, the drastic draft budget was passed by the Diet, with the result that inflation was checked and prices stabilized, though the ensuing recession led to a large number of bankruptcies.

The series of mysterious incidents that occurred in 1949 was in one sense an aftereffect of the Dodge plan. In order to cut down on expenses, JNR and the various government agencies were obliged to make major personnel cuts—which were, quite naturally, opposed by the unions. The Communist party took advantage of this in an attempt to disrupt society and create a situation favorable to revolution.

The Japan Communist party at the time was isolated internationally and in an awkward predicament. It had hoped to bring about revolution via elections—in other words, by peaceful means—but this policy had been subjected to severe criticism from both the Soviet Union and China in turn. Stalin and Mao Tse-tung, who saw the world situation as moving favorably toward Communist revolution, accused the Japan Communist party of lethargy and demanded that it too should join actively in the fight. Under Tokuda's leadership, the party switched to a radical policy and clashed head-on with the government. It ignored the claims of law and order: its members ran trains without taking fares, while in one town in northern Honshu a group of demonstrators led by the Communist party occupied the city offices. It was amid such a menacing atmosphere that the sinister incidents described above occurred.

The summer of 1949 was a major turning point for occupied Japan. Whatever may have been the true origins of these incidents, a majority of the Japanese people were convinced that they were the work of the Communist party, and this had a decisive effect in divorcing the party from the public's affections. Perceiving this, the Occupation authorities, in much the same way as the Imperial Japanese government before them, set about suppressing the Communist party. The party, violating a longstanding taboo, launched into criticisms of the Occupation, but the outcome was a foregone conclusion. In June the following year, the Occupation authorities purged leading members of the Communist party—including Diet members—from public office. Within the same month, a new war broke out on the Korean Peninsula.

Around the time that Japan was experiencing a succession of perturbing incidents, former Army General Imamura Hitoshi was in a Javanese jail awaiting the verdict of a Dutch court. At the outbreak of hostilities his forces had occupied Indonesia; then, as fighting between the Japanese and the Americans grew fiercer in the Pacific area, he took command of the Eighth Army on Rabaul and directed the withdrawal operations from Guadalcanal. The situation was worsening day by day, so Imamura directed that Rabaul should be fortified even more stoutly than Iwo Jima and that a large area of ground should be cleared to enable his forces to become self-sufficient in food. Having had the bitter experience, while commander of a division in south China, of being surrounded for several months with supplies cut off by superior enemy forces, he knew how dire was the threat of hunger to an army. He had perceived, moreover, that in a struggle with U.S. forces in which he had already lost control of the skies, there was no alternative but to do battle mainly from caves. In order to cut their losses, the American forces bypassed the area where he was entrenched without attacking it directly, advancing instead to the west so that Imamura's forces were still left there when the war ended. After his troops had been disarmed by Australian units, Imamura was sentenced by an Australian military tribunal to ten years in prison. Following this, he was sent from the camp on Manus Island in the Pacific to another camp in Java, in order to be tried by Holland also.

Indonesia was in the midst of a war of independence. Just before the defeat, Japan had given Indonesia independence, and Sukarno, as president, had formed a government. Holland, however, had not the slightest intention of letting Indonesia go, and fighting broke out between the newly landed Dutch forces and the Indonesian army of independence. The Japanese forces had been ordered to hand over their arms to the Allied forces and surrender, but it was not possible to enforce the order completely among the lower ranks, and a considerable amount of arms went over to the Indonesian side. Several thousand Japanese troops escaped and joined forces with the independence fighters. The young Japanese soldiers preferred to find scope for their enthusiasm and sense of adventure in fighting for the liberation of Asia rather than return to a defeated fatherland.

In the jail to which Imamura was sent were also incarcerated a large number of officers and men of the army of independence. Word that a general of the Japanese army had arrived spread overnight throughout the jail, and prisoners who recognized him showed their respect and friendliness by calling out in Japanese: "Salute to the supreme commander!" At night, Japanese songs mingled with those of the independence movement, sung in chorus, that resounded through the jail.

Imamura had many different experiences in the jail. A lieutenant of the Dutch army who was in the same jail—he had been confined himself for breaking into a storehouse on behalf of his men because they were so short of supplies—and who had previously fought in the European theater and had been in a German camp, told him indignantly that the way the Dutch forces treated generals was terribly poor compared with the German army. Another acquaintance, a man of mixed blood who worked in the general affairs section of the jail, had been captured by Imamura's forces in the early stages of the war and sent to Japan, where he was put to work for three years in a mine—yet he had, he told Imamura, nothing but pleasant memories of the time. "The supervisor and the engineers all treated me well and invited me to their homes for meals. When I arrived back home and heard so many people say they were ill-treated by the Japanese, I found it almost difficult to believe."

Thanks to their superiority in modern weapons, the Dutch forces succeeded in quelling Indonesia temporarily, but the army of liberation, acting now as guerrillas, fought on persistently with the support of a large segment of the populace. The young soldiers brought to the prison informed Imamura proudly that they were members of suicide squads. In their unshakable determination to secure independence they were ready, even, to throw themselves at the Dutch forces clasping bombs to their bodies, in the same way as Japanese troops had done earlier.

One day, Imamura was contacted by Sukarno himself, via officers of the independence army who had gotten themselves jailed in order to save Imamura and who now urged him to escape along with them.

"The Dutch court is certain to condemn you to death," they said. "The arrangements for a jailbreak are already made."

Imamura refused courteously. He did not doubt the success of the cause of Indonesian independence, and to escape would be one way of saving his own life. Yet he did not feel it right that he, as a former commander of the Japanese forces, should get himself involved in such a dispute. Even though the Dutch might condemn him to death, he accepted the prospect philosophically.

The prosecution, as expected, demanded the death penalty. Yet after a long trial, which was interrupted on the way because the Dutch authorities had their hands too full with the war against the guerrillas and the tense negotiations, he was finally, after Holland had recognized Indonesian independence, pronounced not guilty.

It was in February 1950, four and a half years after the end of the war, that Imamura was sent back to Japan. However, he still had time to serve at Sugamo prison. He personally requested of the Australian

On January 23, 1950, Imamura Hitoshi (saluting) was repatriated from Java along with 692 other war criminals and sent to Sugamo prison.

forces that he be sent to Manus Island. On Manus, an isolated tropical island of fierce heat, some four hundred Japanese officers and men were still imprisoned, including one hundred of Imamura's former subordinates. In Java, letters from Manus had reached Imamura via the Red Cross, and he had learned thereby that, following his own departure, working conditions had suddenly become more severe and the quality of the food had declined excessively. His former subordinates even wondered, they complained, how many of them would live out their terms and get back to Japan alive. At this point Imamura decided that it was his duty to live with his subordinates on the island. His request was granted, and the following day he was transported to "Hell Island."

In Asia as a whole, the waves of nationalism and independence were rising and spreading. Nowhere, unfortunately, was independence achieved peacefully and through negotiations. In Vietnam, Ho Chi Minh proclaimed the nation's independence simultaneously with the defeat of Japan, but French forces soon launched a counterattack. Vo Nguyen Giap, Ho's right-hand man, established a school to provide crash courses for potential officers for the independence army and at the same time launched a guerrilla campaign. Cooperating with the guerrillas as instructors and fighters were some four thousand Japanese officers and men—including Colonel Nakagawa Lang Son—who had deserted from the Japanese army.

In Burma, the Burmese army led by Aung San, which since the outbreak of the war had been cooperating with the Japanese forces, switched sides toward the end as the British forces gained the upper hand, cooperated with them in driving the Japanese off Burmese soil, and gained their independence. The Philippines too, under the leadership of Manuel Roxas, whose life was saved by Lieutenant Colonel Jimbō, gained its independence once more.

In India, where almost no blood had been shed on account of the war, the situation was complex. During the war, in order to secure Indian cooperation, Britain had hinted at autonomy following the war. The "promise," however, was cleverly hedged with traps, and the actual negotiations did not go well. The leaders of the Indian National Congress led by Gandhi passed a resolution calling for Britain to "quit India." The British authorities replied by having them arrested. As the news spread, the whole Indian populace broke into riots demanding Gandhi's release. It was the first revolt of the Indian people for over eighty years, since the Sepoy Mutiny of 1857; at this point, they forgot the doctrine of nonviolence that Gandhi had instilled in them for so long. The British authorities called in troops, slaughtering ordinary citizens mercilessly. Once more, India gave way before military might.

Following the end of World War II, when Churchill left office and the Labour party formed a government, Indian independence came onto the agenda again. (The leaders of the Indian National Army organized in Malaysia were on trial in Singapore, and an extensive movement opposing the trial had developed in India. Nehru, who was among the opponents, praised the INA as having given practical proof that Indians had the ability to unite for a single goal transcending race, religion, and caste.) Here again, however, the British worked skillfully to exploit the antagonism between Hindus and Muslims, and India finally achieved independence, in August 1947, only after bloody civil fighting between the two sides. Pakistan became a separate nation.

A new world was coming into existence as a result of the Second World War. Japan had not, at least in the way that Ishihara Kanji had predicted, "won through in Asia." What Ishihara had overlooked was the broad undercurrent of nationalism in Asia, which the Allies, too, had overlooked in the same way. Another strong current in the world was that of Communist infiltration, and here it was the Soviet Union, as leader of the movement, that "won through." Thus the crucial trends in the new world were to be: the wave of independence movements that overwhelmed first Asia, then Africa; and the confrontation between the United States and the Soviet Union.

At the time of Japan's defeat, President Chiang Kai-shek of China issued a directive to the public and armed forces telling them to repay the past outrages of the Japanese army with virtue. No doubt there was an element of political calculation here; a million armed Japanese troops remained in China, and it was urgently necessary to get them back home without letting them give aid to the Communist forces. Yet Chiang's declaration went beyond mere political expediency, soothing the desire of the Chinese people for revenge and affecting the Japanese with deep emotion. Throughout the whole long war with China, the Japanese forces had shown contempt for the Chinese while giving repeated proofs of their own corruption and depravity. On Japanese at home, who were vaguely aware of these facts, Chiang's words had an electrifying effect, inducing in them a heartfelt searching of their consciences plus a sense of having suffered a moral defeat.

Yet whatever Chiang may have intended, the forces he commanded lacked the capability to appreciate his ideal. The U.S. government, alarmed by the growing ascendancy of the Communist forces, began giving aid to the Chiang Kai-shek regime, but it was too late. Faced with the forces led by Mao Tse-tung—which captured the support of the public by their refusal to indulge in rape and pillaging—Chiang's army looked increasingly like a loser. It is not clear how many former Japanese army officers and men joined forces with these two armies, but it is estimated that at least thirty thousand Japanese went over to the Communists and fought with them in various parts of the country. In particular, Japanese army doctors and nurses in the Manchurian zone were more or less compelled to follow the Communist army and for several years worked for the revolutionary cause. Moreover, once the whole country had been "liberated" and Chinese aid to the Ho Chi Minh forces began, truck transport over the steep mountainous areas between the two countries was almost entirely the work of former Japanese soldiers.

Kasai Jun'ichi, who became an officer in the Communist army and won three medals for his services in battle, eventually applied to be sent back to Japan, but was refused. He threw up all his work, took to drinking even in the daytime, and would stroll about the streets drunk, dangling his medals and demanding loudly to be sent home. It was not until April of the ninth year following the end of the war, when Japan had already gained its independence, that permission for his repatriation was finally given. The Japanese press at the time reported the return of "five hundred Japanese from a China of hitherto unknown prosperity." Unlike earlier repatriates from the continent— who had come back much like beggars, with nothing but the clothes they stood up in—they, at least, brought home with them severance allowances from the Chinese government.

In Manchuria, the worst possible fate awaited Japanese residents and military men. The Soviet forces that on August 9, 1945, broke the neutrality pact and came pouring over the frontier from three sides advanced toward the heart of Manchuria in a great torrent, with armored units in the van. The Kwantung Army had already switched its main force to the South Pacific front and was, moreover, in the process of shifting to an area near the Korean border in order to shorten its lines.

Taken unawares, the Japanese forces could offer almost no effective resistance. On the day following the Soviet invasion, the Kwantung Army made the decision to evacuate Japanese residents living along the South Manchurian Railway to the Korean area, and early in the morning of the second day the first train left Changchun. On board were the families of army men. Hearing of what had happened, Kwantung Army staff officer Kusachi Teigo showed his displeasure. "How the hell did this happen!" he shouted. "I know what you mean, Colonel Kusachi," replied the lieutenant colonel responsible for the permanent residents, shaking his head. "The permanent residents were supposed to be given priority. I tried to arrange it that way myself. But the Japanese who've settled here are reluctant to leave. There was no hope of getting them on board the evening train. So we put the army dependents on first, since they're more mobile."

The average Japanese citizen in Manchuria did not realize the gravity of the situation, but put his faith in the supposedly invincible Kwantung Army. He had been told over and over again—and believed it—that even should Japan proper be occupied, they could hold out there for another two or three years. By the eleventh day following the start of hostilities, the Soviet forces had not merely reached Changchun but had swept on as far as Mukden in southern Manchuria. Several hundred thousand Japanese were left behind in areas beyond the help of the Japanese military and police.

The greatest tragedy befell the farmers who had settled in Manchuria to open up the remoter areas of the country. Following the establishment of the state of Manchukuo, Japan had sent as many as three hundred thousand farmers there, as part of a government policy with the twin aim of, first, finding some outlet for a huge domestic farming population working an inadequate area of cultivable land, and, secondly, tightening Japan's hold on Manchuria. At first, genuine virgin land was used for the purpose, but subsequently they were given already cultivated land purchased at cheap rates from the Chinese. The industry of these Japanese farmers succeeded in bringing bountiful crops to the areas, but with the defeat of Japan the resentment of the local farmers exploded against them. Isolated and helpless, large numbers of settlements were attacked and wiped out, while many of their inhabitants, rather than wait till their wives and daughters were violated, chose to set fire to their homes and kill themselves and their families. By the time the Soviet forces came in, the young men had without exception been called up into the Kwantung Army, leaving only the aged, women, and children in the villages. Those who managed to escape from the villages in horse-drawn carts or on foot were set on by bandits on the way; other groups, lucky enough to be able to use the railways, were intimidated by local inhabitants at each station on the way and stripped of all their possessions, even the clothes they stood up in, so that they finally reached the reception camps set up in large towns along the line with nothing but hemp sacks covering their nakedness. During their desperate flight young children were sold to enable their families to survive, or to save their own lives, and not a few young women voluntarily became the wives of Chinese in order to secure the safety of their families.

Nor did their trials end when they reached the camps, where the cruel winter cold, hunger, typhus, and rape at the hands of the un-disciplined Soviet soldiery awaited them. Large numbers went to swell the ranks of the dead.

The fate of the troops of the Kwantung Army was equally grim. Five hundred thousand officers and men, disarmed by the Soviet forces, were sent en masse to Siberia to endure long days of forced labor with no prospect of repatriation. Here, too, hunger and bitter cold were their inseparable companions, and some one hundred thousand former soldiers succumbed in all. They were set to work by the Soviet forces, but they were also hard driven by brainwashed "democratic elements" from their own ranks. Made leaders overnight by the Communist education that the Soviet Union gave them, these men watched over their colleagues, egging them on to work ever harder. The bait offered them as inducement by the Soviet side was the prospect of qualifying, by becoming "Communist fighters," for early repatriation to Japan. The first batch of these "democratic elements" was repatriated to Japan in 1949—just at the height of the Japan Communist party's struggle to bring about revolution in Japan. Arriving in the port of Maizuru, they promptly set about demonstrating their loyalty to the "Soviet fatherland," raising loud complaints against "improper treatment" by local Japanese officials. Ignoring the tearful entreaties of their families, they startled the public by refusing to go first to their home districts, choosing instead to make a beeline for the Communist party headquarters in Tokyo. The repatriation of former officers and men from the Soviet Union continued in completely unpredictable fits and starts, and some of them remained in detention for as long as thirteen years.

The prisoners of war taken by the American forces, together with the former Japanese troops disarmed by them at the end of the war, were returned to Japan promptly and smoothly, transport ships being provided generously for the purpose. Treatment of prisoners during the war was, in a word, good; here, it was, rather, a spiritual problem that troubled them. They feared that if they returned to Japan they would be subjected to strict punishment and ostracization by the inhabitants of their home districts. In fact, nothing of the kind occurred. The majority of Japanese condemned the former Japanese army and navy out of hand, and looked askance at all the men who until only a short while before had fought, as they thought, for the sake of the fatherland. No one was in the slightest interested in whether they had distinguished themselves in the field or whether they had been prisoners.

The British forces subjected the former Japanese troops to nearly two years of more or less punitive hard labor, or sent them to an uninhabited island off Singapore known as Death Island to taste the pains of hunger before returning them to Japan. The unit that had been responsible for supervising Allied prisoners during construction of the railroad between Thailand and Burma was not among those returned. The railroad in question, designed to provide overland transport between the two countries, was completed during the war by 10,000 Japanese troops, 55,000 prisoners of war, and 70,000 laborers recruited locally. This labor in the tropical heat of an area where malaria was rampant claimed a large number of human lives. The figures for the dead—1,000 Japanese troops, 12,000 prisoners of war, and 30,000 local laborers—speak eloquently of the position of each group and the treatment accorded it. More than half the deaths were due to epidemics of cholera.

After the war, thirty-two members of the unit connected with the construction work, including the commander, were sentenced to death. The unit that had supervised the prisoners was kept isolated in a roughly constructed building on a shoal in the Irrawaddy River, where its rations were reduced progressively. The river contained a large number of river crabs—carriers of amebic dysentery—and though the English troops put up a notice forbidding the Japanese to catch and eat them, the latter were too close to starvation to pay any attention. The result was that the whole unit, like the English troops who had died of cholera before them, succumbed to disease.

On June 21, 1950, Secretary of State John Foster Dulles visited Japan for the first time. The aims of his trip—he had already conceived the idea of a peace settlement with Japan—were to make a tour of Asia and to seek the views of the Occupation in Japan. The greatest problem, if Japan was to be given independence, was what to do about its defense. Meeting Prime Minister Yoshida, Dulles sounded him out concerning the rearmament of Japan, but Yoshida objected on two grounds: that it would not go down well with the Japanese public in its present mood, when the scars of defeat still lingered, and that the Japanese economy could not bear the enormous strain that would be imposed by the acquisition of advanced modern weapons. Instead, Yoshida proposed an alternative plan: that Japan's defense should be taken care of by the stationing of U.S. forces, in which arrangement Japan should cooperate. Talks between the two men had not reached any conclusion when the internal war broke out in Korea.

Without consulting Congress, President Truman promptly directed General MacArthur in Tokyo to send units under his command to the "aid" of South Korea. MacArthur, who dreamed of a triumphal return to America as the general who had succeeded in occupying and ruling Japan, was fired with fresh energy at thus encountering another war. The seventy-year-old warrior promptly flew to the front where, seeing for himself the collapse of the South Korean forces, he on his own initiative ordered the bombing of military targets in North Korea— beyond the 38th parallel to the south of which the president had ordered him to restrict operations. The report of the bombing of Pyongyang by B-29s startled Washington. Next, MacArthur sought permission to throw in land forces. Truman reluctantly agreed to the sending of one regiment, but in no time at all this became first one division, then two.

In the meantime, the sending of U.S. forces into action had created a vacuum in Japan, and MacArthur sent a letter to Prime Minister Yoshida ordering him to found a 75,000-man "National Police Reserve." Whatever it might be called, the proposed force was in essence an army, and as such marked the beginning of Japan's rearmament. A mere four years after it had established a constitution in which, in accordance with MacArthur's ideal, it had renounced all arms, Japan had, on orders from the same man, set about arming itself.

On the Korean Peninsula 65,000 American troops had been thrown into the fray, but by now they were in danger of being driven into the Sea of Japan by the superior North Korean forces. General MacArthur, newly appointed supreme commander of the United Nations forces, devised a grandiose strategic plan whereby the Americans would land at Inchon, behind the enemy's lines to the west of Seoul, thereby catching the other side in a pincer movement and recovering the situation in one fell swoop. On August 20, General J. Lawton Collins, army chief of staff, and Admiral Forrest P. Sherman, chief of naval operations, flew into Tokyo in an attempt to make MacArthur give up this excessively dangerous plan. "Gentlemen," said MacArthur in effect, "the various aspects that you have cited as impossible in practice mean, looked at in a different way, a correspondingly greater effect as a surprise move. Surprise is the greatest guarantee of success in war. The landing operation will succeed, I assure you."

In the end, the joint chiefs of staff gave permission for his operation. The landing at Inchon, carried out before dawn on September 15, was a brilliant success. As they fled in disorder to the north, the North Korean forces put to death the leaders of the areas they had occupied, together with their families, including women and children. The number of prisoners taken by the U.S. army totaled one hundred and thirty thousand. Further emboldened, MacArthur proposed that the attack be carried beyond the 38th parallel, and Washington immediately acquiesced.

It was in mid-October that President Truman and General MacArthur met for talks on Wake Island. The president, with an eye to the approaching midterm elections, felt it advisable to meet with a general at the front whose brilliant victories had won him such widespread popularity. The two men engaged in a little one-upmanship at the airfield, each trying to get the other to come to meet him. By circling a full twenty minutes over the island, Truman's plane succeeded in being the second to land, but when it did so MacArthur was tardy in putting in an appearance, and the president was obliged to wait forty-five minutes cooped up in his plane. When the general finally turned up, he failed to give the president a military salute, instead stretching out his hand in leisurely fashion.

The thing that most worried Truman was possible intervention by Chinese forces. Such a thing, MacArthur asserted, was impossible. The U.S. forces would be able to return to Tokyo by Christmas.

The rout of the North Korean forces continued, with the U.S. and South Korean armies pressing on in hot pursuit toward the Yalu River on the Manchurian border. Now, however, a huge Chinese force, which already had finished assembling in Manchuria around the time that the two leaders were conferring on Wake Island, came pouring over the frontier. The Chinese, unhampered by modern arms, approached the American forces silently along the mountains, encircling them two or three times over, then fell on them like a swarm of locusts. This time it was the turn of the Americans to flee in disorder, in the greatest rout in the history of the U.S. army. Harassed as they fled by guerrillas, they slaughtered civilians and set fire to houses on the way.

In order to cut the Chinese forces' supply lines, MacArthur sought Washington's permission to blow up the bridge over the Yalu River. The president gave permission—but only where the southern half of the bridge was concerned. Pressed back temporarily beyond the 38th parallel, the American forces eventually retrieved the situation, pushed their opponent back in his turn, and recaptured Seoul, but at this point the front became deadlocked. In this way, the brutal fighting rolled back and forth over the Korean Peninsula, involving its citizens indiscriminately in the horrors of war.

With the outbreak of the Korean War, Japanese industry was stimulated by an unprecedented rush of special procurement orders from the U.S. forces. The country became one vast repair and supply base for those forces, which were fighting a modern war in which wear and tear was even more severe than in World War II. The new conflict occurred just at a time when industry, deprived of its subsidies by Dodge's stringent financial policies, was struggling in the depths of a recession. Huge numbers of guns, motor vehicles, and the like were ordered, and large numbers of factories sprang to new life as they set about repairing jeeps, trucks, and armored vehicles. The same invigorating effect extended to other industries in their turn. As the signs of a world arms race encouraged the development of the Japanese economy, stockpiles melted away, and Japan came to life again. By the year following the outbreak of the Korean War, production indices in the Japanese mining and manufacturing industries had already returned to the prewar (1934—36) levels.

The Japanese of the immediate postwar years, their incomes leveled by an all-embracing poverty, experienced an odd sense of equality such as they had never known before. And the threat of starvation obliged them, willy-nilly, to work desperately whatever the task. The labor unions that had been organized on a firm-by-firm basis had passed through a period of frequent strikes but had also learned by now that unless they ensured that their own firms prospered, their own shares too would be small. Accumulated funds were reinvested by firms in equipment based on new technology—whether developed by themselves during the war or introduced from America did not matter. At this point, the fact that almost all factories had been reduced to scrap as a result of a long war and repeated air raids proved, if anything, favorable to the renewal of equipment. For a Japanese economy thus reborn, the Korean War was a springboard from which to launch itself toward further development in the future.

MacArthur had not given up hope of victory in the field and was convinced that such a victory could be won only by bombing military bases in Manchuria—that is, China—and extended the scope of the war as a whole. Between the commander in the field and Washington there loomed the threat of a drama similar to that once enacted by Japan in Manchuria. It was averted, however, by Truman's resolute action in relieving MacArthur of his post.

Around noon on April 16 (Japan time), 1951, the military aircraft *Bataan* carrying MacArthur on his way to America and the plane with special envoy John Foster Dulles on board passed each other over the Pacific. Dulles, who was on his way to Japan to prepare for the peace conference, had been due to meet MacArthur in Tokyo. Now, though, there was no need, and instead they spoke to each other by radio from their respective planes. Dulles said that he still looked forward to advice and support from the general; MacArthur replied by urging him to see that a peace treaty with Japan came into effect just as soon as possible and assuring him of his continued support. The exchange however was, in essence, no more than a formal courtesy.

The peace conference opened in San Francisco in September 1951. Fifty-two members of the United Nations gathered there for it, and, with U.S. Secretary of State Dean Acheson presiding, the proceedings went ahead peaceably. The nations were still inclined to look with less than warmth on Japan as it was readmitted to international society, but apart from the intrusion of the Cold War, there were no particular hitches. President Truman extolled the achievements of General MacArthur in administering the Occupation, together with the efforts made by the Japanese people in cooperating actively with him. "During these six years," he said, "Japan has become a new Japan."

The Soviet delegate criticized Japan as an aggressor and stressed the legitimacy of the Soviet claim to Soviet-occupied Sakhalin and the Kurils. Plenipotentiary Yoshida was obliged to point out that the southern Kurils had in fact been peaceably recognized as Japanese territory ever since the days of Imperial Russia. The Soviet Union and its satellites refused to sign the treaty, but this development had been on the cards from the outset.

Neither the Communist Chinese government nor the Chiang government—by now expelled to Taiwan—was invited to send delegates to the conference. The restoration of diplomatic relations with China was thus left as a task for the future. The Ceylonese delegate, J. R. Jayewardene—later to become his country's president—congratulated Japan on its restoration to international society, saying in part, "Before the war, Japan alone was strong and free in Asia. The slogan of coprosperity in Asia was attractive to the subject peoples. I still recall how certain leaders of Burma and Indonesia cooperated with Japan in the hope of liberating their countries." He also referred to the fact that both Japan and Ceylon were Buddhist nations and concluded as follows: "Hatred cannot be conquered by hatred. Only love conquers hatred."

The warmth of the Ceylonese delegate's words both moved and heartened Yoshida; they were the best possible gift for a Japan about to launch forth once more into international society. At the same time, he had a distinct feeling that the appearance of Asian countries in such a forum as nations with free, independent voices of their own was a new phenomenon of the postwar world.

In his personal habits, Prime Minister Yoshida tended to be self-indulgent, but two months or so before going to San Francisco he resolved to forswear completely the alcohol and cigars of which he was so fond until the day when the peace treaty should be signed. After the signing of the treaty, when he returned to the Palace Hotel, where he was staying, he found on his table a box of the best cigars together with a note. "I hear," said the note, "that you've been going without your favorite cigars for some time. Now the signing is safely over, why not let yourself go?" The sender was none other than the chairman of the conference, Acheson.

The peace treaty formally came into effect in April 1952. With the regaining of Japan's independence, staff officer Tsuji, who had attracted attention so many times on the South Pacific front and had attained notoriety as "war criminal No. 1," emerged from his long

Prime Minister Yoshida and his entourage at San Francisco airport in September 1951, on their way home after the signing of the peace treaty.

hiding. He had been in Saigon at the end of the war but had become a Buddhist monk, in which guise he had smuggled himself into China, where he was given protection by a secret agency of Chiang's, then later on had lived in hiding in occupied Japan. During these years, he wrote a succession of thrilling records of his own experiences, all of which became best sellers. Despite criticism and suspicion directed at him by a large number of people, he became one of the more famous figures of the postwar years and successfully stood for election to the Lower House of the Diet.

Imamura was still on Manus Island. He had brought with him from Tokyo a batch of seeds of the long onion and other vegetables. Rather than protest the poor quality of the provisions, he asked for permission to let the older men engage in crop cultivation. The vegetables planted by the Japanese all gave plentiful yields. The Australian officers and men at the base, many of whom had been in stationed in

Japan and had acquired a taste for sukiyaki, would come to get Japanese onions from them. The prisoners also worked hard making souvenirs for the Australians to take home. The fine craftsmanship appealed to the men stationed at the base, who gave the prisoners so much chocolate and other foods in "payment" that they could not eat it all and had to use one room as a store. This was discovered by the base commander one day, on an unheralded tour of inspection. Furious, he threatened to punish the prisoners to a man. But when Imamura was summoned he said firmly, "It won't stop unless you forbid your own subordinates to order the souvenirs in the first place."

In the end, the punishment was never carried out. Instead, the Australian military authorities on Manus decided to take advantage of the manual skills of the Japanese and have them build such structures as a church, assembly hall, and cinema. The results were excellent; the authorities were delighted and, thanks to this peaceful, constructive project, finally came to feel a kind of affection for the prisoners. Eventually, the authorities realized the pointlessness of keeping Japanese in captivity on that torrid island any longer. The camp was closed, and all its inmates sent home to Japan.

On the morning of August 8, 1953, the transport vessel bringing the last batch of former prisoners from Manus was slowly approaching the wharves of Yokohama. On board was former general Imamura, who for eight years past had had recourse to both Bible and Buddhist scriptures in trying to comfort the other prisoners, including the men condemned to death. As his homeland came into view, he looked back over the experiences of his own long life and prayed that Japan's future would be a peaceful one. At the sight of the Japanese flag fluttering over the harbor, his eyes smarted with tears.

Chronology

Meiji era (1868—1912)

1894—95 Sino-Japanese War
1898   Spain cedes the Philippines to U.S.
1900   Japanese and European troops crush Boxer Rebellion in China
1902   Anglo-Japanese Alliance
1904—5 Russo-Japanese War
1906   School segregation in San Francisco
1910   Annexation of Korea

Taishō era (1912—26)

1913   Alien Land Law signed by governor of California
1914   World War I begins. Japan declares war on Germany
1918   World War I ends
1919   Paris Peace Conference
1922   Washington Naval Limitation Treaty

Shōwa era (1926—)

1929   Great Depression begins
1930   London Naval Limitation Treaty
1931   Manchurian Incident
1932   May 15 Incident
1933   Japan withdraws from League of Nations
1936   February 26 Incident. Germany and Japan sign Anti-Comintern Pact
1937   China Incident
1939   World War II begins in Europe
1940   *Sep.:* Japanese army moves into north Indochina. Tripartite Pact between Germany, Italy, and Japan. U.S. bans export of scrap iron to Japan
1941   *Apr.:* Neutrality Pact between Japan and Soviet Union *Jul.:* Vichy government agrees to Japanese occupation of bases in south Indochina. All Japanese assets in U.S. and Britain frozen *Aug.:* U.S. bans export of oil to

Japan. All U.S., British, and Dutch assets in Japan frozen *Oct.:* Prime Minister Konoe resigns and Tōjō succeeds to premiership *Dec.:* Japanese forces attack Pearl Harbor. Outbreak of Pacific War. *Prince of Wales* and *Repulse* sunk. Fall of Hong Kong

1942 *Jan.:* Fall of Manila. Fall of Kuala Lumpur *Feb.:* Fall of Singapore. Executive Order 9066 for relocation of Japanese-Americans issued *Mar.:* Fall of Rangoon *Apr.:* U.S. bombers' first raid on Tokyo *May:* Battle of the Coral Sea. Fall of Corregidor *Jun.:* Battle of Midway *Aug.:* U.S. marines land on Guadalcanal and take airfield

1943 *Jan.:* Allied forces capture Buna in New Guinea *Feb.:* Japanese army evacuated from Guadalcanal *Mar.:* Battle of the Bismarck Sea *Apr.:* Admiral Yamamoto Isoroku dies when plane shot down on Bougainville *May:* Americans capture Attu in the Aleutian Islands *Jul.:* Evacuation of Japanese army from Kiska completed *Sep.:* Allied forces capture Lae in New Guinea. Italy surrenders *Nov.:* Greater Eastern Asian Conference held in Tokyo. Cairo Conferences. Tehran Conference. Allied forces capture Makin and Tarawa in Gilbert Islands

1944 *Feb.:* Fall of Kwajalein, Marshall Islands *Jul.:* Fall of Saipan. Prime Minister Tōjō resigns and General Koiso succeeds to premiership *Sep.:* Tinian and Guam in Mariana Islands taken by Allied forces *Oct.:* Battle of Leyte Bay. Kamikaze units organized and Japanese Combined Fleet defeated *Nov.:* B-29s bomb Tokyo for first time

1945 *Jan.:* Americans land in Lingayen Gulf in Philippines *Feb.:* Yalta Conference *Mar.:* Allied forces take Manila. Iwo Jima taken by Americans *Apr.:* Americans land on Okinawa. Fall of Japanese government; Suzuki replaces Prime Minister Koiso. President Roosevelt dies and Truman succeeds to presidency *May:* Germany surrenders *Jun.:* Americans take Okinawa *Jul.:* Allies issue Potsdam Declaration *Aug.:* First and second atomic bombs dropped on Hiroshima and Nagasaki. Soviet Union declares war on Japan and invades Manchuria. Japan accepts unconditional surrender *Sep.:* Document of surrender signed on *Missouri* *Oct.:* SCAP suggests five major reforms

1946 *Feb.:* First land reforms put into effect. SCAP delivers draft constitution to Japanese government *Apr.:* General election held for Lower House *May:* International Military Tribunal for the Far East opens. Yoshida forms first cabinet *Aug.:* Economic Stabilization Board established

1947 *May:* Promulgation of new Constitution of Japan

1948 *Mar.:* SCAP issues anti-strike order *Nov.:* International Military Tribunal for the Far East delivers verdicts

1949 *Mar.:* Dodge Plan released *Jul.:* Shimoyama incident. Mitaka incident *Oct.:* People's Republic of China established

1950 *Jun.:* War in Korea begins *Aug.:* National Police Reserve created

1951 *Sep.:* San Francisco Peace Treaty and U.S.-Japan Security Pact signed

1952 *Apr.:* Occupation ends

Bibliography

Agawa, Hiroyuki. *Yamamoto Isoroku*. Tokyo: Shinchō-sha, 1965.

Aida, Yūji. *Prisoner of the British*. London: Cresset Press, 1966.

Arima, Yorichika. *Saishō Konoe Fumimaro no Shōgai*. Tokyo: Kōdan-sha, 1970.

Bōei-chō Bōei Kenshū-jo Senshi-shitsu. *Senshi Sōsho*. 66 vols. Tokyo: Asagumo Shimbun-sha, 1966–72.

Chuman, Frank F. *The Bamboo People: The Law and Japanese-Americans*. Del Mar, California: Publisher's Inc., 1976.

Fujishima, Taisuke. *Chūsei Tōroku*. Tokyo: Yomiuri Shimbun-sha, 1967.

Hatoyama, Ichirō. *Hatoyama Ichirō Kaiko-roku*. Tokyo: Bungeishunjū-sha, 1957.

Hattori, Takushirō. *Dai-Tōa Sensō Zen-shi*. Tokyo: Hara-shobō, 1965.

Hayashi, Shigeru. *Taiheiyō Sensō*. A History of Japan, vol. 25. Tokyo: Chūōkōron-sha, 1967.

Honjō, Shigeru. *Honjō Nikki*. Tokyo: Hara-shobō, 1967.

Ikuta, Makoto. *Rikugun Tokubetsu Kōgekitai-shi*. Tokyo: Bijinesu-sha, 1977.

Imai, Seiichi. *Taishō Demokurashii*. A History of Japan, vol. 23. Tokyo: Chūōkōron-sha, 1966.

Imamura, Hitoshi. *Yūshū Kaiko-roku*. Tokyo: Akita-shoten, 1966.

———. *Imamura Hitoshi Kaiko-roku*. Tokyo: Fuyō-shobō, 1970.

Jōhō, Yoshio. *Tōjō Hideki*. Tokyo: Fuyō-shobō, 1964.

Kasai, Jun'ichi. *Dare mo Shira-nai Chūgoku*. Tokyo: Gunji Kenkyū-sha, 1971.

Kido, Kōichi. *Kido Kōichi Nikki*. University of Tokyo Press, 1966.

Kojima, Noboru. *Taiheiyō Sensō*. Tokyo: Chūōkōron-sha, 1966.

———. *Tokyo Saiban*. Tokyo: Chūōkōron-sha, 1971.

Konoe, Fumimaro. *Konoe Nikki*. Tokyo: Kyōdō Tsūshin-sha, 1968.

Lindbergh, Charles A. *The Wartime Journals of Charles A. Lindbergh*. New York: Harcourt Brace Jovanovich Inc., 1970.

Matsuda, Nobuo, ed. *Nihon no Rekishi*. Vols. 11–12. Tokyo: Yomiuri Shimbun-sha, 1968.

Matsumoto, Seichō. *Shōwa-shi Hakkutsu*. Vols. 3—8. Tokyo: Bungeishunjū-sha, 1965—69.
Misuzu-shobō. *Nitchū Sensō*. Vol. 2. Gendai-shi Shiryō. Tokyo: Misuzu-shobō, 1964.
———. *Taiheiyō Sensō*. 5 vols. Gendai-shi Shiryō. Tokyo: Misuzu-shobo, 1968.
Miwa, Kimitada. *Matsuoka Yōsuke*. Tokyo: Chūōkōron-sha, 1971.
Nakamura, Kikuo. *Shōwa Rikugun Hishi*. Tokyo: Banchō-shobō, 1968.
Nitta, Mitsuo, ed. *Kyokutō Gunji Saiban Sokki-roku*. 10 vols. Tokyo: Yūshōdō-shoten, 1968.
Oka, Yoshitake. *Konoe Fumimaro*. Tokyo: Iwanami-shoten, 1972.
Ōmori, Minoru. *Ho Chi Minh*. Tokyo: Kōdan-sha, 1979.
———. *Nehru*. Tokyo: Kōdan-sha, 1979.
Ōtani, Keijirō. *Gun-batsu*. Tokyo: Tosho Shuppan-sha, 1971.
Ōuchi, Tsutomu. *Fashizumu eno Michi*. A History of Japan, vol. 24. Tokyo: Chūōkōron-sha, 1967.
Ōya, Sōichi. *Ōya Sōichi Senshū*. Vol. 12. Tokyo: Chikuma-shobō, 1960.
———, ed. *Nihon no Ichiban Nagai Hi*. Tokyo: Bungeishunjū-sha, 1965.
Rōyama, Masamichi. *Yomigaeru Nihon*. A History of Japan, vol. 26. Tokyo: Chūōkōron-sha, 1967.
Sakomizu, Hisatsune. *Kikanjū-ka no Shushō-kantei*. Tokyo: Kōbun-sha, 1964.
———. *Dai-Nippon Teikoku Saigo no Yon-ka-getsu*. Tokyo: Oriento-shobō, 1973.
Sanbō-honbu, ed. *Sugiyama Memo*. Tokyo: Hara-shobō, 1967.
Satō, Kenryō. *Satō Kenryō no Shōgen*. Tokyo: Fuyō-shobō, 1976.
Shidehara, Kijūrō. *Gaikō Gojū-nen*. Tokyo: Hara-shobō, 1974.
Shigemitsu, Mamoru. *Shōwa no Dōran*. 2 vols. Tokyo: Chūōkōron-sha, 1952.
Shimada, Toshihiko. *Kantō-gun*. Tokyo: Chūōkōron-sha, 1965.
Shūkan Shinchō Henshū-bu. *MacArthur no Nihon*. Tokyo: Shinchō-sha, 1970.
Sodei, Rinjirō. *MacArthur no Nisen-nichi*. Tokyo: Chūōkōron-sha, 1974.
Sugano, Shizuko. *Saipan-tō no Saigo*. Tokyo: Shuppan Kyōdō-sha, 1959.
Suzuki, Tsutomu, ed. *Nihon-jin no Hyaku-nen*. Vols. 10—16. Tokyo: Sekai-bunka-sha, 1972—73.
Takagi, Hajime. *Hijō no Sora*. Tokyo: Kōdan-sha, 1970.
Takahashi, Masae. *Shōwa no Gun-batsu*. Tokyo: Chūōkōron-sha, 1969.
Takushima, Norimitsu. *Ikō: Kuchinashi no Hana*. Tokyo: Daikō-sha, 1967.
Tanaka, Shin'ichi. *Tanaka Sakusen-buchō no Shōgen*. Edited by Matsushita Yoshio. Tokyo: Fuyō-shobō, 1968.
Tanemura, Sakō. *Dai-Hon'ei Kimitsu Nisshi*. Tokyo: Daiyamondo-sha, 1952.
Tateno, Nobuyuki. *Hanran*. Tokyo: Rokkō Shuppan-sha, 1952.
———. *Shōwa Gun-batsu: Bokkō-hen*. Tokyo: Kōdan-sha, 1963.
———. *Shōwa Gun-batsu: Gekidō-hen*. Tokyo: Kōdan-sha, 1963.
Togawa, Isamu. *Sengo Fūzoku-shi*. Tokyo: Sekka-sha, 1960.
Toland, John. *The Rising Sun*. New York: Random House, Inc., 1970.
Toyoda, Minoru. *Matsuoka Yōsuke*. Tokyo: Shinchō-sha, 1979.

Tsunoda, Fusako. *Issai Yume ni Goza-soro*. Tokyo: Chūōkōron-sha, 1972.

Tsunoda, Jun, ed. *Ishihara Kanji Shiryō: Sensōshi-ron*. Tokyo: Hara-shobo, 1968.

————, ed. *Ishihara Kanji Shiryo: Kokubo-ronsaku-hen*. Tokyo: Hara-shobo, 1971.

Tsurutani, Hisashi. *Amerika Seibu Kaitaku to Nihon-jin*. Tokyo: Nihon Hōso-kyokai, 1977.

Usui, Katsumi. *Nitchu Jihen*. Tokyo: Chūokoron-sha, 1967.

————. *Manshu Jihen*. Tokyo: Chuokoron-sha, 1974.

Yokoyama, Shimpei. *Hiroku: Ishihara Kanji*. Tokyo: Fuyō-shobo, 1964.

Yoshida, Shigeru. *Kaiso Ju-nen*. 4 vols. Tokyo: Shincho-sha, 1957—58.

Index

PLACE NAMES